"*Early in this century philosophy rapidly descended down the black hole of logical positivism where God was seemingly erased from the universe. Few could have imagined that by the end of this century breakthroughs in science—quantum mechanics and astrophysics—would ascend out of this abyss to posit the existence of God in the magnificent and endless cathedral of the cosmos. With admirable lucidity, Dr. Hugh Ross navigates through breathtaking panoramas of scientific evidence upon which he builds a compounding case for the biblical worldview. With the integrity and credibility of the devoted scientist, he handles a broad range of considerations, giving us invaluable apologetic material—from the design argument, probability, to the facts of physics—that bears witness to the existence of a Creator who is personal and transcendent, whom we can glimpse with a new awe.*"

Tal Brooke
Author of *When the World Will Be as One*
President of Spiritual Counterfeits Project
Berkeley, California

THE CREATOR AND THE COSMOS

THE
CREATOR
AND THE
COSMOS

HOW THE GREATEST
SCIENTIFIC DISCOVERIES OF
THE CENTURY REVEAL GOD

HUGH ROSS, Ph.D.

NAVPRESS

Bringing Truth to Life
P.O. Box 35001, Colorado Springs, Colorado 80935

OUR GUARANTEE TO YOU

We believe so strongly in the message of our books that we are making this quality guarantee to you. If for any reason you are disappointed with the content of this book, return the title page to us with your name and address and we will refund to you the list price of the book. To help us serve you better, please briefly describe why you were disappointed. Mail your refund request to: NavPress, P.O. Box 35002, Colorado Springs, CO 80935.

The Navigators is an international Christian organization. Our mission is to reach, disciple, and equip people to know Christ and to make Him known through successive generations. We envision multitudes of diverse people in the United States and every other nation who have a passionate love for Christ, live a lifestyle of sharing Christ's love, and multiply spiritual laborers among those without Christ.

NavPress is the publishing ministry of The Navigators. NavPress publications help believers learn biblical truth and apply what they learn to their lives and ministries. Our mission is to stimulate spiritual formation among our readers.

Library of Congress Catalog Card Number: 92-64094
ISBN 1-57683-288-0

Photograph: © Stock Imagery

Unless otherwise identified, all Scripture quotations in this publication are taken from the *HOLY BIBLE: NEW INTERNATIONAL VERSION*® (NIV®). Copyright © 1973, 1978, 1984 by International Bible Society. Used by permission of Zondervan Publishing House. All rights reserved. Another version used is the *King James Version* (KJV).

Ross, Hugh (Hugh Norman), 1945-
        The creator and the cosmos : how the greatest scientific discoveries of the century reveal God / Hugh Ross.
        p.   cm.
Originally published: Colorado Springs, Colo.: NavPress, c1993.
Includes bibliographical references and index.
ISBN 1-57683-288-0 (pbk.)
1. Creation.   2. Anthropic principle.   3. God—Proof, Cosmological.   I. Title.
BS651.R76 2001
231.7'652—dc21   2001030509

Printed in the United States of America

1 2 3 4 5 6 7 8 9 10 / 07 06 05 04 03 02 01

FOR A FREE CATALOG OF
NAVPRESS BOOKS & BIBLE STUDIES,
CALL 1-800-366-7788 (USA)
or 1-416-499-4615 (CANADA)

CONTENTS

LIST OF FIGURES
AND TABLES

Figures

Tables

PREFACE TO
THE THIRD EDITION

The first and second editions of *The Creator and the Cosmos* focused attention on twentieth-century scientific discoveries that contributed most profoundly to the credibility of faith in the God of the Bible. Since the dawn of the twenty-first century, several more scientific discoveries of great theological importance have been made. Therefore, I have rewritten much of the book, giving it a twenty-first century facelift.

This third edition includes more than seventy pages of new content. Three new chapters and an appendix have been added. The number of references to the scientific literature has nearly doubled.

This edition has benefited significantly from the comments and suggestions of people who were compelled by their reading of the second edition to commit their lives to Jesus Christ. Thanks to them and to the many other friends who recommended improvements, readers will, I trust, find much in this third edition to further inspire and strengthen their faith in the awesome Creator.

ACKNOWLEDGMENTS

My wife, Kathy, deserves the most credit for this book's timely publication. Her support and encouragement during times of stress and deadlines for this and other projects allowed me to persevere. In addition to doing the majority of the editing and rewriting, she spent many hours discussing with me the points of this book and helping me to communicate them more clearly.

Janet Kobobel, former director of publications for Reasons To Believe, was also a major contributor to the editing and rewriting. Several of the word pictures used to clarify technical points are hers. She also kept us coordinated and handled communications with the publisher, artists, and others.

I benefited greatly from discussions with Drs. David and Lynn Carta, Sam Conner, and Allan Sandage. And all of them provided me with important research papers and references. Mal Scharer spent many hours in various libraries hunting down additional references.

Sheila Cherney obtained all of the photographs and permissions. Patty Bradbury provided extra care for my sons, Joel and David, enabling Kathy and me to work as a team. Thanks to Tani Trost and Sandra Frantz for their tireless work in proofreading the text and in updating the indexes.

Lastly, I want to thank Lauren Libby and Dr. Jerry White of The Navigators and Melissa Munro, Greg Clouse, and Pat Miller of NavPress for their enthusiasm and support of this third edition.

CHAPTER ONE

THE AWE-INSPIRING NIGHT SKY

When I was eight, I started saving to buy a telescope. It took several years, but finally I pulled together enough coins to purchase the optics. With my father's help, I designed and built a mount and, at last, peered through the telescope to the heavens above.

I was stunned. I had never seen anything so beautiful, so awesome. The spectacle was too good not to share. I carried my instrument from the back yard to the front so I could invite my neighbors to join me. But no invitation was necessary. No sooner had I planted my telescope on the sidewalk than an enthusiastic crowd formed, a crowd that stayed late into the night.

That evening I began to realize many people, maybe all people, are fascinated with the starry hosts. I once thought that the sheer immensity of the heavens was responsible for that fascination. That's part of it, but there's more. There's the mystery of what's really out there, what those specks of light may be, the mystery of how they all got there and of what lies above and beyond. Gazing at the night sky seems to raise profound questions not only about the universe but also about ourselves.

The Universe and You

Cosmology is the study of the universe as a whole—its structure, origin, and development. It's not a subject just for ivory tower academics. Cosmology is for everyone.

In the words of historian, economist, and college president Dr. George Roche, "It really does matter, and matter very much, how we think about the cosmos."[1] Roche's point is that our concept of the universe shapes our worldview, our philosophy of life, and thus our daily decisions and actions.

For example, if the universe is not created or is in some manner accidental, then it has no objective meaning, and consequently, life, including human life, has no meaning. A mechanical chain of events determines everything. Morality and religion may be temporarily useful but are ultimately irrelevant. The Universe (capital U) is ultimate reality.

On the other hand, if the universe is created, then there must be reality beyond the confines of the universe. The Creator is that ultimate reality and wields authority over all else. The Creator is the source of life and establishes its meaning and purpose. The Creator's personality defines personality. The Creator's character defines morality.

Thus, to study the origin and development of the universe is, in a sense, to investigate the basis for any meaning and purpose to life. Cosmology has deep theological and philosophical ramifications.

Unfortunately, many researchers refuse to acknowledge this connection. In the name of objectivity, they gather and examine data through a special pair of glasses, the "God-is-not-necessary-to-explain-anything" glasses. It's tough for them to admit that such lenses represent their theological position, their personal faith. I've also met researchers who read the universe through the "God-is-whoever-or-whatever-I-choose" glasses.

Though no one is perfectly objective, some researchers are willing to gather and integrate the data to see which theory of origins is most consistent with the facts—whatever that theory may say about the necessity and characteristics of an Originator.

Cosmological Chauvinism
Because cosmology probes such weighty and personal matters, it has evoked possessiveness and competition. This is perhaps more evident today than ever. Three groups vie for supreme authority on the subject: scientists, theologians, and philosophers.

The chauvinism of scientists is exemplified by a pep talk I heard in my undergraduate days at the University of British Columbia. "Not only can a good physicist do physics better than anyone else," said the professor, "he can do anything better than anyone else." He expressed the belief that science training is essential for grappling with the challenges of modern life. In a graduate course on relativity, my professor lamented theologians' past meddling in cosmology. "Today," he boasted, "we have been able to scare most of the ministers out of cosmology with a straightforward application of tensor calculus."[2]

At a meeting of philosophers, I heard a distinguished speaker commiserate with his peers over scientists' bungling intrusion into cosmology. "Even the best physicists," he said, "are lousy philosophers."

At a theology colloquium, I heard from the podium that theologians alone have the right to interpret all science since they are trained in the mother of the sciences, theology. The speaker ended on a dramatic note: "Scientists have only observations. We have revelation!"

Cosmological chauvinism is not simply a manifestation of academic pride. It reflects decades of increasing specialization in education. Universities long ago dropped theology from their science curriculum. Few, if any, seminaries draw students with a background in science. Philosophy students may touch upon theology and science, but usually not in depth. Theology and philosophy students may study the history of their disciplines, science students rarely do.

The inevitable fruits of such specialization are polarization, conflict, and misunderstanding, not to mention neglect of the ordinary people whose tax dollars support much of the research in cosmology. I realize that specialization is necessary to push forward the frontiers of knowledge, but imagine how much more efficiently and effectively we could learn about reality if we were to take an interdisciplinary approach, giving adequate attention to historical context.

If specialists will stop intimidating each other and lay people and start dialoguing in understandable terms, anyone who wants to can explore and integrate the facts about our universe. Then we all, novices included, can enrich our understanding of the meaning and purpose for the universe, for life, for humanity, and for every person.

CHAPTER TWO

MY SKEPTICAL INQUIRY

My own thinking about the meaning of life began with my wonderment about the cosmos. I was born shortly after World War II in Montreal, Canada. My father was a self-taught engineer, and my mother a nurse. Before and during my early years my father founded and built up a successful hydraulics engineering business. The company's rapid financial growth proved too great a temptation for Dad's financial partner, who one day withdrew all the funds and vanished. With his last few dollars, my dad brought my mother, my two sisters, and me to Vancouver, British Columbia. The neighborhood in which we settled was poor but culturally diverse. Our neighbors were mostly refugees from eastern Europe and Asia—people who, like my parents, had tasted success but either lost it or left it for survival's sake.

Are Stars Hot?

My parents say they could see in me an intense curiosity about nature from the time I started to talk. I recall one starlit evening when I was seven, walking along the sidewalk with my parents and asking them if the stars are hot. They assured me that they are very hot. When I asked them why, they suggested I go to the library. They knew I would.

My elementary school library was well stocked with books on astronomy. As I read, I was amazed to discover just how hot the stars are and what makes them burn so brightly. I found out that our galaxy contains a hundred billion suns and that our universe holds more than a hundred billion galaxies. I was astonished by the immensity of it all. I was compelled to find out everything I could about it.

In my eighth year I read every book on physics and astronomy

I could find in our school library. The next year I began to do the same in the children's section of the Vancouver Public Library.

By that time I knew I wanted to be an astronomer. Many of my friends also were reading incessantly and choosing career directions. We didn't think of ourselves as precocious. The nonstop rainfall in Vancouver encouraged a lot of indoor activity and provided plenty of time to think.

At age ten I had exhausted the science resources of the children's and youth sections of the Vancouver Public Library and was granted a pass to the adult section. A few years later I was given access to the library of the University of British Columbia. By the time I was sixteen, I was presenting public lectures on astronomy and at seventeen won the British Columbia Science Fair for my project on variable stars. Also at seventeen I became the director of observations for the Vancouver branch of the Royal Astronomical Society of Canada (an organization of primarily amateur astronomers). I felt glad to have found so early in life a pursuit I loved.

Who Did All This?
Even as a child I always felt a sense of awe concerning nature. Its beauty and harmony, combined with its staggering complexity, left me wondering who or what could be responsible for it all.

By age fifteen, I came to understand that some form of the big bang theory provided the only reasonable explanation for the universe. If the universe arose out of a big bang, it must have had a beginning. If it had a beginning, it must have a Beginner.

From that point on, I never doubted God's existence. But, like the astronomers whose books I read, I presumed that the Beginner was distant and noncommunicative. Surely, I reasoned, a God who built a universe of more than ten-billion-trillion stars would not concern Himself with events on an insignificant speck of dust we call Earth.

Ruling Out Holy Books
My high school history studies bothered me because they showed me that the peoples of the world typically take their religions seriously. Knowing that the European philosophers of the Enlightenment largely discounted religion, I first looked for insight from their works. What I discovered, however, were circular arguments, inconsistencies, contradictions, and evasions. I began to appreciate nature all the more, for it never presented me with such twists.

Just to be fair and not to build a case on second-hand resources, I determined to investigate for myself the holy books of the world's major religions. I figured if God, the Creator, was speaking through any of these books (I presumed He was not), then the communication would be noticeably distinct from what human beings write. I reasoned that if humans invented a religion, their message would contain errors and inconsistencies, but if the Creator communicated, His message would reflect His supernature. It would be consistent like nature is. I chose history and science as good ways to test the revelations on which various religions are based.

In the first several holy books I examined, my initial hunch was confirmed. I found statements clearly at odds with established history and science (see chapter 8, page 97, for an example). I also noted a writing style perhaps best described as esoteric, mysterious, and vague. My great frustration was having to read so much in these books to find something stated specifically enough to be tested. The sophistry and the incongruity with established facts seemed opposite to the Creator's character as suggested to me by nature.

A Word from God?

I was getting a little smug until I picked up a Bible I had received (but not read) from the Gideons at my public school. The book's distinctives struck me immediately. It was simple, direct, and specific. I was amazed with the quantity of historical and scientific references and with the detail in them.

It took me a whole evening just to investigate the first chapter. Instead of another bizarre creation myth, here was a journal-like record of the earth's initial conditions—correctly described from the standpoint of astrophysics and geophysics—followed by a summary of the sequence of changes through which Earth came to be inhabited by living things and ultimately by humans. The account was simple, elegant, and scientifically accurate. From what I understood to be the stated viewpoint of an observer on Earth's surface, both the order and the description of creation events perfectly matched the established record of nature. I was amazed.

That night I committed myself to spend at least an hour a day going through the Bible to test the accuracy of all its statements on science, geography, and history. I expected this study to take about four weeks. Instead, there was so much to check it took me eighteen months.

At the end of the eighteen months, I had to admit to myself that I had been unsuccessful in finding a single provable error or contradiction. This is not to say that there were not any passages in the Bible I did not understand or problems that I could not resolve. The problems and passages I couldn't yet understand didn't discourage me, however, for I faced the same kinds of things in the record of nature. But, just as with the record of nature, I was impressed with how much could be understood and resolved.

I was now convinced that the Bible was supernaturally accurate and thus supernaturally inspired. Its perfection could come only from the Creator Himself. I also recognized that the Bible stood alone in revealing God and His dealings with humans from a perspective that demanded more than just the dimensions we mortals can experience (length, width, height, and time). Since humans cannot visualize phenomena in dimensions they cannot experience, finding these ideas in the Bible also argued for a superhuman author.

As a final exercise, I mathematically determined that the Bible was more reliable by far than some of the laws of physics. For example, I knew from studying physics there is roughly a one in 10^{80} (that's the number one with eighty zeros following) chance of a sudden reversal in the second law of thermodynamics. But I had calculated (with the help of skeptical friends) the probability of the chance fulfillment of thirteen Bible predictions about specific people and their specific actions. My conservative estimate showed less than one chance in 10^{138} that such predictions could come true without supernatural intervention.[1] That meant the Bible was 10^{58} times more reliable than the second law of thermodynamics on just this one set of predictions. I also derived a similar conclusion based on the many instances in which the Bible accurately forecasted future scientific discoveries.[2]

Acknowledging that my life depended moment by moment on the reliability of the second law of thermodynamics, I saw that my only rational option was to trust in the Bible's Inspirer to at least the same degree as I relied on the laws of physics. I realized, too, what a self-sufficient young man I had been. After a long evening of studying the salvation passages in the New Testament, I humbled myself before God, asking Him to forgive me of my self-exaltation and all the offenses resulting from it, and committed myself to follow His directives for my life. At 1:06 in the morning I signed my name on the back page of my Gideon Bible, stating that I had received Christ as my Lord and Savior.[3]

New Evidences

All of the scientific and historical evidences I had collected deeply rooted my confidence in the veracity of the Bible and convinced me that the Creator had indeed communicated through this holy book. I went on to become an astronomer, and my investigations into both the cosmos and the Bible have shown me a more wondrous, personal God behind nature than I could ever have imagined.

Through the years, new evidences have consistently arisen in various fields of science, making the case for Christianity even stronger. By 1986, several breakthrough discoveries uncovered proofs for the God of the Bible so convincing that together with others I formed an organization, Reasons To Believe, to communicate these new evidences to as many people as possible.

Now, several years later, an even more dramatic set of scientific discoveries has come. One of them was called the greatest discovery of the twentieth century. Secular scientists actually reported to the media that these new findings reveal the face of God more clearly than ever. The following chapters explore how and why normally reserved scientists have been moved to speak in such ecstatic terms.

CHAPTER THREE

BIG BANG—THE BIBLE TAUGHT IT FIRST!

Note: This chapter was composed at the suggestion and with the assistance of Dr. John Rea, professor emeritus of Old Testament at Regent University, Virginia Beach, Virginia.

Most science textbooks on cosmology credit Arno Penzias and Robert Wilson with the discovery that the universe began with a hot big bang creation event. While they were the first (1965) to detect the radiation left over from the creation event,[1] they were not the first scientists to recognize that the universe is expanding from an extremely hot and compact beginning. In 1946 George Gamow calculated that only a universe expanding from a near infinitely hot beginning could account for the existing abundance of elements.[2] In 1929 observations made by Edwin Hubble established that the velocities of galaxies result from a general expansion of the universe.[3] Beginning in 1925 Abbé Georges Lemaître, who was both an astrophysicist and a Jesuit priest, was the first scientist to promote the idea of a big bang creation event.[4]

The first theoretical scientific evidence for a big bang universe dates back to 1916. That is when Albert Einstein noted that his field equations of general relativity predicted an expanding universe.[5] Unwilling to accept the cosmic beginning implied by such expansion, Einstein altered his theory to align with the common wisdom of his day. He capitulated with an eternally existing universe.[6]

Biblical Claims for a Transcendent Cosmic Beginning
All these scientists, however, were upstaged at least 2,500 years earlier by Job, Moses, David, Isaiah, Jeremiah, and other Bible authors. The

Bible's prophets and apostles stated explicitly and repeatedly the two most fundamental properties of the big bang, a transcendent cosmic beginning a finite time period ago and a universe undergoing a general, continual expansion. In Isaiah 42:5 both properties were declared: "This is what the Lord says—He who created the heavens and stretched them out."

The Hebrew verb translated "created" in Isaiah 42:5 is *bara'* which has as its primary definition "bringing into existence something new, something that did not exist before."[7] The proclamation that God created (*bara'*) the entirety of the heavens is stated seven times in the Old Testament (Genesis 1:1, 2:3, 2:4; Psalm 148:5; Isaiah 40:26, 42:5, 45:18). This principle of transcendent creation is made more explicit by passages like Hebrews 11:3 which states that the universe that we humans can measure and detect was made from that which we cannot measure or detect. Also, Isaiah 45:5-22, John 1:3, and Colossians 1:15-17 stipulate that God alone is the agent for the universe's existence. Biblical claims that God predated the universe and was actively involved in causing certain effects before the existence of the universe is not only found in Colossians 1 but also in Proverbs 8:22-31, John 17:24, Ephesians 1:4, 2 Timothy 1:9, Titus 1:2, and 1 Peter 1:20.

Biblical Claims for Continual Cosmic Stretching

The characteristic of the universe stated more frequently than any other in the Bible is its being "stretched out." Five different Bible authors pen such a statement in eleven different verses: Job 9:8, Psalm 104:2, Isaiah 40:22, 42:5, 44:24, 45:12, 48:13, 51:13, Jeremiah 10:12, 51:15, and Zechariah 12:1. Job 37:18 appears to be a twelfth verse to make this statement. However, the word used there for "heavens" or "skies" is *shehaqîm* which refers to the clouds of fine particles (of water or dust) located in Earth's atmosphere,[8] not the *shamayim*, the heavens of the astronomical universe.[9] Three of the eleven verses— Job 9:8, Isaiah 44:24, and 45:12—make the point that God alone was responsible for the cosmic stretching.

What is particularly interesting about the eleven verses is that different Hebrew verb forms are used to describe the cosmic stretching. Seven verses—Job 9:8, Psalm 104:2, Isaiah 40:22, 42:5, 44:24, 51:13, and Zechariah 12:1—employ the Qal active participle form of the verb *natah*. This form literally means "the stretcher out of them" (the heavens) and implies continual or ongoing stretching. Four verses—Isaiah 45:12, 48:13, and Jeremiah 10:12, 51:15—use the Qal perfect form. This form literally means that the stretching of the heavens was completed or finished some time ago.

That the Bible really does claim that the stretching out of the heavens is both "finished" and "ongoing" is made all the more evident in Isaiah 40:22. There we find two different verbs used in two different forms. In the first of the final two parallel poetic lines, "stretches out" is the verb *natah* in the Qal active participle form. In the second (final) line the verb "spreads them out" (NASB, NIV, NKJV) is *mathah* (used only this one time in the Old Testament) in the waw consecutive plus Qal imperfect form, so that literally we might translate it "and he has spread them out." The participles in lines one and three of Isaiah 40:22 characterize our sovereign God by His actions in all times, sitting enthroned above the earth and stretching out the heavens, constantly exercising His creative power in His ongoing providential work. This characterization is continued with reference to the past by means of waw consecutive with the imperfect, the conversive form indicating God's completed act of spreading out the heavens. That is, this one verse literally states that God is both continuing to stretch out the heavens and has stretched them out.

This simultaneously finished and ongoing aspect of cosmic stretching is identical to the big bang concept of cosmic expansion. According to the big bang, at the creation event all the physics (specifically, the laws, constants, and equations of physics) are instantly created, designed, and finished so as to guarantee an ongoing, continual expansion of the universe at exactly the right rates with respect to time so that physical life will be possible.

This biblical claim for simultaneously finished and ongoing acts of creation, incidentally, is not limited to just the universe's expansion. The same claim, for example, is made for God's laying Earth's foundations (Isaiah 51:3, Zechariah 12:1). This is consistent with the geophysical discovery that certain long-lived radiometric elements were placed into the earth's crust a little more than four billion years ago in just the right quantities so as to guarantee the continual building of continents.[10]

Biblical Claims for Cosmic Cooling

Finally, the Bible indirectly argues for a big bang universe by stating that the laws of thermodynamics, gravity, and electromagnetism have universally operated throughout the universe since the cosmic creation event itself. The principle here is that any physical system that continually expands under the operation of the laws of thermodynamics, gravity, and electromagnetism must be cooling down. That is, it must be much hotter in the past than it is in the present.

In Romans 8:20 we are told that the entire creation has been subjected to "frustration" or "futility." The next verse declares that all of creation was and currently exists in a state of "slavery to decay" or "bondage to corruption." Ecclesiastes 1 and Revelation 21 also support the conclusion that the whole universe suffers from progressive decay. Genesis 2 and 3 teach that work and pain are part of the creation, both before and after Adam's rebellion in Eden. Such ongoing slavery to decay describes well the second law of thermodynamics, the law of physics which states that as time proceeds, the universe becomes progressively more disordered, decayed, and run down.

In Genesis 1 and in many places throughout Job, Psalms, and Proverbs we are informed that stars and living organisms have existed since the early times of creation. As explained later in this book (see chapter 16), even the slightest changes in either the laws of gravity, electromagnetism, or thermodynamics would make the stars that are necessary for physical life and physical life itself impossible.

Big Bang Fundamentals

That gravity, electromagnetism, and thermodynamics are consistent with a big bang universe should come as no surprise to scientists. As explained in chapter 5 of this book, stable orbits of planets around stars and of stars around the centers of galaxies are possible only in a universe described by three very large rapidly expanding dimensions of space.

Many big bang theories exist. What they all share in common, however, are three fundamental characteristics: (1) a transcendent cosmic beginning that occurred a finite time ago, (2) a continuous, universal cosmic expansion, and (3) a cosmic cooling from an extremely hot initial state. All three of the fundamental characteristics of the big bang were explicitly taught in the Bible two to three thousand years before scientists discovered them through their astronomical measurements. Moreover, the Bible alone among all the scriptures of the world's religions expounds these three big bang fundamentals. Scientific proofs for a big bang universe, therefore, can do much to establish the existence of the God of the Bible and the accuracy of the words of the Bible.

Beginner's Guide to Modern Big Bang Cosmology
Big bang cosmology has become an explosive topic. Heated reactions—and bitter resistance—have arisen from opposite directions in the last century but, ironically, for the same type of reasons: religious reasons. One group of big bang opponents includes those who understand the theory's implications, and the other, those who *mis*understand.

People in the first group understand that the big bang denies the notion of an uncreated or self-existent universe. The big bang theory points to a supernatural beginning and a purposeful (hence personal), transcendent (beyond the boundaries of space, time, matter, and energy) Beginner. Anyone who rejects the reality of God or the knowability of God would, of course, find such an idea repugnant, an affront to his or her religious or philosophical worldview. Similarly, it would offend anyone who wants to spell *universe* with a capital *U*, who has been trained to view the universe itself as ultimate reality and as the totality of all that is real. Again, a religious response.

People in the second group hate the big bang because they mistakenly think it argues *for* rather than *against* a godless theory of origins. They associate "big bang" with blind chance. They see it as a random, chaotic, uncaused explosion when it actually represents exactly the opposite. They reject the date it gives for the beginning of the universe, thinking that to acknowledge a few billion years is to discredit the authority of their holy books, whether the Koran, the Book of Mormon, or the Bible. Understandably, these people either predict the theory's ultimate overthrow or choose to live with a contradiction at the core of their belief system.

Despite opposition from outspoken enemies, the fundamentals of the big bang model, which is actually a cluster of slightly differing models, stands secure. In fact, it stands more firmly than ever with the aid of its most potent and important allies: the facts of nature and the technological marvels that bring them to light, as well as the men and women who pursue and report those facts. The following chapters offer a summary of the accumulated data supporting the big bang.

A Problematic Term
The big bang is NOT a big "bang" as most lay people would comprehend the term. This expression conjures up images of bomb blasts or exploding dynamite. Such a "bang" would yield disorder and destruction. In truth, this "bang" represents an immensely powerful

yet carefully planned and controlled release of matter, energy, space, and time within the strict confines of very carefully fine-tuned physical constants and laws that govern their behavior and interactions. The power and care this explosion reveals exceeds human potential for design by multiple orders of magnitude.

Why, then, would astronomers retain the term? The simplest answer is that nicknames, for better or for worse, tend to stick. In this case the term came not from proponents of the theory but rather, as one might guess, from a hostile opponent. British astronomer Sir Fred Hoyle coined the expression in the 1950s as an attempt to ridicule the big bang, the up-and-coming challenger to his "steady state" hypothesis. He objected to any theory that would place the origin, or Cause, of the universe outside the universe itself, hence, to his thinking, outside the realm of scientific inquiry.[11]

For whatever reasons, perhaps because of its simplicity and its catchy alliteration, the term stuck. No one found a more memorable, short-hand label for the "precisely controlled cosmic expansion from an infinitely or near infinitely compact, hot cosmic 'seed,' brought into existence by a Creator who lives beyond the cosmos." The accurate but unwieldy gave way to the wieldly but misleading.

A Multiplicity of Models

The first attempts to describe the big bang universe, as many as a dozen, proved solid in the broad simple strokes but weak in the complex details. So, they have been replaced by more refined models. Scientists are used to this process of proposing and refining theoretical models. News reporters—even textbook writers—sometimes misunderstand, though, and inadvertently misrepresent what is happening.

Reports of the overthrow of the "standard big bang model" illustrate the point. That model, developed in the 1960s, identified matter as the one factor determining the rate at which the universe expands from its starting point. It also assumed that all matter in the universe is ordinary matter, the kind that interacts in familiar ways with gravity and radiation. Subsequent discoveries showed that the situation is much more complex. Matter is just one of the determiners of the expansion rate, and an extraordinary kind of matter (called "exotic" matter) not only exists but more strongly influences the development of the universe than does ordinary matter.

The reported demise of the "standard big bang" model was interpreted by some readers as the end of the big bang. On the contrary, the discoveries that contradicted the standard model gave rise to a more robust model, actually a set of models attempting to answer new questions. More than once, as one of these models has been replaced with a more refined variant, news articles heralded the overthrow of *the* big bang theory when they should have specified *a* big bang model.

Currently, cosmologists (those who study the origin and characteristics of the universe) are investigating at least three or four dozen newer variations on the big bang theme. Scientists expect still more to arise as technological advances make new data accessible. This proliferation of slightly variant big bang models actually speaks of the vitality and viability of the theory.

It makes sense that the first models proposed were simple and sketchy. The observations at that time, while adequate to support the fundamental principles of the big bang, were insufficient to explore and account for the details. As the evidences have become more numerous and more precise, astronomers have discovered additional details and subtleties, features previously beyond their capability to discern.

New details, of course, mean more accurate "reconstructions" of what actually occurred "in the beginning." Each generation of newer, more detailed big bang models permits researchers to make more accurate predictions of what *should be* discovered with the help of new instruments and techniques.

As each wave of predictions proves true, researchers gain more certainty that they are on the right track, and they gain new material with which to construct more accurate and more intricate models. The testing of these models, in turn, gives rise to a new level of certainty and a new generation of predictions and advances. This process has been ongoing for many decades now, and its successes are documented not only in the technical journals but in newspaper headlines worldwide. Let's take a look.

CHAPTER FOUR

THE DISCOVERY OF THE TWENTIETH CENTURY

On April 24, 1992, newspapers around the world heralded a breakthrough by an American research team. The discovery made the front-page headlines of *The London Times* for five consecutive days. American TV networks gave the story as much as forty minutes of prime-time news coverage.

Reactions by Scientists
What was all the fuss about? A team of astrophysicists had reported the latest findings from the Cosmic Background Explorer (COBE) satellite—stunning confirmation of the hot big bang creation event.

Scientists extolled the event with superlatives. Carlos Frenk, of Britain's Durham University, exclaimed, "[It's] the most exciting thing that's happened in my life as a cosmologist."[1] Cambridge University's Lucasian professor of mathematics, Stephen Hawking, known for understatement, said, "It is the discovery of the century, if not of all time."[2] Michael Turner, astrophysicist with the University of Chicago and Fermilab, termed the discovery "unbelievably important. . . . The significance of this cannot be overstated. They have found the Holy Grail of cosmology."[3]

Turner's metaphor echoed a familiar theme. George Smoot, University of California at Berkeley astronomer and project leader for the COBE satellite, declared, "What we have found is evidence for the birth of the universe."[4] He added, "It's like looking at God."[5]

Theistic pronouncements abounded. According to science historian Frederic B. Burnham, the community of scientists was prepared to consider the idea that God created the universe "a more respectable hypothesis today than at any time in the last hundred years."[6] Ted

Koppel on ABC's "Nightline" began his interview of an astronomer and a physicist by quoting the first two verses of Genesis. The physicist immediately added verse three as also germane to the discovery.

Astronomers who do not draw theistic or deistic conclusions are becoming rare, and even the few dissenters hint that the tide is against them. Geoffrey Burbidge, of the University of California at San Diego, complains that his fellow astronomers are rushing off to join "the First Church of Christ of the Big Bang."[7]

Proofs of the Big Bang

All this excitement was generated because findings from the COBE satellite helped solve a haunting mystery of the big bang model for the origin and development of the universe, thus confirming that model (actually a set of models) and refining it.

Basically the hot big bang model says that the entire physical universe—all the matter and energy, and even the four dimensions of space and time—burst forth from a state of infinite, or near infinite, density, temperature, and pressure. The universe expanded from a volume very much smaller than the period at the end of this sentence, and it continues to expand.

Before April 1992, astrophysicists knew a great deal about how the universe began. Only one small but important component was missing. It was as if they knew how the machine was assembled and how it worked except for one part. They knew what that part should look like, and they knew approximately where to look for it. The COBE satellite (see figure 4.1, page 33) was designed specifically to find this missing part—namely, the explanation for how galaxies form out of a big bang.

Actually, the entire machine itself and many of its basic components were predicted by physicists working in the early part of the twentieth century. Richard Tolman in 1922 recognized that since the universe is expanding, it must be cooling off from an exceptionally high initial temperature.[8] The laws of thermodynamics say that any expanding system must be cooling simultaneously. George Gamow in 1946 discovered that only a rapid cooling of the cosmos from near infinitely high temperatures could account for how protons and neutrons fused together, forming a universe that today is about 72% hydrogen, 25% helium, and 3% heavier elements.[9]

The Cosmic Oven

Astronomers knew, based on the deductions by Tolman and Gamow, that the universe's beginning and subsequent development resembled a hot kitchen oven. When the door of the oven is opened, heat that was trapped inside escapes. Dissipation of the oven's heat takes place as the heat expands outward from the oven. Radiant energy that was confined to a few cubic feet now spreads throughout the kitchen's several hundred cubic feet. As it does, the oven cavity eventually cools down to the temperature of the room, which is now just a little warmer than it was before.

If one knows the peak temperature of the oven cavity, the volume of that cavity, and the volume of the room throughout which the oven's heat is dissipated, then the amount by which the room will warm up can be determined.

Figure 4.1: The Cosmic Background Explorer (COBE) Satellite
—Courtesy of Jet Propulsion Laboratory, NASA.

If one were using the opening of the oven door to dry out some wet towels, it would be important to control the temperature of the oven as well as the rate at which the oven disperses its heat to the room. If the oven were too hot, or the dispersion too slow, the towels would scorch. But, if the oven were too cool, or the heat dissipation too rapid (say the room was too large or the towels too far away), the towels would stay wet.

Similarly, if the universe were to expand too slowly, too many of the nucleons (protons and neutrons) would fuse together to form heavier elements. This would result in too few of the lighter elements essential for life chemistry. On the other hand, if the expansion were more rapid, too many of the nucleons would fuse into lighter elements. This would result in too few of the heavier elements essential for life chemistry.

Following this oven analogy, Gamow's research team in 1948 calculated what temperature conditions would be necessary to yield the currently observed abundances of elements. They concluded that a faint glow measuring only about 5° Centigrade above absolute zero (that's -273° Centigrade or -460° Fahrenheit) should be found everywhere throughout the universe.[10]

At the time, such a low temperature was hopelessly beyond the capabilities of telescopes and detectors to measure. But by 1964 Arno Penzias and Robert Wilson put together an instrument that successfully measured at radio wavelengths the cosmic background radiation (i.e., heat) to be at a temperature about 3° Celsius above absolute zero.[11] Since that initial discovery, the cosmic background radiation has been measured to much greater accuracy and at many more wavelengths.[12] But at most of the wavelengths the cosmic background radiation remained blocked out by the earth's atmosphere and, therefore, was beyond detection. Only a telescope operating in outer space could see well enough.

First COBE Discovery

The first COBE results, reported in January 1990,[13] showed the universe to match a perfect radiator, dissipating virtually all its available energy (see figure 4.2, page 35). The data showed the background radiation temperature to be very low and smooth. No irregularities in the temperature larger than one part in 10,000 were detected.

This extraordinarily low and smooth temperature in the cosmic background radiation convinced astronomers that the universe must have had an extremely hot beginning about 15 to 20 billion years ago. The finding essentially ruled out many alternative models for the universe's beginning such as the steady state model (see chapter 7). How were scientists able to conclude from these COBE findings a hot and relatively recent beginning for the universe? For some clues, let's return to our analogy of the kitchen oven.

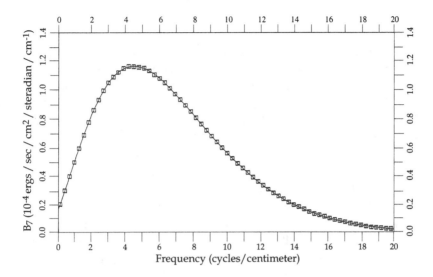

Figure 4.2: COBE's First Measurements of the Spectrum of the Cosmic Background Radiation at the North Galactic Pole of the Heavens
The measured temperature for the background radiation was 2.735° Centigrade above absolute zero. Deviations between COBE's results and the spectrum for a perfect radiator (curve) measured less than 1% over the entire range of observed frequencies.
—Courtesy of John Mather, Goddard, NASA.

Suppose the oven were surrounded by thousands of thermometers, each placed at exactly the same distance from the oven. Suppose also that some time after the oven had been heated, turned off, and its door opened, each thermometer indicated exactly the same temperature. The only possible conclusion we could draw would be that heat flow from the oven cavity to the room totally dominated the normal temperature-disturbing air flows in the room. Such dominance would imply that the original temperature of the oven cavity must have been very much greater than the room's temperature. In addition, if all those thousands of thermometers indicated a very low temperature, we would conclude that considerable time had passed since the opening of the oven door.

The Fantastic Explosion

The temperature measurements from COBE provide convincing evidence of a hot origin for the cosmos some billions of years in the past. Astronomers normally refer to this hot beginning as the big bang for a very good reason.

The cool and uniform temperature of the cosmic background radiation and its close fit to the spectrum of a perfect radiator establishes that the universe has suffered an enormous degradation of energy, typical of a large explosion. Energy degradation is measured by a quantity called entropy. Entropy describes the degree to which energy in a closed system disperses, or radiates (as heat), and thus ceases to be available to perform work. Specific entropy is the measure for a particular system of the amount of entropy per proton.

A burning candle is a good example of a highly entropic system, one that efficiently radiates energy away. It has a specific entropy of about two. Only very hot explosions have much higher specific entropies. The specific entropy of the universe—about one billion— is enormous beyond all comparison. Even supernova explosions, the most entropic (and radiant) of events now occurring in the universe, have specific entropies a hundred times less.

Only a hot big bang could account for such a huge specific entropy for the universe. (Let me be quick to add for those bothered to learn that the universe is so "inefficient" a machine, that only a universe with a huge specific entropy can produce the observed abundances of elements, that is, the elements necessary for life.[14] It can also be shown that if the specific entropy were any greater or any less, stars and planets would never have existed at any time in the universe's history.[15])

Second COBE Discovery

The smoothness of the cosmic background radiation helped confirm a hot big bang beginning for the universe. But it posed a potential problem for a stage of development that scientists estimated would occur roughly a half billion to a billion years after the creation event. Astronomers knew that the background radiation could not be perfectly smooth. At least some level of non-uniformity in the cosmic background radiation would be necessary to explain the formation of star clusters, galaxies, and clusters of galaxies. The whole range of reasonable theories for how galaxies can come together required temperature fluctuations roughly ten times smaller than what COBE had the capability to detect in 1990. Fortunately, the results announced on April 24, 1992, were between ten and a hundred times more precise than the measurements from 1990.

These newly refined COBE measurements showed irregularities in the background radiation as large as about one part in 100,000,[16] just what astrophysicists thought they would find.[17] That missing piece of the machinery was located exactly where they suspected it might be. What's more, the measurements solved some intriguing mysteries about the piece itself—what it's made of and how it works. They could narrow the galaxy formation theories to those that include both ordinary matter and an amazing component called exotic matter. More on this in chapter 5, "Twenty-first Century Discoveries."

Confirmations

To be complete I must report that these dramatic COBE results (see figure 4.3, page 38) did meet with some initial challenges from a few astronomers, including Geoffrey Burbidge.[18] But their skepticism seemed unwarranted to other astronomers since the temperature irregularities showed up at three different wavelengths of observation.

Within a few months, corroborative evidence began to accumulate. A balloon-borne experiment, making measurements at four different wavelengths that were shorter than the three measured by COBE, showed temperature fluctuations lining up perfectly with those in the COBE maps. Edward Cheng, leader of the experiment, concluded, "With two totally different systems, it's very unlikely that random noise would give rise to the same lumps at the same places in the sky."[19]

Twelve months later, two radiometers operating in Tenerife, Spain, detected actual structure in the cosmic background radiation. Whereas the COBE and balloon measurements were sensitive enough to establish that fluctuations in the cosmic background radiation did indeed exist, they could not delineate with any accuracy the location and size of individual features. This delineation was achieved through fully independent radiometers operating at three different wavelengths, longer than the wavelengths observed by COBE and the balloon-borne instruments. The angular scale (size of the angle in the sky over which measurements were made) was 5.5°. Fluctuation structures as large as ten degrees across were found, and the amplitude of these structures is completely consistent with the earlier statistical detections by COBE and the balloon-borne experiment.[20]

A few weeks after the release of the Tenerife results, cosmic background radiation fluctuations on angular scales of about 1° were detected. These measurements also are consistent with the detections by COBE and the balloon-borne experiment.[21]

Since then, over a dozen different sets of new observations have confirmed the cosmic background radiation fluctuations.[22] In fact, the latest observations are of such high quality that they are shedding light as well on other creation parameters, such as the values of the cosmic mass density, the cosmological constant, and the quantities of various forms of exotic matter (see the following two chapters).

Independent confirmation comes from a variety of recent detections of exotic matter (see chapter 5, "Twenty-first Century Discoveries"). The important point to remember is that galaxy formation no longer casts a shadow of doubt on the big bang scenario.

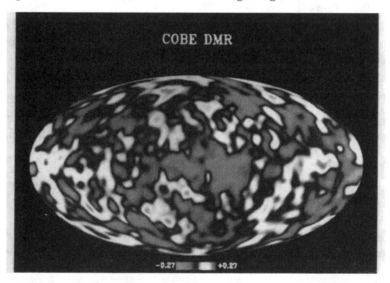

Figure 4.3: Microwave Map of the Whole Sky Made from One Year of Data Taken by COBE's Differential Microwave Radiometers (DMR)
The Milky Way galaxy lies horizontal across the middle of the map. Data from all three DMR wavelengths were used to model and remove emission from our galaxy. This map revealed for the first time temperature fluctuations in the cosmic background radiation. The amplitudes of the fluctuations are consistent with explaining the birth and growth of galaxies using large amounts of exotic matter.

—Photo courtesy of Jet Propulsion Laboratory, NASA.

Third COBE Discovery

Deviations between the 1990 COBE results and the spectrum for a perfect radiator measured less than 1% over the entire range of observed frequencies (see figure 4.2, page 35). Data released from the COBE research team (see figure 4.4, below) at an American Astronomical Society meeting in January 1993 reduced the deviation to less than 0.03%. The new data also yields the most precise measure to date of the temperature of the cosmic background radiation, 2.726° Kelvin (that is 2.726° Centigrade above absolute zero), a measure that is accurate to within 0.01°K[23] and completely consistent with newer independent measurements.[24]

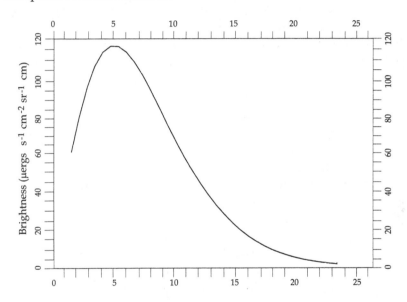

Figure 4.4: The Latest COBE Satellite Results of the Spectrum of the Cosmic Background Radiation
Deviations between COBE's measurements and the spectrum for a perfect radiator (curve) are less than 0.03% over the entire range of observed frequencies. This is the strongest direct evidence to date for a hot big bang creation event.
— Courtesy of John Mather, Goddard, NASA.

These new results do more than just prove that the universe began with a hot big bang. They tell us which kind of hot big bang. The 1990 results left room for the possibility that the big bang could have been a tightly spaced succession of "little" bangs. The new results rule out that possibility. The universe must have erupted from a single explosive event that by itself accounts for at least 99.97% of the radiant energy in the universe.

With a single explosive creation event accounting for so much of the radiation in the universe, astronomers can conclude that the temperature fluctuations in the cosmic background radiation, not disturbances arising from smaller events, must have transformed the smooth primordial cosmos into today's universe of clumped clusters of galaxies.

Watching the Universe Cool Down

Astronomers now have optical telescopes so large they can directly witness the universe getting colder and colder as it gets older and older. That is, they can demonstrate through direct observations that the universe was hotter in the past than it is in the present. By comparing the actual past temperatures of the universe with the temperatures predicted by a hot big bang creation event, astronomers can offer a simple and dramatic proof for cosmic creation.

Let me clarify that the temperature 2.726°K for the cosmic background radiation is for nearby regions of space. Because radiation from great distances takes much longer to reach us, temperatures at such distances reveal the heat of the cosmos at earlier times. If the hot big bang model is correct, observations at great distances should yield significantly higher temperatures for the cosmic background radiation. For this reason, astronomers for many years have desired to measure the cosmic background radiation at great distances.

In September 1994 that desire was fulfilled. The newly opened Keck Telescope, the world's largest optical instrument, enabled astronomers to measure spectral lines of carbon in two gas clouds so distant that their radiation represents an epoch when the universe was about one-fourth its present age. They were able to select lines that would provide a sensitive measure of the temperature of the cosmic background radiation. According to the hot big bang model, the background radiation for the universe at this early epoch should be 7.58°K. The Keck Telescope observations indicated 7.4±0.8°K.[25] In the words of David Meyer, Northwestern University astrophysicist, these measurements are "strikingly consistent with the Big Bang theory."[26]

In December 1996 the same team of astronomers made a second measurement using the identical technique on a more distant gas cloud.[27] The measured temperature was just slightly above 8°K. The hot big bang model predicts a temperature of 8.105°K. Recently, a different team measured a gas cloud whose distance shows us the universe at about one-sixth its present age. The detected background radiation temperature of just under 10°K matched that predicted by the hot big bang.[28] Once again, all the measurements are strikingly consistent with a big bang creation event.

A Big Bang Picture Album

The simplest-to-grasp evidence in support of the big bang comes from pictures. With the help of various imaging devices, one can actually enjoy a kind of time-lapse photo of the big bang. The images show the universe in its various "growing up" stages, much as a time-lapse camera captures the opening of a flower, or as a photo album documents the development of a person from birth onward.

Such an album is made possible by light (or radiation) travel time. Observing a distant galaxy, for example, some 5 billion light-years distant is equivalent to seeing that galaxy 5 billion years ago, when the light now entering an Earth-based telescope began its journey through space. In one sense, astronomers can only capture glimpses of the past, not of the present, as they peer out into space.

Thanks to the Keck and Hubble Space Telescopes, astronomers now have a photo history of the universe that covers nearly 14 billion years. It begins when the universe was only about half a billion years old and follows it to "middle age," where it yet remains. The sequence of images in figure 4.5 presents highlights from this cosmic photo album. Photo (A) shows the universe at the equivalent of infancy, before galaxies exist. The images in (B) depict the "toddler" stage, when newly-formed galaxies are so tightly packed as to rip the spiral arms off one another; the youthful universe, a time when most of the galaxies are still actively generating new stars and galaxy collisions are frequent; and the universe's entrance to middle age, a time when nearly all galaxies have ceased forming new stars and galaxy collisions are rare (C).

Figure 4.3 (see page 38) deserves special attention. It captures that moment in cosmic history when light first separated from darkness, before any stars or galaxies existed. It shows us the universe at just 300,000 years of age, only 0.002% of its current age.

These images testify that the universe is anything but static. It expanded from a tiny volume and changed according to a predictable pattern as it grew, a big bang pattern. A picture is still worth a thousand words, perhaps more.[29]

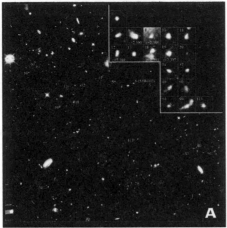

–Courtesy of R. Windhorst (Arizona State University) and NASA

–Courtesy of STScI/NASA

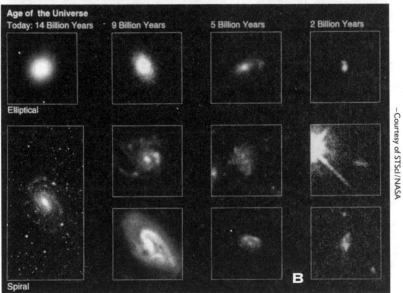

–Courtesy of STScI/NASA

Figure 4.5: A Photo Album History of the Universe

(A) The eighteen dim clumps of stars shown above are in the process of coming together to form a proto-galaxy. The look-back time is about 12 billion years.

(B) These Hubble Space Telescope images show elliptical and spiral galaxies at stages roughly equivalent to infancy, childhood, youth, and middle age (its current developmental stage).

(C) As the two galaxies of the Antennae collide, they rip material away from each other. Such collisions were common in the past but are less common now that the universe is more spread out.

TEN-DIMENSIONAL CREATION

Throughout the 1980s and early 1990s theoretical physicists recognized that there simply was not enough room within the dimensions of length, width, height, and time for all the symmetries demanded by both gravity and quantum mechanics. In 1996 a team led by Andrew Strominger discovered that only in ten space-time dimensions (nine space and one time) could gravity and quantum mechanics successfully coexist at all epochs of cosmic history. This theoretical calculation was subsequently supported by several observational confirmations.

The picture of creation that arises out of this new result proceeds as follows:

1. At the creation event ten space-time dimensions instantly and transcendently appear. They reside within an infinitesimal volume.
2. All nine space dimensions rapidly expand.
3. At 10^{-43} seconds (a ten millionth of a trillionth of a trillionth of a trillionth of a second) after the creation event, six of the nine space dimensions cease expanding.
4. Thereafter, the space dimensions of length, width, and height continue to rapidly expand.

Presently, the six tiny space dimensions are very tightly wrapped up around the three large space dimensions. Except for the interiors of black holes, the tiny space dimensions today play no role in the dynamics of the universe. For more details on the discovery that creation is ten- rather than four-dimensional and the significance of this discovery for establishing the Christian faith, see my book, *Beyond the Cosmos*.[30]

Stability of Stars and Orbits Proves Big Bang

Perhaps the most concrete big bang evidence is that stable orbits and stable stars are possible *only* in a big bang universe. Physical life would be impossible unless planets orbit with stability, stars burn with stability, and stars orbit galaxy cores with stability.[31]

Such stability demands gravity, not just any force of gravity, but gravity operating according to the inverse square law. Gravity operating at that level demands three large rapidly expanding dimensions of space—the big bang universe.

In two dimensions of space, gravity would obey a different law (objects with mass would attract one another in proportion to the inverse of the distance separating them). In four space dimensions, gravity would obey a different law (massive bodies would attract one another in proportion to the inverse of the cube of the distance separating them). Such distinct laws guarantee, for example, that planets either would be ejected away from their stars or gobbled up by them.

Stability under the influence of gravity, in turn, demands that the three dynamic space dimensions be large (significantly unwound from their original tight curl).[32] Otherwise galaxies would be so close together as to wreak havoc on stellar orbits, and stars would be so close together as to wreak havoc on planets' orbits. When galaxies are too close together, galaxy collisions and close encounters catastrophically disturb stars' orbits. Likewise, when stars are too close together, their mutual gravitational tugs catastrophically disturb the orbits of their planets.

The three dimensions of space must be expanding at a particular rate, as well. A universe that expands too slowly will produce only neutron stars and black holes. A universe that expands too rapidly will produce no stars at all and thus no planets and, of course, no stable orbits.

The simple fact is this: humans do observe that galaxies, stars, and planets exist, and that they exist with adequate stability to allow humans to exist and observe them. This fact, in itself, argues for the big bang. In fact, it argues for a specific subset of big bang models.

Mounting Evidences

These twentieth-century evidences for a big bang creation event are impressive enough by themselves. The dawn of the twenty-first century brings even more spectacular evidences to an already overwhelming vindication of the Bible's doctrine of cosmic creation. Such evidences are the subject of the next chapter.

CHAPTER FIVE

TWENTY-FIRST CENTURY DISCOVERIES

The journal *Science* gave "the discovery of the cosmological constant" the "breakthrough of the year" award for 1998.[1] It turns out the announcement was premature. Not until April of 2000 did it become clear that such a constant must exist.

That the cosmological constant qualifies as the breakthrough of the year, if not the decade or the century, arises from its implication that the big bang is the most exquisitely designed entity known to man. In the words of physicist Lawrence Krauss, a self-described atheist, the cosmological constant "would involve the most extreme fine-tuning problem known in physics."[2]

What Is the Cosmological Constant?

When Albert Einstein first proposed his theory of general relativity he immediately noted that it predicted that the universe was expanding from a beginning, from an infinitesimal volume. This flatly contradicted the reigning cosmological model of his day. That model proposed an infinitely old universe held in a static state throughout infinite time.

There were several philosophical biases expressed in this infinitely old, static universe. One was to give the mechanisms of natural evolution ideal chemistry for infinite time so that God need not be invoked to explain life.[3]

To save the static universe model, Einstein introduced ad hoc into his general relativity equations a cosmological constant to perfectly cancel off the effects of gravity everywhere in the universe.[4] When astronomers proved that the universe indeed was and is expanding from a cosmic beginning, Einstein rejected his proposed cosmological constant calling it "the greatest blunder of his scientific career."[5]

Now, more than 60 years later astronomers have resurrected Einstein's constant from oblivion. However, the value they are attaching to it is very different and their rationale for it likewise very different.

What exactly is this cosmological constant? It is best described as a self-stretching property of the space-time fabric of the universe. The constant would imply that space, independent of matter and independent of any heat or light, stretches itself. Moreover, the larger the space-time envelope of the universe grows, the more stretching energy that it gains. It is this gaining of stretching energy that causes some science writers to refer to the cosmological constant as an anti-gravity factor. The effect of the cosmological constant on the space-time envelope of the universe is to make two massive bodies appear to repel one another. Moreover, the farther apart two bodies are from one another the more strongly they will appear to repel one another. It is this outcome of the cosmological constant that prompted Stephen Hawking to joke that the cosmological constant is repulsive in both senses of the word.

In contrast, gravity acts as a brake on cosmic expansion. In junior high physics classes we all learned that, according to the law of gravity, two massive bodies attract one another and that the closer two massive bodies are to one another the more strongly they will attract. Since the universe contains a lot of mass, gravity works to pull the massive bodies together and thereby slows down cosmic expansion.

When the universe is young and, therefore, more compact, gravity's effect on cosmic dynamics would be powerful while a cosmological constant's would be weak. However, when the universe is old and, therefore, more spread out, a cosmological constant's effect would be strong while gravity's would be weak. Thus, if gravity alone influences cosmic dynamics, astronomers will observe that throughout cosmic history the expansion of the universe slows down. The slowing down effect will be seen to get progressively weaker as the universe ages. However, if both gravity and a positive cosmological constant are operable, astronomers will see cosmic expansion transition from slowing down to speeding up.

The Discovery

The yardstick of choice for measuring cosmic expansion throughout the past history of the universe are type Ia supernovae (see box, "Type Ia Supernovae," on page 49). Type Ia supernovae are very bright and thus can be seen at great distances that correspond to when the universe was billions of years younger than it is now.

All type Ia supernovae have the identical brightness. So, astronomers, by comparing the light they actually see from different type Ia supernovae, can determine how far away each type Ia supernova is from us. The spectral lines astronomers measure in the light from a particular supernova tell them how fast that supernova is moving away from us (see box, "Redshift Velocities," on page 49). Thus, with measurements on dozens of type Ia supernovae of widely differing brightnesses astronomers can determine the universe's expansion rate over a broad range of look-back times. (The look-back time is how much time it takes light to travel from the supernova to us.)

The results from a supernova research team led by Adam Riess[6] prompted the 1998 breakthrough of the year award. However, no attempt was made in their analysis to take into account the clumpy character of the universe (the observation that matter in the universe is clumped into galaxies, stars, and dark matter of various forms). As noted by cosmologists six decades ago, any departure from a perfectly uniform universe (smooth matter distribution) will result in a slightly faster expansion rate.[7] Therefore, before one can claim the discovery of a cosmological constant, one must separate the faster expansion due to cosmic clumping from that due to a cosmological constant.

A second team of thirty-one astronomers cooperating in what is called The Supernova Cosmology Project published results in the June 1, 1999 issue of the *Astrophysical Journal*.[8] With forty-two type Ia supernovae in their data bank they were able to consider the effect of small-scale clumping of matter. They demonstrated that for all realistic models of cosmic clumping a cosmological constant must exist. Also, the uncertainties in their measurements were much less than that of the previous attempt. Given that type Ia supernovae are reliable distance indicators, there was no little basis for doubting the existence of a cosmological constant.

A possible hitch in the reliability of type Ia supernovae as distance indicators was raised just days after the second team published their paper. Three astronomers from the University of California, Berkeley and one from Mount Stromlo Observatory in Australia noted that for ten nearby type Ia eruptions the time it took for the explosions to reach their peak brightness was about two days longer than for type Ia supernova at much greater distances.[9] During the next eight months similar concerns and concerns about the effects of intergalactic dust and other environmental differences for distant supernovae were raised by five other research teams.[10] By mid 2000, however, these concerns were largely allayed by astronomers at Lawrence Berkeley National Laboratory and the Space Telescope Science Institute, who demonstrated that the small discrepancies between distant and nearby type Ia supernovae made no significant difference in the reliability of type Ia supernovae as distance indicators.[11]

What the type Ia supernova observations demonstrated is that the universe's rate of expansion was slowing down for the first 8 or 9 billion years of its history and speeding up for the last 6 or 7 billion years. The latest data were precise enough to yield, as well, the best measurements to date on the age of the universe (14.5 or 14.9 billion years depending on the method of calculation)[12] and the cosmic mass density (0.28 of what would be necessary to halt the expansion of the universe).[13]

Remarkably, in the same issue of the *Astrophysical Journal* in which The Supernova Cosmology Project's paper appeared were other papers which independently confirmed both of the SCP group's measurements on the age and mass density of the universe.[14] Three additional papers in recent issues of the *Astronomical* and *Astrophysical* journals give the most accurate measurements to date on the ages of the oldest stars in our galaxy, in the supergiant galaxy M87, and in the Fornax dwarf galaxy. These ages are all at slightly more than 13 billion years.[15] As such, they resolve the widely publicized problem when, in 1995, certain measurements of cosmic expansion rates appeared to make the universe about a billion years younger than the oldest stars.[16]

A Canadian team of astronomers lead by Richard Richer has recently produced evidence that the population of white dwarf stars in the halo of our galaxy is much larger than what had previously been presumed.[17] This would imply that the universe cannot be younger than 14.5 billion years.[18] This, in turn, means that a cosmological constant approximating the value determined by The Supernova Cosmology Project must exist.

TYPE IA SUPERNOVAE

A supernova is the catastrophic explosion that occurs at the end point of stellar burning for very massive stars. At the brightest part of its explosion a supernova will outshine a galaxy of a hundred billion stars.

The more massive the exploding star, the brighter the explosion. A star will not become a supernova unless its mass at the end of its burning cycle exceeds 1.4 solar masses.

A type Ia supernova is a burnt out star (called a white dwarf) whose mass lies just below the 1.4 solar mass limit that gains mass by accretion from a companion star (its gravity is strong enough to tear mass away from its companion). When the mass of the white dwarf reaches the 1.4 solar mass limit it becomes a supernova. Because all type Ia supernovae have the same mass, they all manifest the same peak brightness. Therefore, they are good indicators of distance.

REDSHIFT VELOCITIES

The lines that astronomers see in a star's spectrum indicate the wavelengths at which certain elements and compounds in the star are either emitting or absorbing light. If the star is moving toward us, the wave crests become bunched together and thus appear to us at shorter wavelengths. If the star is moving away from us, the wave crests become stretched out and thus appear to us at longer wavelengths. By measuring the amount by which a star's spectral lines are shifted toward longer (that is, redder) wavelengths, astronomers can determine the velocity at which that star is moving away from us.

Figure 5.1:
The Sky Over Mt. Erebus?
If a 35-mm camera could detect microwave light, this would be the view from the Boomerang launch site in Antarctica.

The shaded splashes show temperature fluctuations in the cosmic microwave background radiation from the cosmic creation event (two images combined for illustration).

Flat-Out Confirmed

At an April 25, 2000 news conference, NASA announced the eagerly awaited results of the "Boomerang" experiment. Using high altitude balloons sent up from Antarctica, where the cold, dry, thin, stable air permits the most accurate measurements, NASA researchers gathered sufficient data to determine that the universe's geometry is very nearly flat. Details appeared in the April 27 issue of *Nature*[19] and some spectacular graphics and video clips were featured on the web site of one of the researchers.[20] The bottom line of this highly technical, hard-to-explain discovery is this: the shortest distance a beam of light can travel between two distant galaxies is a straight (or nearly straight) line, rather than a curved line. The universe, though four-dimensional, is flat in that the four-dimensional system lacks curvature.

This discovery of a flat or nearly flat universe yielded three important affirmations of the biblical creation account. First, it confirmed a prediction astronomers made about the cosmic background radiation, a prediction arising from the current best model for the origin of the universe, a model perfectly aligned with biblical cosmology. Second, in combination with the measurements of the mass density of the universe, it established a value for the cosmological constant. This value, in turn, established more powerfully than ever the high degree of design and fine-tuning the universe required in its moment of origin. Third, it revealed that we humans have the "good fortune" to exist at the one moment in cosmic history when the universe is most completely and clearly detectable.

Shortly after the Cosmic Background Explorer (COBE) satellite established the existence of temperature fluctuations in the cosmic background radiation, astrophysicists predicted a pattern for these fluctuations that a transcendent cosmic creation leading to the possibility of physical life would produce. Researchers showed that the amplitude of the temperature differences in the cosmic background radiation would show up in a particular pattern, a bell curve pattern, determined by the "slice of space" studied—*and* depending on the geometry of the universe. Here is a word sketch of the details (see graph on page 53 for clarification):

A telescope with the capacity to distinguish temperature details ten "moon diameters" apart would detect less temperature variation than would a telescope capable of seeing temperature details just one "moon diameter" apart. But, that's roughly where the curve should turn around. A temperature variation peak at one, two, or three moon diameters resolution is what we would expect from a hot big bang creation event. Thus, a telescope capable of measuring details in a smaller sky segment, say a tenth of a moon diameter across, should detect less temperature variation than would the one-moon-diameter detector.

The predicted pattern is precisely what many independent research groups have observed.[21] In particular, the Boomerang measurements were made at so many different angular resolutions and with such precision that the team has been able to make, for the first time ever, an accurate determination of the geometry of the universe. This breakthrough caused quite a stir in the media.

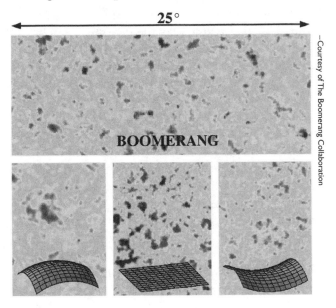

Figure 5.2: Simple Geometry
Cosmological simulations predict that if the universe has a flat geometry (in which standard high school geometry applies), the greatest differences between "hot spots" and "cold spots" will be observed when the telescope is tuned to 1 degree of angular resolution (bottom center). If, on the other hand, the geometry of space is curved, the greatest temperature differences will appear at angular resolutions either much larger or smaller than 1 degree (bottom left and right). Comparison with the Boomerang image (top) indicates that space is very nearly flat.

Why the Excitement Over "Flatness"?

Few news reporters have been able to explain for lay readers the scientific significance of the Boomerang findings—only that they *are* significant. Fewer still, perhaps, are those who grasp the theological significance. In a nutshell, the findings answer questions about what the universe contains and how it develops over time. These answers, in turn, magnify the accuracy of biblical cosmology and the necessity of the biblical Creator.

Research through the past decade had already yielded a relatively precise measure of the mass density of the universe. That measure took into account both ordinary matter (matter that strongly interacts with radiation—for example, protons, neutrons, and electrons) and exotic matter (matter that very weakly interacts with radiation—for example, neutrinos), and the total fell short—by some 67 to 85%—of the mass density that would give the universe a flat geometry.[22]

The Boomerang results showed that the total density of the universe—mass density plus another type of density called "space energy" density, also known as the cosmological constant—add up to a value somewhere between 88 and 112% of what would be necessary for a flat geometry cosmos. Another high altitude balloon experiment performed over Texas determined a value for the space energy density term between 85 and 125% of cosmic flatness.[23] From these numbers we know the possible range of variation from perfect flatness and we know that the space energy component is about 70 to 80% of the total content of the cosmos.

Within three months additional confirmation was achieved. Astronomers measured the velocities of various galaxies over a broad range of distances to determine how much the individual velocities differed from the big bang expansion velocity of the universe.[24] As noted by Jewish astronomers Idit Zehavi and Avishai Dekel, much of the relative differences in velocity only could be attributed to the space energy density, or the cosmological constant. They were able to conclude, roughly, that the space energy density term is about four to five times greater than the mass density term.

The Boomerang findings have propelled this investigation far forward. They provide a measurement so accurate as to remove any reasonable doubt about the existence of a space energy density term. They provide a measurement so accurate as to provide new details about what makes up the cosmos. It shows us that most of the mass of the universe is "exotic" in nature and that, most likely, most of that exotic matter is "cold" (made up of particles that move much more slowly than the speed of light). These new details give us a clearer picture of the characteristics of our cosmic home and, at the same time, add to the body of evidence supporting the biblical creation model.

Establishing that the expansion of the universe is governed by two factors, mass density *and* space energy density, points to an astonishing degree of fine-tuning. In fact, for life to be possible in the universe, that is, to obtain the stars and planets necessary for physical life, the value of the mass density must be fine-tuned to better than one part in 10^{60} and the value of the space energy density to better than one part in 10^{120}. Again, in the words of Lawrence Krauss, this is "the most extreme fine-tuning problem known in physics."[25] Just how extreme is noted in the box, "Extreme Design," on page 54.

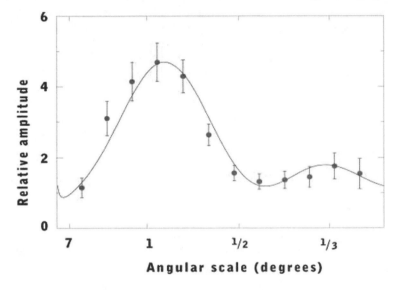

Figure 5.3: Just As Predicted
The points on this graph indicate the temperature differences between the "hot spots" and "cold spots" that dominate the Boomerang images. The line shows the curve predicted by the model for a geometrically flat, hot big bang universe. Given the close fit between the data points and the predicted curve, the model's accuracy is affirmed.

Looking Ahead
If the hot big bang creation model where cold dark exotic matter is the dominant form of matter is correct, we can anticipate that ongoing measurements of the temperature differences in the cosmic background radiation will reveal not just one well-defined peak in the amplitude of those differences but several. Two experiments have already been scheduled. One is simply a more advanced version of

the Boomerang study, and it should produce results as early as 2003. The other, which promises yet another breakthrough in precision, is a NASA satellite scheduled for launch in 2007 with the first results due as early as 2008.

EXTREME DESIGN

Theologically, the space energy density demonstrates that for physical life to be possible at any time or place in the history of the universe the value of the mass density of the universe must be fine-tuned to within one part in 10^{60}, and the value of the cosmological constant must be fine-tuned to within one part in 10^{120}.[26] To put this in perspective, the best example of human engineering design that I am aware of is a gravity wave telescope capable of making measurements to within one part in 10^{23}. This implies that the Creator at a minimum is ten trillion trillion trillion trillion trillion trillion trillion trillion times more intelligent, knowledgeable, creative, and powerful than we humans.

To word it another way, before this discovery the most profound design evidence scientists had uncovered in the cosmos was a characteristic that had to be fine-tuned to within one part in 10^{40}. Thanks to this twenty-first century discovery, the evidence that God created and designed the universe for the benefit of life and human beings in particular has become 10^{80} times stronger (a hundred million trillion trillion trillion trillion trillion trillion trillion times stronger).

Given how spectacularly research on the cosmic background radiation has confirmed the hot big bang creation model, not to mention all the other confirmations of that model (see Appendix "Summary of Scientific Evidences for a Big Bang Creation Event" on page 221), astrophysicists eagerly anticipate the success of these experiments. Some hints of a second amplitude peak, for example, have already been observed.[27] What fuels their excitement is the possibility that we will soon be able to make very precise determinations of
- the age of the universe
- the universe's expansion rate at various epochs since creation
- the mass density of the universe
- the space energy density of the universe
- how much of the various forms of ordinary and exotic matter exist, and
- whether or not the universe manifests a "quintessence" property.

Such an accurate and detailed picture of cosmic creation holds powerful potential to promote a Christian worldview amid a secularist society, most importantly to encourage personal faith in Jesus Christ. It may also help in settling creation disputes within the Christian community. We need not wait for these new advances, however. The information already at hand can make a mighty impact!

Facing a New Challenge

Quintessence is the term some physicists have attached to a hypothesized phenomenon that would reduce, they suggest, the necessity of extreme design inherent in the cosmic density terms. Non-theistic astronomers' disdain for the implications of those measurements becomes evident in abstracts of their most recent research papers. Astronomers Idit Zehavi and Avishai Dekel write, "This type of universe . . . requires a degree of fine tuning in the initial conditions that is in apparent conflict with 'common wisdom.'"[28] Physicist N. Straumann says, "We are . . . confronted with a disturbing cosmic coincidence problem."[29]

Quintessence, they hope, may offer an escape—or will it? If quintessence represents a variation over time in the term describing the pressure of the universe divided by the term describing its density, *and* if one carefully chooses the initial value of this pressure-to-density ratio, *and* if one sets its rate of variation to a specific value, *then* perhaps a significant amount of the apparent design in the cosmic density terms could be removed.

To date no evidence for quintessence exists. However, we know the universe contains exotic matter. If the right kind of exotic mass particles exist, and if they exist in the just right abundance with the just right distribution, then the desired quintessence would become possible.

At this point most readers will have figured out that this appeal to quintessence is simply a design trade-off. Design eliminated from the cosmic density terms would be replaced, at least in part, by new design in the pressure-to-density ratio or in the kind, amount, and distribution of exotic mass particles. As one group of astronomers has pointed out, the discovery of quintessence could actually confront non-theists with even more evidence for design than it would eliminate.[30]

Human limitations will always hinder our assessment of cosmic design. Researchers will either underestimate or overestimate the true level of design in any given characteristic. Sometimes they will see it where it is not manifest; sometimes they will overlook it where it is. However, the more we learn about the universe, the more indications of design we discover (see chapters 14 "A 'Just Right' Universe," and 16 "Earth: The Place for Life"). The more we learn about the universe, the more accurate our estimates of the level of design in its characteristics. The strength of the case for the God of the Bible can be judged by the direction of the trend line. Through the years, as we learn more and more about the universe, the longer—not shorter—grows the list of features that reflect fine-tuning *and* the more exquisite that fine-tuning appears.

A Precise Moment in Time

In a recent *Astrophysical Journal* article, Lawrence Krauss and Glenn Starkman together lament the future of astronomy.[31] Why the despair? The value of the space energy density tells us that from now on the universe will expand faster and faster. This accelerating expansion implies that more and more objects in the universe will eventually disappear from our view. Distant objects currently observable will be moving away from us at velocities exceeding the velocity of light. Thus, they will be beyond the theoretical limits of any existing *or possible* telescopes. Astronomers will have less and less of the universe to look at and enjoy.

Contemplation of this fact gives Christians a sense of wonder, not despair. It shows that God created humanity at the precise moment in history and enabled us to develop the necessary standard of living and technology when we would have the optimal view of the extent and splendor of His creation. If we had arrived earlier in cosmic history, we would see less since the age of the universe limits both the distance out to which we can see and the numbers and kinds of objects that would have formed in the universe. If we had arrived later, we would see less because of the accelerating expansion of the universe.

Now is the best possible time to be an astronomer. *Now* "the heavens declare [more loudly than ever] the glory of God." (We also are at the best possible location. See chapter 14.) We have hope, not despair. God, the Creator, has written that as soon as He completes the conquest of evil, He will replace this awesome universe with one even more glorious, far beyond our capacity to think or imagine.[32]

Helium Abundance Matches Big Bang Prediction

While the discoveries of the cosmological constant (space energy density term) and a nearly flat geometry for the universe easily rank as the most dramatic cosmic discoveries of the dawn of the twenty-first century, they are by no means the only new evidences for a big bang creation event. The big bang theory says that most of the helium in the universe formed very soon after the creation event. According to the big bang, the universe was infinitely or nearly infinitely hot at the creation moment. As the cosmos expanded, it cooled, much like the combustion chamber in a piston engine.

By the time the universe was one millisecond old it had settled down into a sea of protons and neutrons. The only element in existence at that time was simple hydrogen, described by a single proton. For about twenty seconds, when the universe was a little less than four minutes old, it reached the right temperature for nuclear fusion to occur. During that time, protons and neutrons fused together to form elements heavier than simple hydrogen.

According to the theory, almost exactly one-fourth of the universe's hydrogen, by mass, was converted into helium during that twenty-second period. Except for tiny amounts of lithium, beryllium, boron, and deuterium (which is hydrogen with both a proton and a neutron in its nucleus), all other elements that exist in the universe were produced much later, along with a little extra helium, in the nuclear furnaces at the cores of stars.

One of the ways astronomers can test the big bang theory is to measure the amount of helium in objects that are so far away (and, hence, are being viewed so far back in time) that they predate significant stellar burning. A second way is to examine objects in which little stellar burning has ever occurred. That is, astronomers can find and make measurements on relatively nearby objects in which star formation shut down quickly, too quickly to contribute significantly to the total helium abundance.

In 1994 astronomers measured for the first time the abundance of helium in very distant intergalactic gas clouds.[33] These measurements, confirmed by additional measurements,[34] revealed the presence of helium in the quantity predicted by the big bang model.

In the last 1999 issue of the *Astrophysical Journal*, a team of American and Ukrainian astronomers published yet another proof for the hot big bang creation event.[35] The six researchers used the Multiple Mirror and Keck telescopes to check the quantity of helium in two of the most heavy-element-deficient galaxies known (blue compact galaxies I Zwicky 18 and SBS 0335-052). They determined that helium comprised 0.2462 ± 0.0015 of the total mass of those galaxies. After subtracting the tiny amount of star-produced helium in the two galaxies, they derived a primordial helium abundance of 0.2452 ± 0.0015, consistent with the findings in distant, ancient objects. This value is so close to the big bang prediction that the team concluded it "strongly supports the standard big bang nucleosynthesis theory."[36]

During the months since that publication was released, Canadian astronomers have refined the data of the American-Ukrainian team.[37] Their correction (based on the elimination of data from hot-star-excited nebulae within the galaxies) yielded a primordial helium abundance 1.5% higher and 20% more accurate than the first set of figures. The new value (0.2489) is so very close to the theoretically expected value as to be indistinguishable.[38]

As an added bonus, the data that led to the calculation of the primordial helium abundance yielded a determination of the number of "species" of light neutrinos (that is, low mass neutrinos) = 3.00 ± 0.15.[39] This number supports yet another new evidence for the big bang creation event described later in this chapter (see "Neutrino Mass," on page 64).

Deuterium and Lithium Abundances
Whatever quantity of deuterium (heavy hydrogen) and lithium exists today was produced during the first four minutes of creation, the big bang theory tells us. Not all that deuterium and lithium remains, however, for stellar burning gobbles up those elements, rather than producing more.

In seeking to measure the abundance of deuterium and lithium and to compare that amount with the amount predicted by the big bang model, astronomers focused again on extremely distant systems, also on nearer systems in which little stellar burning has occurred.

With significant help from the Keck telescopes[40] and from the "Hubble Deep Field" image (a "picture" assembled from layers upon layers of Hubble Space Telescope exposures to the same part of the sky),[41] seven different teams produced measurements.[42] In their words, the deuterium and lithium abundances fit the big bang predictions "extremely well."[43]

Density of Protons and Neutrons

The big bang theory fails to produce the stars and planets necessary for life and the elements necessary for life unless the cosmic density of baryons (protons and neutrons) takes on a specific value. This value is about 4 or 5% of the maximum mass density that would still permit the universe to continue expanding forever, what astronomers call the critical density. Therefore, an obvious test of the big bang would be to see if the baryon density is close to this 4 to 5% of the critical density.

Until recently, the determination of primordial helium, deuterium, or lithium abundances was the only reliable way to get a measure of the density of baryons in the universe. The best results came from the seven teams mentioned in the two sections above. They determined that the cosmic baryon density is equal to 0.04 to 0.05 of the critical density.

During the last year astronomers have developed three new and independent methods for measuring the cosmic baryon density. The most spectacular and accurate of these three new methods comes from the Boomerang maps of the temperature fluctuations in the cosmic background radiation. From the North American test flight of the Boomerang balloon the cosmic baryon density was measured at 0.05 of the critical density.[44] The other two methods gave an average value of roughly 0.03.[45] These independent confirmations of the cosmic baryon density deduced from primordial helium, deuterium, and lithium abundances give yet more evidence for a big bang creation event.

Cosmic Expansion Velocity Matches Big Bang Prediction

An obvious way to test the big bang is to affirm that the universe is indeed expanding from an infinitesimal volume and to measure the rate of its expansion from the beginning up to the present moment. While this task may seem simple in principle, in practice it is not. Measurements of adequate precision are enormously difficult to make. Only in the last few years have measurements as accurate (or nearly so) as the other big bang proofs become possible.

Five methods (some independent, some slightly dependent) for measuring the cosmic expansion rate have now been developed and applied (see table 5.1). The average of the five yields a rate of 64 kilometers per second per megaparsec (a megaparsec = the distance light travels in 3.26 million years). Running the expansion backward at this rate implies that the universe is approximately 14.6 billion years old.

The newly discovered space energy density term adds another half billion years, suggesting that the universe is about 15.1 billion years old. This figure serves as a confirmation of the model because of its consistency with other age indicators, including the cosmic background radiation, the abundance of various radiometric elements,[46] and the measured ages of the oldest stars (see below).

Table 5.1: Latest Measurements of the Cosmic Expansion Rate
Astronomers have developed and refined five measuring tools for determining the rate of expansion for the universe, or what they call the "Hubble Constant." A megaparsec = the distance light travels in 3.26 million years.

Method	Hubble Constant Value
gravitational lensing	66 km/sec/megaparsec[47]
Tully-Fisher	61 km/sec/megaparsec[48]
cepheid distances to galaxies	62 km/sec/megaparsec[49]
type Ia supernovae	61 km/sec/megaparsec[50]
geometric distance measures	69 km/sec/megaparsec[51]
average of measured values	64 km/sec/megaparsec
age calculation based on average of values	14.6 billion years
correction for energy density term	+0.5 billion years
corrected age calculation	15.1 billion years

Star Populations Fit Big Bang

Big bang theory proposes that three distinct generations of stars formed at certain intervals after the creation event. Astronomers creatively refer to these generations as Population III, Population II, and Population I stars. The numbering system seems reversed, since Population III stars are the oldest, but the latter were the last to be discovered and studied; hence, the confusing numbering system.

According to the big bang, Population III stars formed when the universe was barely a half billion years old. By that time, matter had condensed adequately for stars to begin coalescing. However, since the universe had expanded so little as yet, the average density of gases was much higher than today's observed density. Thus, nearly all of the earliest stars were supergiant stars.[52] Such stars burn up very quickly (astronomically speaking), in less than 10 million years. They end with catastrophic explosions, dispersing their ashes throughout the cosmos.

Given the brief burning time and early formation of such stars, big bang theorists conclude that few, if any, Population III stars should still be observable. However, their remains should be. Population III stars leave a distinctive signature of elements in their scattered ashes. This signature is found in all the distant gas clouds of the universe.

Recently, there has emerged evidence that some of the rare low-mass Population III stars may have been found.[53] Their low mass means that they can burn long enough for astronomers to be able to find them today. They have been difficult to detect, though, because they absorb the ashes of the giant Population IIIs, thus taking on a disguise. Recently, however, stellar physicists have developed tools for distinguishing Population III survivors from the younger Population II stars that form from the ashes of Population III supergiants.[54]

The big bang theory makes three major predictions about Population II stars: (1) this group should be the largest of the star populations, given that it formed when galaxies were young and at their peak star-forming efficiency; (2) they should be more numerous in certain locations, such as globular clusters, where early star formation proceeds most efficiently, and (3) they should come in all sizes, all mass categories from low to high, not favoring one category over another. All three predictions are borne out by astronomers' observations over the last few decades.

The third generation of stars, the Population I stars (including Earth's sun), formed from the scattered ashes of the largest Population II stars. These ashes are easy to distinguish from Population III ashes because they are at least 50% richer in heavy elements (those heavier than helium). The gaseous nebulae (or gas clouds) scattered throughout the spiral arms of the Milky Way and the gas streams the Milky Way galaxy steals from nearby dwarf galaxies are actually "ash heaps" of giant Population II stars.

The big bang theory says that star formation shut down for the most part shortly after the formation of Population II stars. Thus, most galaxies are devoid, or nearly devoid, of Population I stars. The big bang also says that in the few galaxies where Population I stars do form, the most intense period of star formation was the past few billion years, and the most intense regions of star formation are the densest areas, such as the nuclei and spiral arms. (Some also would have formed in what astronomers call "irregular" galaxies.) All these characteristics have proved true, confirmed by observations.

Does the big bang allow for Population IV stars to form in the future? Yes, it does. But, it predicts that this population should be tiny compared to the other three. Everywhere astronomers look in the universe, they see signs that star formation will soon shut down totally, even in those galaxies still active in forming stars. ("Soon" to an astronomer is not tomorrow or next year but a few billion years hence.) Astronomers anticipate, for example, that the Milky Way galaxy will experience a "brief" burst of star formation when it pulls the Large Magellanic Cloud (its companion galaxy) into its core region some 4 or 5 billion years from now. Already the universe is old enough to make such incidents rare.

Oldest Stars Tell Their Story

Since the big bang theory indicates when the Population II stars formed—the era when galaxies began to take shape, roughly .5 billion to 1.5 billion years after the creation event—astronomers can test the theory by determining the age of the oldest visible stars. By adding .5 to 1.5 billion years to that age, they can compare the sum with the creation dates suggested by other independent measures.

One difficulty of this seemingly simple test is that stars, like some people, sometimes hide their age well. Stars in dense clusters, however, can be more easily dated than others, and globular clusters appear to comprise the oldest of the Population II stars. Table 5.2 lists the most accurate dating of globular cluster stars in five different galaxies. It also includes the limit researchers recently placed on the oldest white dwarf stars in Earth's galaxy.

Table 5.2: Latest Measurements of the Oldest Population II Stars

Star Group	Measured Ages (billions of years)
average of all globular clusters in our galaxy	12.9 ± 1.5[55]
47 Tucanae (oldest globular cluster in our galaxy)	14.1 ± 1.0[56]
Large Magellanic Cloud globulars	same as for Milky Way[57]
globular cluster in WLM dwarf galaxy	14.8 ± 0.06[58]
globular clusters in Fornax dwarf galaxy	same as for Milky Way[59]
average of all globulars in our galaxy	less than 14.0[60]
oldest white dwarfs in our galaxy	more than 12.6[61]
average of all globulars in M87 (a supergiant galaxy)	13.0[62]
average of all results = 13.5 billion years	

The numbers indicate that globular clusters formed within a 2- to 3-billion-year time window, roughly consistent from galaxy to galaxy. If one adds to their ages the years prior to Population II star formation (1 billion ± 0.5 billion years), the derived age fits remarkably well all other methods for determining how long the universe has been expanding from the creation event.

Exotic Matter Measurements

As noted already, the mass density of the universe has two components: (1) ordinary matter, that is, matter that strongly interacts with radiation—for example, protons, neutrons, and electrons and (2) exotic matter, that is, matter that very weakly interacts with radiation—for example, neutrinos. Because of its strong interaction with radiation, astronomers have a relatively easy time detecting and measuring the amount of ordinary matter in the universe (see "Density of Protons and Neutrons" on page 59). An exotic matter particle like the neutrino, however, can travel through 600 trillion miles of liquid water without any interaction. But, all matter, whether ordinary or exotic, exerts a gravitational pull. Therefore, astronomers measure gravitational disturbances throughout the universe to determine the total amount of matter in the universe. Subtracting the measured amount of ordinary matter from the total amount of matter reveals the amount of exotic matter.

As I described in the second edition of this book, astronomers developed eight different methods during the 1990s to measure the total amount of cosmic matter.[63] While all of these methods produced consistent results, the most reliable proved to be gravitational lensing, cosmic expansion rate measures, detection of diffuse hot intergalactic gas, and determinations of the onset of star and galaxy formation in the history of the cosmos. From the nine best measurements based on these methods astronomers have determined that the total amount of matter in the universe adds up to about 29% of the critical density (the maximum mass density that would still permit the universe to expand forever).[64]

To this determination a new method has been added. At the June 2000 meeting of the American Astronomical Society, a large team of American, Australian, and British astronomers announced that they had successfully measured the redshifts (see box "Redshift Velocities," on page 49) of 106,585 galaxies located in a two-degree field (a piece of the sky about four moon diameters wide).[65] Each redshift had two components: one due to the universe's expansion and a second much smaller component arising from the galaxy's individual motion that results from the gravitational tugs it experiences from neighboring galaxies. A straightforward statistical analysis of these individual galaxy motions establishes the total mass density of the universe. The matter density value that comes out of the team's analysis is one-third of the critical density.[65] This value agrees, within the measuring errors, with the previous mass density measurements. It also agrees with an analysis of the relative velocities of galaxy pairs in the Mark III survey[66] and with the results from detailed simulations for the formation and clustering of galaxies.[67]

The good news is that the Two Degree Field Survey is just the beginning. By the end of 2001 the same team will have measured 250,000 galaxies. Come 2004, the Sloan Digital Sky Survey will complete redshift measures on a million other galaxies. Then, astronomers will get their wish—a truly accurate cosmic mass density measurement.

The currently available mass density measurements, nonetheless, leave little doubt that most of the matter in the universe is exotic. The ratio of exotic matter compared to ordinary matter is roughly five to one. This ratio is just what is needed in a big bang scenario to explain the observed characteristics and populations of the stars and galaxies.

Neutrino Mass

For astronomers the icing on the cake of their exotic mass density measurements would be to actually detect some specific exotic mass particles. For over a decade physicists have noted that probably the easiest candidate would be neutrinos. Here, detecting neutrinos is not the problem. Physicists have been detecting them since 1956. The challenge is to prove that neutrinos have mass and, if possible, to accurately measure the mass of the neutrino.

From a 1997 physics conference in Italy came the news that different research groups independently detected neutrino mass. To be more precise, they observed neutrinos oscillating, that is, spontaneously switching from one flavor to another.[68] (Neutrinos come in three different varieties or flavors, namely, electron, muon, and tau.)

Oscillation means mass. Neutrinos can oscillate only if they have mass.

The case for neutrino mass was made more compelling because two radically different types of detectors came up with the same result. One was a 50,000-ton water tank surrounded by 13,400 photo detectors. The other was a thousand tons of corrugated iron interspersed with charged particle detectors.[69] Additional evidence came in 1998 when the group using the 50,000-ton water tank confirmed neutrino oscillation from two sources: solar neutrinos[70] and neutrinos in the earth's atmosphere.[71]

Confirming the results from the two different oscillation experiments is what is called the "missing solar neutrinos" problem. Solar physicists now can understand why their neutrino detectors have found only a third of the neutrinos that they calculate the sun's nuclear furnace must produce. Their detectors are tuned to pick up just one flavor of neutrino. The "missing" neutrinos apparently were missed when they oscillated. The neutrino "deficit" is no deficit at all.

Neutrino oscillations only tell us that neutrinos have mass, not how much mass. But, they do establish the lower limit of that mass—at least a few billionths the mass of an electron, and potentially they can reveal the differences in mass among the three neutrino flavors.

Several research labs are attempting to make direct measurements of neutrino mass, using something called "neutrinoless double beta decay" experiments. In 1997 a Russian-German collaboration determined that the neutrino mass can be no greater than 0.48 electron volts (that's slightly less than a millionth of an electron mass).[72]

The difference between the lower and upper limits on the neutrino mass is nearly a factor of a thousand times. Fortunately, a new experiment was devised in 1999 that holds the promise of an accurate measure of the neutrino mass. It is a beta decay experiment based on the emission spectrum of the element rhenium. An Italian research team showed that there is enough detail in the rhenium beta decay emission spectrum to measure the neutrino mass.[73] Within a year or two of the publication of this book a reasonably precise determination of the neutrino mass should be available.

Even the presently available neutrino mass limits, however, have cosmological significance. Neutrinos are copiously produced in both the big bang creation event and in stellar burning. The big bang by itself generates about ten billion neutrinos for every baryon (proton or neutron) that exists in the universe. Thus, neutrinos add up to at least 0.05 to 5% of the critical density.

The bottom line, then, is that not only have astronomers shown that exotic matter exists in the cosmos, they also have identified a particle that contributes a small fraction of that exotic matter. And, a small fraction contribution is consistent with the best available cosmological models. Those models predict that most of the exotic matter should be "cold" and only a small fraction "warm" or "hot." Hot exotic matter is made up of particles traveling at velocities close to that of light. Such particles typically have masses far below that of a proton. Cold exotic mass particles are particles moving at low velocities. Typically, their masses are much above that of a proton. As such, they are much more difficult to detect. Nevertheless, experiments are underway with the possibility of finding them.[74]

Table 5.3: Exotic Matter Candidates
These candidates could make up the proportion of the mass of the universe that does not strongly interact with radiation (note: $10^{-5} = .00001$ and $10^6 = 1,000,000$).

Exotic Matter Candidate	Mass Relative to a Proton	Density (number per cm^3)	Velocity Profile
axions, majorons	10^{-4}–10^{-10}	10^9	cold
low mass neutrinos	10^{-8}	100	hot
gravitinos	10^{-6}	10	warm
axinos, mirror particles	10^{-6}	10	warm/cold
photinos, higgsinos, gluinos	10^{-1}	10^{-4}	cold
heavy neutrinos	1	10^{-5}	cold
magnetic monopoles	10^{16}	10^{-21}	cold
newtorites	10^{19}	10^{-24}	cold
maximons and pyrgons	10^{19}	10^{-24}	cold
supersymmetric strings	10^{19}	10^{-24}	cold
quark nuggets	10^{39}	10^{-44}	cold
primordial black holes	10^{40}	10^{-45}	cold

Theological Reaction to Big Bang Cosmology

Though the case for the big bang, that is, a transcendent cosmic creation event, rests on compelling, some might say *overwhelming*, evidence, the theory still has its critics. Some skepticism may be attributable to the communication gap between scientists and the rest of the world. Some of the evidences are so new that most people have yet to hear of them. Some of the evidences, including the older ones, are so technical that few people understand their significance. The need for better education and clearer communication remains. In fact, it motivates the publication of this book.

Communication and education gaps explain only some of the skepticism, however. Spiritual issues are also involved. The few astronomers who still oppose the big bang openly object not on scientific grounds but on personal, theological grounds.

In my first book, *The Fingerprint of God*, I tell the story of astronomers' early reaction to findings that affirmed a cosmic beginning, hence Beginner.[75] Some openly stated their view of the big bang as "philosophically repugnant." For decades they invented one cosmic hypothesis after another in a futile attempt to get around the glaring facts. When all their hypotheses failed the tests of observational checks, many of those astronomers conceded, perhaps reluctantly, the cosmic prize to the big bang.

Today, only a handful of astronomers still hold out against the big bang. Their resistance, however, is based not on what observations and experiments can test but rather on what observations and experiments can never test. Though their articles appear in science journals, they engage in metaphysics rather than in physics, in theology (more accurately, anti-theology) rather than science. These metaphysical gymnastics disguised as science are the subject of chapters 6, 7, 8, 11, and 12. In chapters 9 and 10 I describe powerful new evidences that the CAUSE of the universe transcends matter, energy, and the ten space-time dimensions associated with matter and energy. In chapters 13–17 I look at how new scientific discoveries identify many of the personal attributes of the universe's CAUSE. We will see how the new science reveals not only that a god exists but exactly what kind of God created the universe.

CHAPTER SIX

EINSTEIN'S CHALLENGE

Until Albert Einstein's theory of general relativity came along in the early part of the twentieth century, scientists saw no reason to question the notion that the universe is infinite and everywhere the same. After all, the philosophical and scientific underpinnings of this view had been hammered into place by one of the most influential thinkers of all time, Immanuel Kant (1724–1804).

An Infinite Perspective

Kant reasoned that an Infinite Being could be reflected in nothing less than an infinite universe.[1] How the universe came to be is immaterial and therefore unknowable, according to Kant. He concerned himself with how the universe works. His studies convinced him that everything in the universe could be accounted for by the laws of mechanics described by Sir Isaac Newton (1642–1726). On that assumption, he built the first in a series of mechanistic models for the universe.

Kant extended his reasoning beyond physical science into the realm of biology. He saw that a static (life-favorable conditions persisting indefinitely), infinitely old, and infinitely large universe would allow the possibility of an infinite number of random chances. With an infinite number of building blocks (atoms and molecules) and an infinite number of chances to assemble them in random ways (appropriate physical and chemical conditions existing for infinite time), any kind of final product would be possible—even something as highly complex as a German philosopher.[2] His attempt to construct a model for life's origin was abandoned only when he realized that a scientific understanding of the internal workings of organisms was missing.

Perhaps the major credit for Darwinism and the multitude of *isms* that sprang from it belongs to Immanuel Kant.[3]

THE PARADOX OF THE DARK NIGHT SKY

Why does it get dark when the sun sets? This question is not so trite as it sounds. In the context of an approximately static, infinitely old, and infinitely large universe, the light from all the stars would add up to an infinite brightness.

The brightness of a light source is diminished by four for every doubling of its distance. For example, a light bulb at the center of a one-foot diameter globe will illuminate the globe's surface four times brighter than the same bulb at the center of a two-foot diameter. This is because the two-foot diameter globe has a surface area four times larger than the one-foot diameter globe. So, since Jupiter, for example, is five times more distant from the sun than Earth, the sunlight it receives is twenty-five times dimmer.

Consequently, if stars are evenly spaced from one another, the light received from them on Earth doubles for each doubling of the diameter of space. This is because with each doubling of the distance from Earth, the volume of space, and thus the number stars within that volume, increases eight times, while the light received from the stars, on average twice as distant, decreases by only four times. Hence, if the distance from Earth is doubled indefinitely, to an infinite distance, the accumulated light from all the stars must reach infinite brightness. So the night sky should be infintely luminous.

This conclusion, nevertheless, did not stop proponents of an infinite universe. They claimed clouds of dust between the stars would absorb starlight sufficiently to allow the night sky to be dark even in an infinite universe. They overlooked (until 1960), however, a basic principle of thermodynamics that states, given sufficient time, a body will radiate away as much energy as it receives. Therefore, even that interstellar dust eventually would become as hot as the stars and radiate just as much energy. Thus, the universe in some respect must be finite. (See also discussion in chapter 7, page 78.)

As Far As the Eye Can See

As evidence that what we think about the cosmos matters, no century prior to the nineteenth had seen such dramatic change in people's concepts about life and reality. The view of an infinite cosmos in which these changes were rooted received greater and greater theoretical and observational support. As stronger optics carried astronomers deeper into the heavens, all they could see was more of the same kinds of stars and nebulae (gas clouds) they had already seen up close.

Thousands of stars and a few dozen nebulae became billions of stars and millions of nebulae. It seemed endless. Astronomers and laypeople alike were boggled by the immensity of it all.

Further support for Kant's model of the universe came from the amazing triumph of Newton's laws of motion. As astronomers documented the motions of planets, of satellites orbiting the planets, of comets and asteroids, of binary stars, and of stars in star clusters, everything matched what those laws predicted. Kant's claim that everything about and in the universe could be accounted for by the laws of mechanics was substantially bolstered.

The combination of the astronomers' observations and an apparent answer to the paradox of the dark night sky (see box on page 70) resulted in the elevation of Kant's cosmological model from an hypothesis to a theory. By the end of the nineteenth century it was cast in concrete.

Einstein Discovers Relativity

The concrete began to crack, however, almost before it dried. As physicists made their first accurate measurements of the velocity of light, they were taken by surprise (see figure 6.1, below). A revolution was beginning. Here is what would be deduced: (1) No absolute reference system exists from which motions in space can be measured; and (2) the velocity of light with respect to all observers never varies. The velocities of the observers are irrelevant.

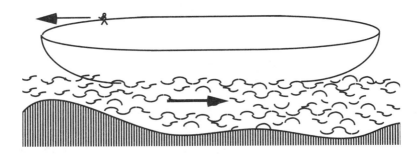

Figure 6.1: The Principle of Invariance
If a ship's captain were jogging around his vessel at 10 mph while the current flowed at 10 mph, the captain would be moving at 20 mph (relative to the ground) when jogging in the direction of the current, and 0 mph when jogging in the opposite direction. This law we have known since the days of Galileo. However, in velocity of light experiments, the motion of the observer proves entirely irrelevent. The velocity of light does not vary with the motion of the observer.

In 1905 a German-born Swiss engineer named Albert Einstein (1879–1955), who studied physics in his spare time, published several papers of enormous significance. Two of them spelled out these conclusions about the constancy of the velocity of light.[4] He called the findings the principle of invariance, but others referred to them as relativity, and that name stuck.

Once this initial theory of relativity (later dubbed "special" since it focused only on velocity) was solidly established,[5] Einstein went to work on the extension of the theory, an effort that demanded every ounce of his genius. The results, published in 1915 and 1916,[6] were the equations of general relativity, equations that carry profound implications about the nature and origin of the universe.

Einstein Discovers the Beginner

For one, these equations show that the universe is simultaneously expanding and decelerating. What phenomenon behaves this way? There is one: an explosion.

When a grenade, for example, is detonated, the pieces of the grenade expand outward from the pin assembly. As they do, they collide with material (air molecules, buildings, furniture, etc.) that slows them down (deceleration). If the universe is the aftermath of an explosion, then there must have been a beginning to the explosion— a moment at which the pin was pulled. By the simple law of cause and effect, it must have had a Beginner—someone to pull the pin.

Einstein's own worldview initially kept him from adopting such a conclusion. Rather, he hypothesized in 1917 a self-stretching property of space that would perfectly cancel out the deceleration and expansion factors[7] (see box "Einstein's Repulsive 'Force,'" page 74). This perfect cancellation would permit the universe to remain in a static state for infinite time.

Einstein's attempted patch job did not hold up, however. Astronomer Edwin Hubble (1889–1953) in 1929 proved from his measurements on forty different galaxies that the galaxies indeed are expanding away from one another. Moreover, he demonstrated that expansion was in the same manner predicted by Einstein's original formulation of general relativity[8] (see figure 6.2, page 73). In the face of this proof, Einstein grudgingly abandoned his hypothesized self-stretching space property and acknowledged "the necessity for a beginning"[9] and "the presence of a superior reasoning power."[10] As noted in chapter 5 (see pages 47-48), however, an international team of astronomers has discovered that Einstein was right about the existence of a self-stretching property of space but quite wrong about the value of the constant governing the self-stretching property. The discovery establishes that the universe always has been expanding and will continue to expand at an ever accelerating rate.

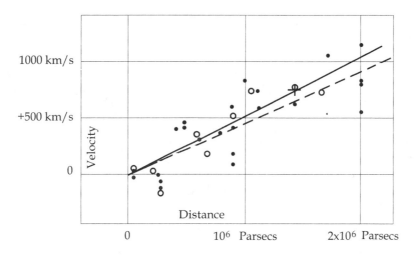

Figure 6.2: Hubble's Original Velocity-Distance Relation[11]
The velocities (kilometers per second) at which several galaxies are moving away from us are plotted against estimated distances. One parsec equals 3.26 light years, where one light year equals 5.9 trillion miles. The cross represents the mean of measurements made on twenty-two other galaxies. All measurements shown here were made before 1929.

As Hubble's plot demonstrates, the more distant the galaxy, the faster it moves away from us. Such a relationship between velocity and distance implies that the entire universe must be experiencing a general expansion.
    —From the Proceedings of the National Academy of Sciences.

Einstein's God

Einstein's "superior reasoning power," however, was not the God of the Bible. Though he confessed to the rabbis and priests who came to congratulate him on his discovery of God that he was convinced God brought the universe into existence and was intelligent and creative, he denied that God was personal.

Of course, those clergy had a stock response to Einstein's denial: How can a Being who is intelligent and creative not also be personal? Einstein brushed past their objection, a valid one, by raising the paradox of God's omnipotence and man's responsibility for his choices:

If this Being is omnipotent, then every occurrence, including every human action, every human thought, and every human feeling and aspiration is also His work; how is it possible to think of holding men responsible for their deeds and thoughts before such an almighty Being? In giving out punishment and rewards He would to a certain extent be passing judgment on Himself. How can this be combined with the goodness and righteousness ascribed to Him?[12]

EINSTEIN'S REPULSIVE "FORCE"

Einstein's equations of general relativity predicted an exploding universe and, hence, the need for a beginning. To avoid the conclusion of a beginning (and thus a Beginner), Einstein suggested, through an added term to his equations, that there might exist the equivalent of an undiscovered force of physics operating everywhere in the universe.

Gravity tells us that two massive bodies will attract one another. It also tells us the strength of the attraction will increase the closer the two bodies approach one another.

Einstein's added term is really a hypothesized self-stretching property of the space dimensions or space fabric of the universe. The larger the universe grows, that is, the more stretched out the space fabric of the universe becomes, the more energy that fabric gains to continue the stretching.

The net effect of Einstein's added term (neglecting the fundamental forces) is that all bodies would appear to repel one another. Moreover, the strength of the apparent repulsion increases the more apart bodies are from one another. Einstein proposed a value for the constant (he labeled it the "cosmological constant") governing the self-stretching property of space so that everywhere and at every time in the universe the self-stretching property would perfectly cancel out the effects of gravity. Thereby, the universe would forever remain dynamically static.

Einstein's cosmological constant was a convenient loophole for him for another reason. Though no astronomer had ever detected the constant's effect, Einstein and others could claim that the reason was the limited distance of our probing out into the cosmos. Today that excuse is gone. Astronomers not only are seeing out to the farthest reaches of the cosmos, they are able to make cosmic expansion measures of unprecedented accuracy.

Recently (see pages 47-48), a large team of astronomers discovered that Einstein was right about the existence of a cosmological constant but quite wrong about its value. Their discovery establishes that the universe always has been expanding and will continue to expand at an ever accelerating rate.

None of the clergy Einstein encountered ever gave him a satisfactory answer to his objection. Typically, they responded by saying that God has not yet revealed the answer. They encouraged him to endure patiently and blindly trust the All-Knowing One.

Regrettably, Einstein lacked the persistence to pursue an answer further. He took for granted the biblical knowledge of these religious professionals and assumed that the Bible failed to adequately address this crucially important issue. Of what value, then, could such a "revelation" be?

Lacking a solution to the paradox of God's predestination and human beings' free choice, Einstein, like many other powerful intellects through the centuries, ruled out the existence of a personal God. Nevertheless, and to his credit, Einstein held unswervingly, against enormous peer pressure, to belief in a Creator.

I am grieved that no one ever offered Einstein the clear, biblical resolution to the paradox he posed. (I offer such a resolution in my book, *Beyond the Cosmos*.[13]) I am also sad that Einstein did not live long enough to see the accumulation of scientific evidence for a personal, caring Creator (see chapters 14 and 16). These might have sparked in him a willingness to reconsider his conclusion.

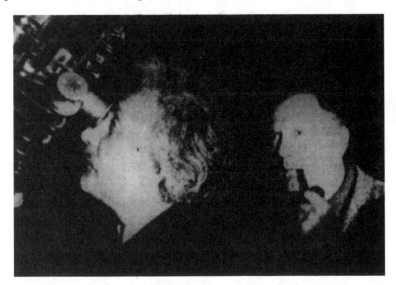

Figure 6.3: Einstein and Hubble
Photo shows (from left) Albert Einstein and Edwin Hubble at the Mount Wilson 100-inch telescope near Pasadena, California, where Hubble made his observations that demonstrated the galaxies are expanding away from one another.
— *Photo courtesy of The Huntington Library.*

CHAPTER SEVEN

CLOSING LOOPHOLES: ROUND ONE

Einstein fought the idea of a beginning, but other researchers fought harder. Why? Consider how much was at stake, how many ideas, theories, and isms had already been built on the foundation of an infinitely old universe. If that foundation was removed and replaced by one with completely different specifications, much or most of what had been built on top of it would come tumbling down or at least require major reconstruction.

Foundational changes of major proportion have occurred in history, but only through time and struggle. The revolution launched by Copernicus (1473–1543), shifting people's concept of reality from an Earth-centered to a sun-centered astronomical system, took well over a century. Some still resist it today. Ironically, the resistance to both Copernicus's and Einstein's work was fueled by fear of what their new view said about God and the Bible. Sixteenth-century scholars feared a loss of respect for both. Twentieth-century scholars feared an increase of respect.

The desire to keep God out of the picture was no hidden agenda but a clearly expressed one. British cosmologist Sir Arthur Eddington (1882–1944) expressed his feelings clearly: "Philosophically, the notion of a beginning of the present order of Nature is repugnant. . . . I should like to find a genuine loophole."[1] "We [must] allow evolution an infinite time to get started."[2]

The battle was on to protect certain belief systems, especially evolutionism (the belief that inorganic material evolves into simple cells and later into advanced life without any input from a divine Being), and to defeat the notion of a beginning, with its obvious implications.

The Hubble Time

Edwin Hubble's research not only confirmed that the universe is expanding but also measured the rate of its expansion. With that measurement (adjusted a little for the slowing down caused by gravity) and a rough estimate of the distance to the farthest-out galaxies, it was no complicated matter to produce a ball-park figure for when the universe began—the Hubble time. It was somewhere in the range of a few billion to several billion years.

HUBBLE TIME AND YOUNG-UNIVERSE CREATIONISM

Ironically, one of the attempted end runs around the Hubble time has been made by a vocal segment of the Christian community. Rather than seeing the Hubble time as a proof for a recent creation event and thus a strike against materialist philosophies, they see it as proof for an ancient cosmos with time enough for strictly natural evolutionary processes to work. Like many people of the nineteenth century, they seem so boggled by the billions of years that they liken such a time frame to infinite time.

This group of creationists insists that a literal reading of the Bible demands a creation date for the cosmos of only some six to ten thousand years ago. They interpret the creation days of Genesis 1 as six consecutive twenty-four-hour periods.

Not all Bible-believing Christians accept this interpretation, however. As many Hebrew scholars point out, a literal reading of Genesis can just as well support six geologic epochs for the creation days. Both a literal and consistent reading of the Bible, an interpretation that integrates all relevant Bible passages, lends ample support for the creation days being long time periods. From this view astronomy and the Bible are not in conflict over the creation date; they agree. Readers interested in more detail about this creation-date controversy from both a biblical and scientific perspective will find it in my book, *Creation and Time* (Colorado Springs, CO: NavPress, 1994).

Whatever illusions certain paleontologists and origin-of-life theorists may have embraced, astronomers recognized that billions of years was hopelessly too brief for atoms to assemble into living things free of any input from a divine Designer (see chapter 16).[3] Therefore, many of them invested enormous energy and creativity in attempts to escape the limits imposed by the Hubble time. Two of these models became especially popular.

Steady State Universe

In 1948 three British astrophysicists, Herman Bondi, Thomas Gold, and Fred Hoyle, circumvented the beginning via "continual creation."[4]

Their models suggested that creation of matter is an act of nature, even a law of nature, not a one-time miracle from outside nature. Skipping past any attempt to explain the expansion of the universe, they proposed that the voids resulting from expansion are filled by the continual, spontaneous self-creation of new matter (see figure 7.1, below).

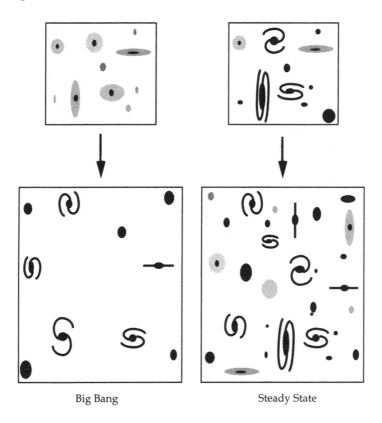

Big Bang   Steady State

Figure 7.1: Big Bang Growth Versus Steady State Growth
In a big bang universe the density of matter thins out and the mean age for the galaxies advances. All big bang models predict a finite age for the universe. In a steady state universe new matter is spontaneously and continuously created. The density of matter remains the same, and the mean age for the galaxies is constant. On a large scale, nothing changes with time. All steady state models assume that the universe is inifinite in age and extent. Since the light of very distant galaxies takes considerable time to reach us, astronomers can look back into the past to see which growth pattern the universe follows.

The champions of this steady state hypothesis made their theological position clear from the start. Bondi and Hoyle declared their opposition to the notion that anything could transcend the realm of nature.[5] Hoyle made no bones about his opposition to Christianity. To his thinking, "the Universe is everything" and to suggest otherwise is "crackpot."[6]

Failing the Test

During the last three decades a series of complex observational and theoretical tests was developed to prove or disprove the steady state model.[7] Amazingly, the simplest test, devised by Sir James Jeans in the 1920s, was applied last of all. Jeans pointed out that a universe that has no beginning and no end should manifest a "steady" population. That is, the number of stars and galaxies in various stages of development should be proportional to the time required to pass through these stages. There should be balanced numbers of newly formed, young, middle-aged, elderly, and extinct stars and galaxies.[8]

What do we find? A host of "youthful" stars, with ages ranging from a few days to about 14 billion years. If 14 billion years seems old, let me assure you, it is not, compared to most stars' life expectancy. The majority of stars in the universe are capable of burning for more than 80 billion years.[9]

In the population of galaxies, the steady state model met with yet more trouble. All, or nearly all, are approximately the same age. We see virtually no newly formed galaxies. The very few that are reported, most astronomers agree, are the aftermaths of collisions between mature galaxies. Galaxies in the universe are so tightly packed that such collisions are expected to occur from time to time.

As for older galaxies, we see none at all. Neither are there any extinct varieties. The death knell rang for steady state models when American astronomer Donald Hamilton determined that all the galaxies were formed at approximately the same time,[10] as the big bang predicts.

Under the weight of these and at least nine other independent refutations,[11] plus new evidence that the darkness of intergalactic space must result from the finite ages of all the galaxies[12] (see the box "The Paradox of the Dark Night Sky," page 70), the steady state models eventually staggered and fell.

Quasi-Steady-State Universe

As noted in books by both Christian[13] and nonChristian astronomers,[14] and even by steady state model proponents themselves,[15] steady state models have been decisively proven wrong by observational advances. In addition to the failures already noted in this chapter, the established character of the cosmic background radiation, the abundance of the elements, the dispersal of galaxies with respect to time, the cosmic entropy measure, and the accelerating expansion of the universe clearly refute the possibility that we live in a steady state universe.

EVOLUTION AS EVIDENCE FOR CREATION

Outside of the context of the physical sciences, and especially in the biological sciences, evolution is seen as the adversary of creation. In the clash between the steady state and big bang models, however, we witness the apparent irony that new evidences for the evolution of the universe actually establish that the universe was created in the relatively recent past.

In the physical sciences evolution typically is defined as change taking place with respect to time. Such a definition is theologically neutral. No claim is made as to whether the observed changes are naturally driven or supernaturally driven. In this respect the Bible is "evolutionary" in its teachings on creation since it frames the creation account into a chronology of change through time—thirteen major creation events sequenced over six creation days.

The theological thrust of the steady state models was that no personal involvement from God was necessary to explain our existence. Steady state says the universe has not evolved and that it has existed for infinite time. Thus, the dice of chance could have been thrown an infinite number of times under favorable natural conditions to explain the assembling of atoms into organisms.

But, observational proofs now affirm that the universe has evolved, very significantly, from a beginning just several billion years ago.[16] Thus, our existence cannot be attributed to the natural realm's lucky throw of the dice (out of an infinite number of throws). Moreover, the big bang determines that the cause of the universe is functionally equivalent to the God of the Bible, a Being beyond the matter, energy, space, and time of the cosmos (see chapters 9 and 10).

Rather than concede a cosmic Beginner, however, proponents of the steady state theory have modified their models into what they term a quasi-steady-state universe. Instead of new matter continuously coming into existence from everywhere in the universe, in the quasi-steady-state model new matter is sporadically created in the nuclei of large active galaxies (galaxies with explosive events occurring in their cores).[17]

In contrast with the big bang interpretation, quasi-steady-state proponents would replace a single primordial fireball arising from a transcendent creation event about 15 billion years ago with a great many time-separated "primordial" fireballs which would result from the creation and ejection of matter from the centers of large galaxies. Rather than attributing the activity in the nuclei of large galaxies to black holes sucking in matter, they claim that these nuclei are spewing out matter as a result of some hidden creation mechanism. Quasars would not be very distant super-energetic galaxies but rather relatively nearby hot spots ejected from regular galaxies. In the quasi-steady-state model, even though the universe continually expands, it maintains roughly the same density through newly created matter filling in the voids of space generated by cosmic expansion. Like in the steady state model, the universe would have an infinite past.

Refutations of Quasi-Steady-State Cosmology

Many quasar images indeed do appear adjacent to galaxy images. However, such appearances are also what one would expect in a big bang universe. With the universe only 15 billion years old, foreground galaxies still so crowd the field of view that it is inevitable for background quasars to appear adjacent to them. Also, it is no longer true that observations of quasars appear only as very bright points of light. With the advent of telescopes as powerful as the 400-inch Keck, astronomers have been able to detect faint wisps of galaxy parts enveloping the quasars. Thus, quasars are not isolated point sources. Apparently, they are the nuclei of enormous galaxies in their early, formative stages.

Big bang astronomers deduce that quasars are giant black holes residing at the centers of supergiant galaxies and are fueled by huge amounts of gas being sucked into the black holes. As the universe expands and galaxies become less crowded together, the amount of gas for a supergiant galaxy reaches a peak in time somewhere between the galaxy's infancy and early adulthood. A problem, however, is that some quasars are so powerful that not even the maximum gas in a supergiant galaxy would provide it with enough fuel. To get the power output up to the observed levels, a young, supergiant galaxy would need to steal a lot of gas from nearby galaxies.

According to recent Hubble Space Telescope images, this latter scenario accurately describes what is taking place. In figure 7.2 (see page 83) we see one large galaxy colliding with a supergiant galaxy at about a million miles per hour. This collision provides all the gas needed to sustain the quasar in the nucleus of the supergiant.[18]

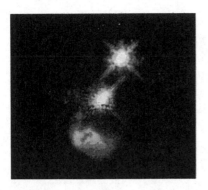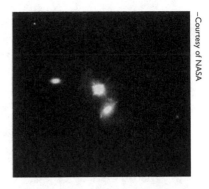

–Courtesy of NASA

Figure 7.2: Images from the Hubble Space Telescope of New-Born Quasars
In the image on the left a large galaxy (center) is colliding with a supergiant galaxy (bottom) at about a million miles per hour.

In a big bang universe we expect young galaxies to be packed together more tightly than they are today. Hubble Space Telescope images provide support for this tighter packing.[19] Therefore, we would expect quasars to be most abundant when the universe is a few billion years old.

Specifically, we would expect no quasars to exist today, that is, at distances corresponding to short light-travel times. This is because too much gas already has been consumed. Consequently, at distances corresponding up to about half the age of the universe, quasars should be rare. However, at distances equivalent to about a fifth the age of the universe, they should be abundant. Finally, at distances equivalent to about a tenth the age of the universe they should, again, be rare. This is because at one-tenth of cosmic history, insufficient condensed gas clouds would have formed to sustain more than a few quasars.

Reliable space density surveys of quasars began to be published in 1994, 1995, and 1996. These surveys confirmed the big bang predictions while contradicting the quasi-steady-state predictions.[20] Since then, newer observations have substantially added to the weight of evidence for the big bang and against the quasi-steady-state.[21]

Quasi-steady-state proponents are forced to deny that giant black holes exist in the central cores of giant active galaxies. While for two decades now astronomers' observations have established that supermassive, supercondensed bodies must exist in the cores of giant galaxies, they could not definitely prove that they were black holes. This changed recently when researches found a way to measure the spin velocities in the inner regions surrounding such supercondensed bodies. These velocities measured close to one-third the velocity of light, a result that can only be explained if the supercondensed bodies are black holes exceeding a million solar masses.[22]

Quasi-steady-state proponents go to extreme lengths arguing that the shifting of the spectral lines of quasars toward longer or redder wavelengths does not imply that the quasars are at great distances. (Remember that in the big bang model, the redshift of an object is an indicator of distance, so that the greater its redshift, the greater its distance.) They claim the high velocities indicated by the redshifts result from the quasars being ejected from galactic nuclei, not from a big bang cosmic expansion. While very few astronomers have ever accepted this proposition for the reasons stated above, a direct refutation has seemed impossible given the extreme distances of quasars implied by the big bang theory. The problem is that the big bang distances are out of reach for all distance measuring methods except for those based on the shifting of spectral lines.

This impasse on distance measuring methods, however, was broken this past June. At radio wavelengths it is possible to link widely separated telescopes together to build an interferometer with the equivalent resolving power of a 6,000 mile diameter telescope. Exploiting such an instrument, a team of American astronomers achieved a direct distance measurement based on the trignometric method familiar to land surveyors for the quasar, 3C 279.[23] They determined that 3C 279 must be at least 5.9 billion light years away. This establishes that the big bang interpretation of quasars is correct and the quasi-steady-state interpretation is wrong.

In the quasi-steady-state model all the helium in the universe comes from nuclear burning that takes place inside stars. To account for all the helium we observe in the universe such burning must proceed for at least a hundred billion years. Astronomers fail to see any stars or galaxies anywhere in the universe older than 14 billion years. Moreover, while stars are efficient in distributing elements heavier than helium to the interstellar medium (through explosions), most of the helium produced by stars remains trapped inside dead stars. The ratio of heavy elements to helium in both the interstellar medium and intergalactic medium is consistent with the big bang. That same ratio contradicts the quasi-steady-state model.

Many other refutations of the quasi-steady-state model abound. The most significant that remain are the density of baryons (protons plus neutrons) in the universe,[24] the density of exotic matter,[25] and the characteristics of the cosmic background radiation.[26] In the face of all this evidence, a major book has just been released by the three remaining proponents of the quasi-steady-state model,[27] namely Fred Hoyle, Geoffrey Burbidge, and Jayant Narlikar. Ironically, further discoveries made since that book went to press now decisively rule out the possibility of a quasi-steady-state universe.

One form of the steady state model that is still seriously entertained by astronomers is what is called the "eternal inflation" model. Here, the continual creation of protons and neutrons is supplanted by the continual creation of entire universes. Big bang universes are presumed to spontaneously appear as expanding bubbles in an infinite and eternal quantum-fluctuating space-time foam. This model is a subset of the multiple universe models. They are discussed in chapter 15 under the subhead, "An Infinity of Universes?" on pages 171–174.

Philosophical End Run

The defeat of the steady state model and its offspring, the quasi-steady-state model, led non-theistic astronomers to express first a momentary lament and then a newfound hope. The prestigious British journal *Nature* published this statement from physicist John Gribbin:

> The biggest problem with the Big Bang theory of the origin of the Universe is philosophical—perhaps even theological—what was there before the bang? This problem alone was sufficient to give a great initial impetus to the Steady State theory; but with that theory now sadly in conflict with the observations, the best way round this initial difficulty is provided by a model in which the universe expands from a singularity [that is, a beginning], collapses back again, and repeats the cycle indefinitely.[28]

Gribbin signaled the change in a new direction for those committed to finding some way around a transcendent cosmic creation event just some 15 billion years ago.

CHAPTER EIGHT

CLOSING LOOPHOLES: ROUND TWO

R esearch that crushed the steady state universe models simultaneously built up the big bang, with its implications of a beginning and a Beginner. Cosmologists who yet resisted this turn of research resurrected a model for the universe proposed thousands of years ago by Hindu teachers and later by Roman philosophers—the reincarnating or oscillating universe. The appeal of this model is that it seems to allow for the relatively recent beginning (as in the Hubble time) while retaining the possibility of infinite or nearly infinite time.

Bouncing Universe

The familiar law of gravity says that massive bodies tend to attract each other. We also know that the mutual attraction of massive bodies in the universe acts as a brake on the expansion of the universe. As you may recall from the earlier discussion of critical mass, the expansion of the universe could be brought to a halt by gravity if the universe contained enough mass. But that's not all gravity could do. It could throw the expansion into reverse and shrink the universe back to a tiny volume.

Here's where the oscillating universe model shows imagination. It suggests that rather than crunching back into a "singularity" (an infinitely shrunken space representing the boundary at which space ceases to exist or at which space comes into existence), the imploding universe somehow bounces back and begins a new cycle of expansion. Some unknown bounce mechanism is invoked to make this happen (see figure 8.1, page 88).

According to Princeton physicist Robert Dicke, an infinite number of these cycles of expansion and contraction of the universe would "relieve us of the necessity of understanding the origin of matter at any finite time in the past."[1] The creation event becomes irrelevant, and our existence could be attributed to one lucky bounce. After all, given an infinite number of cosmic bounces, it is argued that surely one would produce all the conditions necessary to convert particles and atoms into human beings through strictly natural processes.

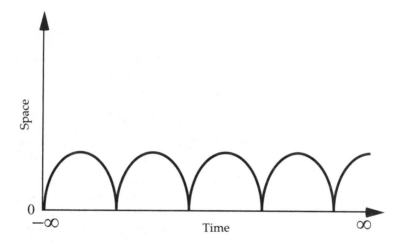

Figure 8.1: The Infinitely Oscillating Universe Model
In the oscillating universe model suggested by physicists like Robert Dicke and John Gribbin, the universe alternates for infinite time between phases of expansion and contraction. Gravity halts the expansion and generates a suc-ceeding phase of contraction. An unknown physical mechanism is proposed to somehow bounce the universe from a period of contraction into a period of expansion, and the characteristics of the contraction and expansion phases are presumed not to vary significantly with time.

In 1965, when the oscillating universe model first emerged as a serious theory,[2] many astronomers launched an all-out effort to find sufficient mass to halt and reverse the expansion of the universe. As noted in chapter 5 (see pages 63-66), however, all the evidence, both observational and theoretical, points in the opposite direction. Even with the consideration of exotic matter, the total mass falls consider-ably short of what would be needed to force an eventual collapse of the universe. The latest measurements establish a cosmic mass den-sity that is 0.3 ± 0.1 of what is needed to reverse cosmic expansion.[3]

The Rebound Problem

But missing mass is not the only difficulty. Even if the universe did contain enough mass to reverse its expansion and even if a bounce mechanism were discovered or devised theoretically, the number of bounces or oscillations would be limited because of entropy (energy degradation).

The second law of thermodynamics tells us that the entropy of the universe increases with time. This entropy increase means a decrease in the energy available to perform mechanical work, such as bouncing. So less and less mechanical energy would be available with each bounce to make the bounce happen.

The decrease in mechanical energy from bounce to bounce has two ramifications. First, it means that with each bounce, the universe expands farther out before it begins collapsing. Picture the action of a ball attached by a rubber band to a wooden paddle. When the rubber band is new, its elasticity is greatest, and it yanks the ball back powerfully. But as it gets warmed up and stretched several times, it loses some of its pull on the ball, and the ball goes out farther from the paddle more easily. The effect for the cosmos is diagramed in figure 8.2.

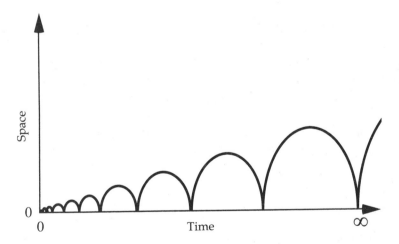

Figure 8.2: Thermodynamic Dissipation Within an Oscillating Universe
Even if the universe conceivably could oscillate, it could not have been oscillating for infinite time. The laws of thermodynamics compel the maximum diameter of the universe to increase from cycle to cycle. Therefore, such a universe could look forward to an infinitely long future but only a finite past. The ultimate moment of creation, at most, could be pushed back only to about a trillion years ago.

Notice that as time goes on the humps grow larger and larger. Looking backward in time, they grow smaller and smaller to a starting point in the not-too-distant past. From the perspective of physics, the universe could not bounce more than about a dozen times—a number far short of infinity.

WILL THE UNIVERSE EVER COLLAPSE?

Discussion of the merits of an oscillating universe model becomes academic if the universe lacks the mass to halt its expansion and force a subsequent collapse.

With every passing year during the past dozen, the observational evidence for a universe that continues to expand forever grew stronger and stronger while the evidence for a universe that subsequently collapses grew weaker and weaker. The latest measurements now establish beyond any reasonable doubt that there is insufficient mass to halt cosmic expansion.[3]

As further proofs against an eventual collapse, the discoveries that the universe's space fabric has an ongoing self-stretching property and that it has a spatially flat geometry establish that the universe will continue to expand forever. Moreover, the universe will expand at a progressively faster and faster rate. For more details see chapter 5, pages 45-53.

The second ramification of entropy lies in its effect on the bounce energy. Not only is mechanical energy for contraction lost with each bounce, but so is energy for rebounding. If a rubber ball is dropped from a height of three feet above a hardwood floor, it will rebound, but it will not come up three feet. Some of the energy in the ball was radiated away through friction into heat when the ball made contact with the floor. In fact, each time the ball hits the floor more mechanical energy is converted into heat, and eventually the ball stops bouncing.

A ball with a high mechanical efficiency, for example a volleyball blown up to a high air pressure, may bounce a dozen times before it comes to a stop on the floor. A ball with a low mechanical efficiency, for example a very soft foam-rubber ball, may bounce only twice before it stops.

But the universe has far less mechanical efficiency than a foam-rubber ball. In 1983 and 1984, American astrophysicists Marc Sher, Alan Guth, and Sidney Bludman demonstrated that even if the universe contained enough mass to halt its current expansion, any ultimate collapse would end in a thud, not a bounce.[4] In terms of mechanical energy, the universe more closely resembles a wet lump of clay than a pumped up volleyball (see table 8.1). Sher and Guth confidently entitled their paper "The Impossibility of a Bouncing Universe."

Table 8.1: Mechanical Efficiencies of Some Common Systems
If the universe oscillates, that means it is behaving like an engine or a system designed to perform work. The ability of a system or engine to perform work or to oscillate depends on its mechanical efficiency. The universe literally ranks as the worst engine in all existence. Its mechanical efficiency is so low that oscillation is impossible.

System or Engine	Mechanical Efficiency
diesel engine	40%
gasoline engine	25%
steam engine	12%
human engine	1%
universe	0.00000001%

Quantum Gravity Speculations

Sher, Guth, and Bludman weren't alone in demonstrating the impossibility of a cosmic bounce. Two Russian physicists, Igor Novikov and Yakob Zel'dovich, developed their own proof based on the geometry of collapsing structures.[5] But none of the five researchers dealt with the theoretical possibilities for oscillation that arise from the quantum gravity era, presumably because so little is yet known about that era (see box "The Quantum Gravity Era," page 92). But it did seem to offer an infinitesimal straw for diehards to grasp.

Arnold Sikkema and Werner Israel grasped it, hypothesizing bizarre effects of merging black holes in that split second when all the matter and energy of the universe would still have been contained in a very tiny volume.[6] These men honestly admitted that no consistent theory of quantum gravity yet exists. It must be noted, too, that the oscillation theory they proposed yields at most only a sharply limited number of bounces. It offers no escape from the notion of a beginning in the not-so-distant past.

That slender straw grasped by Sikkema and Israel was crushed recently by Russian physicist André Linde. At a symposium on the large-scale structure of the universe, Linde demonstrated that the universe, with the characteristics we observe, cannot have arisen from a bounce in the quantum gravity era. Why?

There are two considerations:

1. During the collapse phase toward a hypothetical bounce at least one region or volume (technically called a "domain") in the

universe would utterly resist being crushed to the tiny volume necessary for the exotic effects of quantum gravity to take over.[7]

2. The bounce, if it could take place, would not produce sufficient matter.[8]

Let me explain. The universe, before the hypothetical bounce, begins with a huge amount of space curvature and little or no matter. But, as the universe expands, space is stretched, reducing the curvature. This loss of curvature is transformed into matter, and in the process, a huge amount of entropy is generated. Because of the enormous entropy produced, the process is not reversible. Matter cannot be converted back into the needed space curvature. Thus the universe we live in cannot be the product of oscillation even if the bounces are hypothesized to occur in the quantum gravity era.

THE QUANTUM GRAVITY ERA

Physicists are designing theories to cope with conditions before the universe was even 10^{-43} seconds old (less than a quadrillionth-quadrillionth-trillionth second). At 10^{-43} seconds, the force of gravity within the universe becomes comparable to the strong nuclear force. This force holds protons and neutrons together in the nucleus of the atom. At such a magnitude, gravity may possibly be modified by quantum mechanical effects. Hence this early stage of the universe is called the quantum gravity era.

Since the energy densities that exist during the quantum gravity era lie far beyond the capabilities of even the most powerful particle accelerators, many theoreticians have presumed that they are therefore free to speculate any physical conditions or, for that matter, any physical laws they desire. However, since such physics is obviously beyond "The possibility of observational verification," it would, by definition, fall outside the realm of science and into the realm of metaphysics.

Nevertheless, even though the energies encountered are far beyond current experimental physics, a powerful observational check does exist— the present universe in which we live. If a quantum gravity theory cannot explain how the present universe developed from the initial quantum state, it must be incorrect.

Recently, a string theory solution has established that the current laws of physics framed within ten space-time dimensions, six of which stopped expanding when the universe was only 10^{-43} seconds old, hold all the way back to the very beginning of the universe. The solution successfully predicts the operation of both special and general relativity and contains a number of predictions about conditions in the universe that have proven true. A brief description of the solution and its ramifications is given in the next chapter. A detailed one can be found in my book, *Beyond the Cosmos.*[9]

Scalar Field Speculations

Many theoretical attempts to escape a singular cosmic beginning have shown up lately in the scientific literature.[10] They are all variations on a theme in that they all propose the introduction of some unknown, undiscovered physics to alter the physics we do know, can measure, and understand. To be specific, they speculate that some kind of unknown scalar field (see box, "What Is a Scalar Field?" below) acts as a third factor, in addition to gravity and the self-stretching property of the universe's space fabric. This third factor, they presume, is sufficiently dominant at critical epochs in the universe's history to transform the cosmos from a system manifesting a single transcendent beginning to one that has multiple non-transcendent beginnings.

The transformation from a single transcendent beginning to multiple non-transcendent beginnings implies that the cosmic limits that dictate a CAUSE for the universe indistinguishable from the God of the Bible might possibly be stretched enough to permit alternate explanations. Rather than take the space to respond to every such theoretical attempt, I will pick one here that typifies the whole group.

WHAT IS A SCALAR FIELD?

In cosmology a scalar field is either a force or an energy term in the equations of general relativity that affects the dynamics of the universe. It can be constant or a function of either spatial position or time. As such, it can either augment or subtract from the dynamical effects that would arise from gravity alone. Such adjustments to gravity can be either simple or complex functions of space and time.

In the standard big bang model there are no scalar fields. Gravity alone determines the past, present, and future dynamics of the universe. New observations clearly demonstrate, however, that such a simple interpretation of the universe is incorrect. That is, the big bang is more complex.

The scalar fields that the new observations support pose no threat to the conclusions of a carefully designed singularity beginning and of an equally carefully designed cosmic expansion subsequent to the beginning. In fact, as explained in chapter 5, pages 45-53, they considerably add to the evidence of such designs.

Fakir's "No-Beginning" Model

In an August 2000 issue of the *Astrophysical Journal*, Redouane Fakir, a cosmologist at the University of British Columbia, published an article titled "General Relativistic Cosmology with No Beginning of Time."[11]

The author admits he chose the title for its shock value since astrophysicists for nearly two decades have been convinced that any cosmological model based on general relativity must produce the feature of a singular beginning (that is, a past moment when all the matter and energy in the universe and all the space-time dimensions that can be associated with that matter and energy had a common beginning).

First, Fakir reviews just how strongly the singularity theorems[12] (see chapter 9, pages 107-108) establish the necessity for a transcendent CAUSE for the entire universe. He documents how the theorems prove a cosmic singularity beginning for both a universe governed by classical general relativity and for inflation models (models where a hyper expansion of the universe at many times the velocity of light occurs during a finite period when the universe is very young, younger than 10^{-32} seconds). He also notes how the usual alternatives to general relativity, namely, scalar tensor theories of gravity (see box "What Is a Scalar Field?"page 93), either produced unstable solutions or demand conditions that are contradicted by well established observations.

Fakir states in the abstract of his paper, nevertheless, that he has achieved a cosmic model that is "naturally free of singularities despite the fact that it uses only classical general relativity."[13] A careful read of his paper reveals, though, that Fakir's model is not a no-beginning model. It is, in fact, a multiple-beginning model. Specifically, he tries to revive the oscillating universe model of the 1970s with its infinite number of cycles of cosmic expansion and contraction extending into both the infinite past and the infinite future.

Fakir accomplishes his cosmic oscillations by introducing a time-varying scalar field into his model to supplement the effects of general relativity and the self-stretching property of the cosmic space fabric on cosmic dynamics. (Thus, it is not a purely general relativistic model.) The strength of the scalar field he proposes would rise from a near-zero value to a maximum at the cosmic bounce point and then decline again to a near-zero value.

A crude visual picture of Fakir's model would be a universe that contains enough mass to gravitationally brake the cosmic expansion so that growth of the universe is not only halted but eventually reversed. During the contraction phase of the universe the scalar field would gradually grow until it became strong enough to reverse the effect of gravitational collapse.

Fakir admits that in his model, cosmic re-collapse occurs far too quickly for stars to form unless he introduces a lot more fine-tuning in several of the cosmic parameters.[14] Philosophically, this extra fine-tuning is self-defeating. Any role of God that might have been diminished in monkeying with the beginning is compensated for by a necessarily increased divine role in designing the universe so that physical life becomes possible.

There are much more severe difficulties with Fakir's model. His model only escapes a singular beginning if the universe is dynamically closed, that is, if it is headed for an eventual collapse. However, as described in chapter 5 (see pages 46-51), maps of the temperature fluctuations in the cosmic background radiation, published in 2000, combined with measurements on distant type Ia supernovae, published in 1999, present us with undeniable evidence that cosmic expansion has transitioned from a gradual deceleration to an exponentially increasing acceleration. In other words, the universe will expand forever at an increasingly greater rate. New measurements published since those results went to press further add to the weight of evidence.[15]

As noted already, another severe difficulty is that the thermodynamic state of our universe, or of any universe capable of sustaining physical life, will not permit a cosmic bounce either in the past or the future. One reason for this is that the cosmic entropy necessary for physical life (specifically, for life-suitable stars and planets to form and remain) will not allow the heat energy and matter that was generated from the release of space curvature when the universe was extremely young (less than 10^{-34} seconds old) to be reversed. (That is, this heat energy and matter cannot be converted back into space curvature.) Several more reasons why cosmic bouncing is impossible are described in one of my previously published books.[16]

Alternative Scalar Fields?

The proposal of some kind of scalar field to modify or replace the theological implications of general relativity and the big bang is not new. As noted in chapter 6, Einstein himself made such a proposal in 1917.[17] So did the British mathematician Sir Arthur Eddington in 1930.[18] In 1961 Carl Brans and Robert Dicke claimed that a strong scalar field (specifically, that the strength of gravity varies significantly with time) would alter the beginning implied by general relativity alone.[19]

Such proposals and others like them were subsequently struck down by observational limits established by astronomers. In addition to the observational constraints already described in this book, the near spherical shape of the sun, neutron star tests of general relativity, measures of the cosmic mass density, the cosmic space energy density, and the cosmic baryon (protons and neutrons) density produce tight limits on the degree to which any kind of scalar field can modify the beginning implied by general relativity and the big bang.

The introduction of scalar fields into cosmic models is not always easy for even the educated reader to spot. For example, suggestions that certain constants of physics, like the fine structure constants, the velocity of light, and the electromagnetic and gravitational force constants, took on slightly different values when the universe was much younger are all, in fact, scalar field models. Likewise, the cosmic quintessence discussed in chapter 5 (pages 55-56) is an appeal to a cosmic scalar field.

Much tighter constraints on such proposals and appeals are coming from new measurements of distant galaxies, seismic activity on the sun, and physics laboratory experiments. For example, results from the Global Oscillation Network Group (GONG) and the Birmingham Solar Oscillation Network (BiSON) now establish that the gravitation constant G varies by no more than one part in a trillion per year.[20] Also, the motions of small-mass galaxies severely limit the size of any possible modification of local gravity relative to global gravity.[21] High-resolution spectra of quasars put the variability of the proton-to-electron mass ratio at less than one part in one hundred trillion per year.[22] The electromagnetic fine structure constant can be expressed as a function of either the velocity of light or the value of the electron charge. Laboratory experiments and measures of star formation rate histories in distant galaxies establish that its value departs by no more than one part in a hundred thousand from the modern value at that epoch in the universe when galaxies first formed (about 13.5 to 14.0 billion years ago).[23] Compared to when star formation in galaxies was at its peak (roughly seven to ten billion years ago), the electromagnetic fine structure constant could differ by no more than one part in a million relative to the modern value.[24] Within the last seven billion years essentially no room at all exists for changes in its value. While the average reader may not grasp the exact nature and strength of these evidences, he or she can appreciate that the list is extensive.

These recently established limits are strong enough to eliminate any reasonable possibility for an escape, during cosmically measurable time, from a singular cosmic beginning based on an hypothesized variability of either the gravitation constant, the proton-to-electron mass ratio, the velocity of light, or the electron charge value. It is true, however, that such demonstrations, however, place no limits on what might have occurred before cosmically measurable time, that is, before the universe was 10^{-19} seconds old (a ten millionth of a trillionth of a second old). I will comment in chapters 12 and 15 on speculations about alternate physics during this first miniscule moment.

In a work just submitted for publication, two cosmologists from Tufts University demonstrated that "non-minimally coupled" scalar fields permit violations of the second law of thermodynamics (the law of increasing entropy or increasing disorder) over long periods whereas "minimally coupled" scalar fields do not.[25] Since the possible violation of the second thermodynamic law would place much, if not most, of particle physics, black hole physics, and quantum mechanics in jeopardy, proposing non-minimally coupled scalar fields for our universe must be judged unreasonable. Without getting into all the technicalities of the differences between minimally coupled and non-minimally coupled scalar fields, it is important to note that only appeals to certain kinds of non-minimally coupled scalar fields allow for the possibility of escape from a cosmic singularity beginning. In other words, any reasonable or observationally possible cosmic scalar field leaves the singularity theorems unchallenged. Consequently, it is reasonable to conclude that the universe must have been caused by an ENTITY who transcends matter, energy, and all the space-time dimensions associated with matter and energy.

The Reincarnation Connection

Most Eastern religions, ancient and modern (including Hinduism, Buddhism, and most new age philosophies, among others), are rooted in the doctrine of cosmic reincarnation, the oscillating universe. The popularity of these teachings soared in the West with the popularity of the oscillating universe model.

I watched this phenomenon during my graduate student days at the University of Toronto. When several of my peers embraced one or more of the many Hindu or Buddhist sects in vogue, I asked them why. They quoted passages from their scriptures concerning the never-ending cycles of birth, growth, collapse, death, and rebirth of the cosmos and of ourselves as one with it, the "reality" described by the oscillating universe model.

What clinched their commitment, they said, was the amazing accuracy of Hindu scriptures in predicting the period of oscillation, the time between successive rebirths. These writings said 4.32 billion years.[26] Astrophysicists of the day (the 1970s) said 20 to 30 billion years—*if* the oscillating universe model were to prove correct.

My friends reasoned that for the ancient Hindus to get that close to the right answer, Hinduism must be more than a humanly crafted religion. It must come from some superhuman source. This bit of rational support, combined with the enchantment of anything non-Western and nontraditional and an aversion to the moral values of Christianity, was enough to draw them into one of the daughter faiths of Hinduism.

But the rational rug has now been pulled out. Reality is not described by infinite cycles of cosmic reincarnation. The worldview underlying Hinduism and its many derivatives has proven false.

CHAPTER NINE

SCIENCE DISCOVERS TIME BEFORE TIME

With the collapse of the oscillating universe model, attempts to get around the Hubble time (no more than about 16 billion years since the universe began) turned in a new direction. Holdouts for an infinitely old universe now hypothesize that the fundamental laws of nature as we know them are either incorrect or break down under special conditions.

Escape from Reality

From this new battle front comes the work of amateur plasma physicist Eric Lerner, author of *The Big Bang Never Happened*. Lerner notes that the laws of nature cannot explain the amazing advance in complexity of living organisms that has taken place on Earth over the past 4 billion years.[1] He acknowledges that this advance stands in violation of the second law of thermodynamics, which says that systems tend to degrade from higher levels of order, complexity, and information to lower levels of order, complexity, and information.

Since Lerner rejects the existence of a Creator, he is forced to conclude that the second law of thermodynamics broke down.[2] And if the second law of thermodynamics broke down for organisms on Earth, it could have broken down for the entire physical cosmos, he suggests.[3] Since the second law ties in with one of the ways we measure time (the rate at which entropy, or energy degradation, increases), Lerner concludes that our observations of the age of the universe are incorrect, that they cannot be used to argue for a beginning of the cosmos just some billions of years ago. There was no big bang, he says, thus no Creator.

The circularity of Lerner's reasoning seems obvious. Starting with the supposition that God does not exist, he reinterprets the laws of nature. Then he uses his rewrite of reality to support the conclusion that God does not exist. Another description of his work is "escape from reality."

An observational refutation of Lerner's hypothesis arises from stellar physics. The kinds of stars that are necessary to make physical life possible in the universe are extremely sensitive to even slight changes in the major laws or constants of physics. Therefore, the existence of stable burning stars of all different masses at all different distances from us (see chapter 14 for details) establishes the constancy of physics throughout the history of the universe.

The constancy of physics follows since light from very distant stars takes a much longer time to travel to us than light from nearby stars. Thus, by measuring the physical condition of stars at varying distances astronomers can affirm that Lerner's end-run around a transcendent creation event fails. For that era before stars existed, namely, the first half billion years or so of cosmic history, the measured physical conditions of the cosmic background radiation also affirm no changes have occurred in the physical laws and constants.

No God of the Gaps

Even working within the laws of physics, researchers with an anti-God bias often make blind leaps of faith to escape any evidence of God's involvement in reality. For centuries Christians were criticized for their "God of the gaps." Sometimes that criticism was deserved. Christians tended to use gaps in understanding or data to build a case for God's miraculous intervention. Then, when scientific discoveries uncovered a natural explanation for the "divine phenomenon," ridicule was heaped not only on those proposing the divine explanation but also on belief in God's existence.

In the twentieth century we see the reverse of the God of the gaps. Non-theists, confronted with problems for which ample research leads to no natural explanations and instead points to the supernatural, utterly reject the possibility of the supernatural and insist on a natural explanation even if it means resorting to absurdity.

For example, steady state models were supported by an imagined force of physics for which there was not one shred of observational or theoretical evidence. The oscillating universe model depended on an imagined bounce mechanism for which there was not one shred of observational or theoretical evidence. Similar appeals to imagined forces and phenomena have been the basis for all the cosmological models proposed to avoid the big bang with its implications about God.[4] The disproof of these models and the ongoing appeal by non-theists to more and more bizarre unknowns and unknowables seem to reflect the growing strength of the case for theism (see chapters 7, 8, 12, and 15).

Testing the Gaps

Is it the God-of-the-gaps or the no-God-of-the-gaps? One way to find out is to eliminate the gaps through advancing scientific research. Increased knowledge about the system may reveal a natural explanation for the supposed supernatural phenomenon. Conversely, increased knowledge may demonstrate that the natural explanations fail while the supernatural explanation succeeds.

What matters are not isolated examples of theistic or atheistic researchers being proven wrong in their hypothesized explanations. Christian theists, for example, believe that in the record of nature natural explanations are the norm and divine supernatural explanations are the exception. However, the demonstration that one of their supernatural explorations proves to be a natural one poses no threat to their belief in the God of the Bible.

What counts is the overall trend. As we learn more and more about the universe, Earth, and life, does the evidence for God's existence and design of the natural realm get stronger or weaker? If the atheist is right and the theist is wrong, then the more we discover about the cosmos, Earth, and life, the evidence for divine transcendence and design will become weaker. On the other hand, if the theist is right and the atheist is wrong, the more we learn about the cosmos, Earth, and life, the evidence for divine transcendence and design will become stronger.

Time and Its Beginning

Even before the death of the oscillating universe model, a fundamental reason was uncovered for the failure of cosmological models that rejected the finite age of the universe. In a series of papers appearing from 1966 to 1970, three British astrophysicists, Stephen Hawking, George Ellis, and Roger Penrose, extended the solution of the equations of general relativity to include space and time.[5] The result was called the space-time theorem of general relativity.[6]

This theorem is true under all possible physical conditions given that the universe contains mass and that its dynamics are reliably described by the equations of general relativity. Recent efforts to escape the theological consequences of the theorem has led to the discovery that its conclusions are valid over even broader conditions. Not only does the theorem hold in a universe governed by classical general relativity, it also holds for cosmic inflation models.[7]

Cosmic inflation models are universe models where a scalar field produces a hyper expansion of the universe at many times the velocity of light during a very brief period when the universe is younger than 10^{-33} seconds. As noted in chapters 7 and 8, all possible scalar field adjustments to classical general relativity that are consistent with our observations of the universe are subject to the transcendent cosmic creation event that flows out of the space-time theorems. The theorems state that space and time must have originated in the same cosmic bang that brought matter and energy into existence.

In Hawking's words, time itself must have a beginning.[8] Proof of the beginning of time may rank as the most theologically significant theorem of all time, assuming validity of the theory of general relativity.

Thumbs Up for General Relativity

What was needed to solidify the proof for the beginning of time was evidence that general relativity really does tell the true story about the dynamics of the universe. Fully aware of the importance of observational confirmation, Einstein proposed three tests at the time of his theory's publication.[9] Within two years, in 1919, a team led by British astronomer Arthur Eddington met the conditions for the first test when they proved that the sun's gravity bends starlight by just the amount general relativity predicted.[10] This finding generated some excitement, but with a probable error of about 10% in the measurement, scientists were not satisfied.

In the years following, progress in reducing the errors was frustratingly slow. By 1970 five more tests had been added to Einstein's three. Accuracy of confirmation had improved from 10% to 1%,[11] but still not enough to convince all the skeptics. Some theoreticians began to speculate that the universe, though dominated by general relativity, might also be influenced to a tiny degree by an unknown force field.[12] This speculation and imprecision cast just enough doubt on the space-time theorem to dampen enthusiasm for it, initially.

However, as research has continued that small shadow of doubt has shrunk to the vanishing point. By 1976 an echo delay experiment placed on the moon by Apollo astronauts reduced the uncertainty down to 0.5%.[13] In 1979 measurements of the gravitational effects on radio signals further reduced the uncertainty to just 0.1%.[14] In 1980 a hydrogen maser clock (based on the laser principle and nearly a hundred times more accurate than the best atomic clock) aboard a NASA rocket confirmed general relativity to the fifth place of the decimal.[15] But all these tests have been made in the context of the sun's and the earth's gravity. What if the context were different?

Strong Field Tests

Compared to the gravity of black holes, neutron stars (stars that are solid crystals comprised of neutrons touching one another from the central cores out to their surfaces), and the universe in its earliest moment after creation, the gravity of the sun and the earth are weaker by more than a hundred thousand times. Astrophysicists have wondered for some time if departures from general relativity might be observed for very strong gravitational field events.

Figure 9.1: Binary Pulsar
The large, ordinary star on the left orbits the more massive pulsar on the right. The pulsar is what remains from the supernova explosion of a very large star. During the supernova event, it undergoes a collapse so intense that its protons and electrons are fused into neutrons. A single teaspoonful of its matter would weigh five billion tons. The scale here is underestimated. The partner star typically measures about a million miles in diameter whereas the pulsar typically is only six miles in diameter.

The first such tests were conducted in 1982 on the binary pulsar PSR 1913+16.[16] A pulsar is a rapidly rotating neutron star whose magnetic axis is so offset from its rotation axis that powerful pulses of energy are beamed toward the earth every time it rotates. Most binary pulsars are systems in which an ordinary star orbits a pulsar (see figure 9.1). PSR 1913+16 is unusual in that the star orbiting the pulsar is also a neutron star. (Not all neutron stars emit powerful pulses.) A pulsar's gravitational pull on an ordinary star orbiting about it is very intense. The gravitational interaction between two neutron stars orbiting about one another is more intense yet. Initial experiments showed no departures from the predictions of general relativity. But again the error margin was about 10%.

In January 1992, an international team of astronomers led by Russell Hulse and Joseph Taylor published the results of ten years' high-quality observations not only on this pulsar but also on two others.[17] The team applied three separate tests of general relativity to each of the pulsars. In each case general relativity passed with flying colors. In the case of PSR 1913+16, the observed results agreed with the values predicted by general relativity to an accuracy of better than 0.5%.

The 0.5% accuracy figure for general relativity is based on one set of experimental constraints only. General relativity predicts that, over time, two neutron stars orbiting about one another will radiate so much gravitational energy that they will spiral inward toward one another causing their orbital periods to speed up. Careful measurements of the orbital periods for PSR 1913+16 year by year provide an ever more stringent test of the theory of general relativity. With measurements now extending over twenty years (1974 to 1994), general relativity is confirmed overall to an error of no more than one part in a hundred trillion. In the words of Roger Penrose, "This makes Einstein's general relativity, in this particular sense, the most accurately tested theory known to science!"[18] The rest of the scientific community agreed, awarding to Hulse and Taylor the Nobel Prize in physics for their breakthrough efforts.

General Relativity Confirmed in All Contexts

While Hulse and Taylor's measurements did convince the community of physicists and astronomers of general relativity's reliability, there were still a few doubters among certain theologians and philosophers. They had been waiting for general relativity to be proved in all relevant contexts. But, thanks to additional discoveries, their wait is over.

Previous to Hulse and Taylor's work, general relativity had passed eleven independent experimental tests. What was lacking, however, were tests in and around black holes, the demonstration of perfect or near perfect (and therefore unambiguous) "Einstein rings," and the demonstration of the predicted but elusive "Lense-Thirring effect." These evidences now have been supplied by new scientific observations.

As two Austrian physicists, Joseph Lense and Hans Thirring, pointed out in 1918, general relativity predicts that any spinning massive body will drag or twist the space-time fabric in its immediate neighborhood. Specifically, general relativity states that if a disk of material orbits a very dense body like a neutron star or black hole at an angle to the plane of the star or hole's spin axis, the dragging or twisting of space-time that is predicted will cause the disk to wobble like a child's top. In turn, the wobble will generate oscillations in the intensity of the X-ray radiation emitted from the gas in the disk. The theory even predicts the rate at which the oscillations should occur according to the spin characteristics of the particular neutron star or black hole.

At a 1997 meeting of the American Astronomical Society two separate teams, one from the Massachusetts Institute of Technology and the other from the Astronomical Observatory of Rome and the University of Rome, reported on the first ever detection of such oscillations. The American team observed five black holes and discovered oscillations as rapid as 300 times per second.[19] In each case the oscillation rate was exactly what general relativity predicted. The Italian team observed several black holes and likewise the general relativistic predictions were right on target.[19] Recently, an independent study done with NASA's Rossi X-ray Timing Explorer satellite confirmed the Lense-Thirring effect on neutron stars that spin 1,000 times per second.[20]

A few weeks after the twisting of the space-time fabric was first observed, general relativity passed three more tests. One was the first conclusive proof for the existence of stellar mass black holes. (General relativity predicts that a galaxy of our size and age should contain several stellar mass black holes.) Measurements of the orbital characteristics of an optical star orbiting the x-ray nova, A0620-00, established beyond all doubt that the nova exceeded the maximum mass for a stable neutron star (meaning that the star could not possibly have avoided becoming a black hole).[21] Since then, several more X-ray novae have yielded the same conclusion.[21]

General relativity also predicts the existence of supermassive (exceeding a million solar masses) black holes in the nuclei of very large galaxies. The existence of such supermassive black holes was established several years ago. What is new is the first time measurement of the velocities of the inner regions of the accretion disks surrounding these supermassive black holes.[21] These velocities, measuring close to one-third the velocity of light, are consistent with the predictions of general relativity.

Most people know that general relativity predicts that gravity will bend slightly the light of stars. A much more dramatic and definitive test of general relativity can be had when a massive galaxy lies exactly on the line of sight between the observer's telescope and a distant quasar. In this case general relativity predicts the appearance of an "Einstein" ring centered on the image of the quasar. Now, for the first time, an unambiguous, complete Einstein ring has been seen at optical and infrared wavelengths.[22] The accompanying image (see figure 9.2, below) was made by the Hubble Space Telescope, what physicist Andrew Watson termed a "dazzling demonstration of Einstein's theory at work."[23]

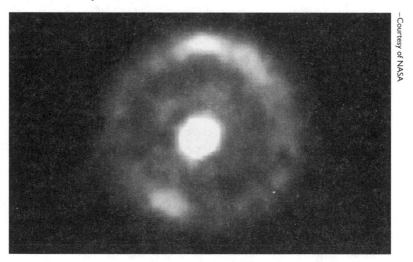

– Courtesy of NASA

Figure 9.2: The First Image of a Complete Einstein Ring at Optical Wavelengths

The last major prediction of general relativity still lacking observational confirmation was the Lense-Thirring effect for relatively weak gravitational fields. The predicted effect is incredibly small and until recently no instruments existed with the necessary sensitivity to either confirm or deny general relativity at this level. What did the trick was a four-year-long study on two laser-ranged satellites, LAGEOS and LAGEOS II, orbiting the earth.[24] Five physicists from Italy and Spain established that the Lense-Thirring effect indeed exists for weak fields of gravity and its value is within 10% of general relativity's prediction with a plus or minus total error of about 20%.[25]

Finally, a hypernova, the first one ever seen, was observed in 1998. A hypernova is an explosion so intense that at certain wavelengths (gamma ray wavelengths) and for a few seconds the energy release is the equivalent of millions of supernovae (a supernova at maximum light outshines a hundred billion ordinary stars). So intense was this explosion that some compared it to the big bang itself and speculated that perhaps its energy output was too much for the laws of physics.[26] Abandoning the laws of physics would open the door to abandoning all the physical evidence for divine creation. But, general relativity provides an easy, albeit dramatic, rescue. According to general relativity, the merger of neutron stars and/or black holes will generate exactly the kind of gamma ray burst that was observed.[27] In fact, if such an event were to take place near our galaxy rather than more than halfway across the universe, it would produce the gravity waves predicted by general relativity and particle physics at a strong enough level for us to detect. Of course, if such an event were much closer than that, the human species would be exterminated!

Today it can be said that no theory of physics has ever been tested in so many different contexts and so rigorously as general relativity. The fact that general relativity has withstood all these tests so remarkably well implies that no basis at all remains for doubting the conclusions of the space-time theorem.

So What?

This combination of tests with their successive shrinking of errors has laid to rest any nagging doubts about Einstein's equations of general relativity. Since general relativity does describe accurately the dynamics of the universe, the space-time theorems can be trusted.

The space-time theorems tell us that the ten space-time dimensions of the universe have existed only for as long as the universe has been expanding, less than 15 billion years. Time really does have a beginning.

The law of causality (or the law of statistical correlation in which quantum or statistical mechanical effects are significant) says that effects emanate from causes and not the other way around. Thus, causes precede their effects. Time, then, can be defined as a dimension along which cause-and-effect phenomena occur.

While a few philosophers might object to this causal time definition, it is a definition that allows all time-dependent phenomena in the sciences to be treated consistently. It is the most common definition of time employed by the popular media and in lay society. Since no physically living human transcends the space-time fabric of the universe (and, therefore, cannot observe time from outside or beyond time), no such human can boast an absolute or complete definition of time.

Such an absolute or complete time definition, however, is unnecessary. We simply need a consistent definition of time, and we need to use that definition consistently. So, whenever I refer to time in this book, I mean physical time, that is, time as defined by cause-and-effect operations.

The lack of physical time, thus, implies no cause and effect. If time's beginning is concurrent with the beginning of the universe, as the space-time theorems say, then the cause of the universe must be some entity operating in the equivalent of a time dimension completely independent of and preexistent to the time dimension of the cosmos. This conclusion is powerfully important to our understanding of who God is and who or what God isn't. It tells us that the Creator is transcendent, operating beyond the dimensional limits of the universe. It tells us that God is not the universe itself, nor is God contained within the universe. Pantheism and atheism do not square with the facts.

Pantheism claims there is no existence beyond the universe, that the universe is all there is, and that the universe always has existed. Atheism claims that the universe was not created and no entity exists independent of the matter, energy, and space-time dimensions of the universe. But all the data accumulated in the twentieth and twenty-first centuries tell us that a transcendent Creator *must* exist. For all the matter, energy, nine space dimensions, and even time, each suddenly and simultaneously came into being from some source beyond itself.

It is valid to refer to such a source, entity, or being as the Creator, for creating is defined as causing something—in this case everything in the universe—to come into existence. Matter, energy, space, and time are the effects He caused. Likewise, it is valid to refer to the Creator as transcendent, for the act of causing these effects must take place outside or independent of them.

Not only does science lead us to these conclusions, but so also does the Bible. It is the only holy book to do so.

CHAPTER TEN

A GOD OUTSIDE OF TIME, BUT KNOWABLE

When the atheist astronomer Geoffrey Burbidge complained that his peers were rushing off to join the First Church of Christ of the Big Bang, he was on the right track. The space-time theorems of general relativity lead not just to a theistic conclusion but specifically to the God of the Bible.

Of all the holy books of the religions of the world, only the Bible unambiguously states that time is finite, that time has a beginning, that God created time, that God is capable of cause and effect operations before the time dimension of the universe existed, and that God did cause many effects before the time component of our universe existed. Some of the Bible verses making such statements are given in table 10.1 (page 110).

Other holy books besides the Bible allude to extra dimensions, trans-dimensional phenomena, and transcendence, but these allusions are inconsistent. The god and the doctrines these books proclaim always are shaped and limited in some way by the dimensions of length, width, height, and time.

The Bible alone describes God as a personal Creator who can act entirely independent of the cosmos and its ten space-time dimensions. The God of the Bible is not subject to length, width, height, and time. He is the One who brought them into existence. Moreover, the Bible alone describes attributes of God that defy explanation in the limited context of four dimensions. Some examples are the description of God as a Being who is singular and plural (the Trinity) and the simultaneity of free will and predestination. God's extra-dimensional attributes are discussed briefly in chapter 17 and in detail in another of my books.[1]

Table 10.1: Some Bible Verses Teaching God's Extra-Dimensional Capacities

In the beginning God created the heavens and the earth. (Genesis 1:1)

By faith we understand that the universe was formed at God's command, so that what is seen was not made out of what was visible. (Hebrews 11:3)

The Hebrew phrase *shamayim erets*, translated "heavens and earth," always refers to the entire physical universe. The Hebrew word for "created," *bara*, means "to make something brand-new or to make something out of nothing." Hebrews 11:3 states that the universe we can detect was made through that which we cannot possibly detect. This means that the universe was made transcendently, that it came from a source independent of matter, energy, length, width, height, and time.

This grace was given us in Christ Jesus before the beginning of time. (2 Timothy 1:9)

The hope of eternal life, which God, who does not lie, promised before the beginning of time. (Titus 1:2)

These verses state that time has a beginning and that God was causing effects before the beginning of time.

"You loved me before the creation of the world." (John 17:24)

He chose us in him before the creation of the world. (Ephesians 1:4)

He was chosen before the creation of the world. (1 Peter 1:20)

The Greek word for "world" in these passages is *kosmos*, which can refer to part of the earth, the whole of planet Earth, or the entire universe. Most scholars agree that the context of these verses implies the latter definition. Thus, God again is seen as causing effects before the creation of the universe, which would include our dimension of time.

Through him all things were made; without him nothing was made that has been made. (John 1:3)

For by him all things were created: things in heaven and on earth, visible and invisible, whether thrones or powers or rulers or authorities; all things were created by him and for him. He is before all things, and in him all things hold together. (Colossians 1:16-17)

These verses declare that Jesus Christ created everything. Nothing was created that He did not create. He existed before anything was created. That is, Christ was not created.

On the evening of that first day of the week, when the disciples were together, with the doors locked for fear of the Jews, Jesus came and stood among them. (John 20:19)
They were startled and frightened, thinking they saw a ghost. He said to them, "Why are you troubled, and why do doubts rise in your minds? Look at my hands and my feet. It is I myself! Touch me and see; a ghost does not have flesh and bones,

as you see I have." When he had said this, he showed them his hands and feet. And while they still did not believe it because of joy and amazement, he asked them, "Do you have anything here to eat?" They gave him a piece of broiled fish, and he took it and ate it in their presence. (Luke 24:37-43)

The disciples understood the impossibility of a physical body passing through physical barriers. That is why they concluded that the form of Jesus in front of them had to be ghostly or spiritual and not physical. But Jesus proved His physical reality by allowing the disciples to touch Him and by eating food in front of them. Though it is impossible for three-dimensional physical objects to pass through three-dimensional physical barriers without one or the other being damaged, Jesus would have no problem doing this in His extra dimensions. Six spatial dimensions would be adequate. He could simultaneously translate the first dimension of His physicality into the fourth dimension, the second into the fifth, and the third into the sixth. Then He could pass through the walls of the room and transfer His three-dimensional body from the fourth, fifth, and sixth dimensions back into the first, second, and third.

Your attitude should be the same as that of Christ Jesus: Who, being in very nature God, did not consider equality with God something to be grasped, but made himself nothing, taking the very nature of a servant, being made in human likeness. And being found in appearance as a man, he humbled himself and became obedient to death—even death on a cross! Therefore God exalted him to the highest place and gave him the name that is above every name, that at the name of Jesus every knee should bow, in heaven and on earth and under the earth, and every tongue confess that Jesus Christ is Lord, to the glory of God the Father. (Philippians 2:5-11)

This passage says that, in coming to Earth, Jesus Christ stripped Himself of the extra-dimensional capacities He shared with God the Father and the Holy Spirit. But these capacities were restored to Him once He had fulfilled His mission of redeeming human beings from their sin.

◆　◆　◆

Religions that view the Bible through the limited dimensionality of the universe inevitably deny portions of God's transcendence. Judaism accepts almost all the teaching of the Old Testament but rejects the New Testament. Islam and Mormonism "accept" both the Old Testament and New Testament but add other holy books to supersede them. The Jehovah's Witnesses accept the Old and New Testaments but choose to change several hundred words in both. Other cults such as Christian Science, Unity, and Religious Science simply ignore "unpleasant" passages in the Old and New Testaments.

The common denominator in all the alternatives to Christianity is a denial, at least in part, of God's transcendence and extra-dimensional attributes. For example, the tri-unity of God is taught only in the Christian faith.

Suffice it to say, Burbidge's conclusion stands. General relativity and the big bang lead to only one possible conclusion: a Creator matching the description of Jesus Christ. He is our Creator-God.

But Who Created God?

A question children often ask about God is, If God created us, who created God? A sophisticated adult might phrase the question this way: Given that Jesus Christ created the universe and everything in it, including all matter, energy, and the ten space-time dimensions, who created Him?

Actually, the question itself yields an elegant proof for creation. The universe and everything in it is confined to a single, finite dimension of time. Time in that dimension proceeds only and always forward. The flow of time can never be reversed. Nor can it be stopped. Because it has a beginning and can move in only one direction, time is really just half a dimension. The proof of creation lies in the mathematical observation that any entity confined to such a half-dimension of time must have a starting point or point of origination. That is, that entity must be created. This necessity for creation applies to the whole universe and ultimately to everything in it.

The necessity for God to be created, however, would apply only if God, too, were confined to half a dimension of time. He is not.

Again, by our definition, time is that realm or dimension in which cause-and-effect phenomena take place. According to the space-time theorems of general relativity, such effects as matter, energy, length, width, height, six other space dimensions, and time were caused independent of the time dimension of the universe. According to the New Testament (2 Timothy 1:9, Titus 1:2), such effects as grace and hope were caused independent of the time dimension of the universe. So both the Bible and general relativity speak of at least the equivalent of one additional time dimension for God.

In the equivalent of two or more dimensions of time, an entity is free from the necessity of being created. If time were two-dimensional, for example, both a time length and a time width would be possible. Time would expand from a line into a plane (see figure 10.1, page 113). In a plane of time, an infinite number of lines running in an infinite number of directions would be possible. If God were to so choose, He could move and operate along an infinite time line that never touches or crosses the time line of our universe. As John 1:3, Colossians 1:16-17, and Hebrews 7:3 say, He would have no beginning and no end. He would not be created.

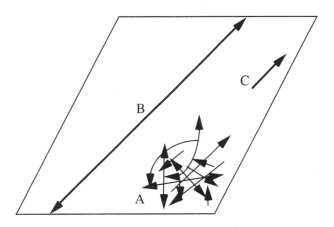

Figure 10.1: God's Time Frame Relative to Our Time Frame
If time were two-dimensional rather than one-dimensional, it would be some kind of plane rather than a line. In this case, an infinite number of time lines (A) would run in an infinite number of directions. This, according to general relativity and the Bible, is the situation with the Creator. If the Creator were to so choose, He could move and operate for infinite time, forward and backward, on a time line (B) that never intersects or touches the time line of our universe (C). As such, He would have no beginning and no end. He would not be created.

Non-Theistic Rebuttals

General relativity and the big bang provide a formidable threat to rational atheism. Committed atheists have recognized the threat and have attempted a response.

The Council for Democratic and Secular Humanism in the winter 1992–1993 issue of their magazine *Free Inquiry* lined up four physicists to write articles under the banner "Does the Big Bang Prove the Existence of God?"[2] The British journal *Nature* enlisted its physics editor, John Maddox, to write an editorial titled "Down with the Big Bang."[3] Atheists have also attempted to revive a plasma model of the universe to replace the big bang.[4]

In the first of the four *Free Inquiry* articles, Jean-Claude Pecker, a theoretical astrophysicist, questions whether the universe is expanding, and if it is, whether it is expanding at a rate consistent with star and galaxy cluster ages.[5] In the second, plasma physicist Milton Rothman claims, "All of the God theories collapse when three serious questions are asked: Where did God come from, where did God exist before the universe existed, and how did this God learn how to create?"[6] In the third, astrophysicist Victor Stenger looks to a natural spontaneous generation process followed by some "natural processes of self-organization" as the way to avoid the need for God's participation.[7] In the fourth article, philosopher Adolf Grünbaum objects to a theistic explanation for the big bang since it "presupposes some completely fictitious super-time for which no evidence at all has been given." He claims that "it makes no sense to trust [the making of] time as being on a par with [the making of] objects like stars or atoms."[8]

In the *Nature* editorial, John Maddox predicts that since young-Earth creationists have "impaled themselves on the hook of trying to disprove the relatively recent geological record," it will be only a matter of time before "the impatient creationists will have to retreat to the Big Bang" to support their belief in creation. Maddox concedes that creationists' beliefs have "ample justification" in the big bang. For this very reason he declares the big bang "thoroughly unacceptable" because it implies "an ultimate origin of our world" whose cause or Causer lies beyond the universe.[9]

What is Maddox's escape plan? He pins his hopes on a paper by British astrophysicists Donald Lynden-Bell, J. Katz, and J. H. Redmount, which shows that the universe might have begun as a line in space-time rather than as a point.[10]

A Point or a Line?

Let's tackle John Maddox's objections first. The space-time theorem of general relativity does imply that the universe originated from a singularity, but Maddox's definition of that singularity is inaccurate. A singularity is not an infinitely small point, as he suggests, but rather the whole of three-dimensional space shrunken down to a size of zero volume.

Thus it does not matter whether the universe expands from a point or a line. Both a point and a line have zero volume. For that matter, any one-, two-, three-, or N-dimensional shape for the origin of the universe that has zero volume yields a theistic conclusion. In all such cases the universe exhibits a big bang and an ultimate origin for all the cosmic space-time dimensions. Therefore, Maddox's argument fails. Based on his own words, Maddox's rejection of the big bang flows from his personal commitment to atheism rather than from scientific considerations.

A Numbers Game

Jean-Claude Pecker points to Halton Arp and William Tifft's observations of abnormal redshifts (redshift values that do not match the distance estimates for the objects in question) for some quasars as evidence that the universe may not be expanding. He ignores the fact that the universe's expansion is well established by the distances and velocities of galaxies where no abnormalities are seen. Moreover, recently, radio astronomers have confirmed the universe's expansion through direct geometric distance measures to both a galaxy and a quasar.[11] These direct measures unequivocally prove that redshift values do match distance estimates. Besides, the peculiar redshifts of Arp and Tifft are well accounted for by the overlap of quasar and galaxy images. Galaxies and quasars so crowd the field of view that inevitably on occasion several will line up in the astronomer's line of sight. What appears to be an anomalous redshift may in fact be another galaxy at a different distance.

Acknowledging that Arp and Tifft's abnormal redshifts may not prove truly anomalous, Pecker nevertheless believes he might still have a loophole. He speculates that the ages of the oldest stars might turn out to be inconsistent with measures of the mass and the expansion rate for the universe.

However, the track record of the observations is just the opposite. As the measuring tools multiplied and precision of measurements progressed, the correlation between the measured ages of the oldest stars and the age of the universe has become much tighter. Since 1992, we have seen a tremendous improvement in the accuracy of age determinations for the cosmos through measurements of the universe's total mass, baryon mass (mass of protons and neutrons), and expansion rates and through measurements of the maximum duration of star burning. Such measures were discussed in chapter 5 (pages 59-60) and remain in complete agreement.

Other Evaporating Concerns

Milton Rothman stumbles over the question, If God created us, who created God? It's the time-line problem. Scientific and biblical answers exist, but Rothman seems unaware of them. His real barrier may be his refusal to accept any reality beyond the concrete and tangible. He states that the only acceptable theory is one which "permits questions to be answered in an empirical manner so that we may understand the answers."[12]

Victor Stenger's appeal to spontaneous self-generation at the moment the universe began, followed by billions of years of self-organization that continues right through to the present, is purely speculative. Not one example of significant self-generation or self-organization can be found in the entire realm of nature. In fact, nature shows us just the opposite. (Examples like snowflakes do not count. They simply manifest order with little accompanying complexity. See chapter 14, page 164.) Without causation nothing happens and without organization by an intelligent being, systems tend toward lower and lower levels of complexity.

Adolf Grünbaum stumbles over the nature of time. No wonder. Two of the *Free Inquiry* authors correctly quote Saint Augustine as stating that time did not exist before the beginning of the universe.[13] Several Christian theologians to this day speak, like Augustine, of God dwelling in timeless eternity. This leads to the very contradictions that Grünbaum addresses. But the Bible claims (see John 17:4, Ephesians 1:4, Colossians 1:16-17, 2 Timothy 1:9, Titus 1:2, Hebrews 11:3), and science confirms, that God was causing effects before the time dimension for our universe existed. ("Time" by our definition is that realm or dimension in which cause-and-effect phenomena occur.) Once this concept of time is understood, Grünbaum's objections to God as the cause for existence of the universe evaporate.

To be fair to Augustine and many Augustinian theologians, Augustine clearly taught that God was fully capable of cause-and-effect phenomenon independent of the time dimension of our cosmos. It would be better to attribute to Augustine that time as we experience it did not exist before the beginning of the universe nor will it exist after God is finished with this universe.

The Biggest Challenger?

What some perceive as a more potent challenge to the big bang comes from Hans Alfvén's plasma theory (plasma refers to high energy charged particles distributed in such a way that they form a neutral gaseous medium). The main point of the plasma model is that gravitational theories alone are inadequate to explain the structure and dynamics of stellar systems, galaxies, galaxy clusters, and even the cosmos itself.

According to Alfvén, electromagnetic effects must play an important role. His point was proven correct for the solar system as far back as the early '60s. At that time it was demonstrated that strictly gravitational treatments could not possibly explain the development of the planets in our solar system. However, the combination of gravity and electromagnetism, as formulated by Alfvén, provided the missing answer.[14]

Along similar lines, Eric Lerner recently has insisted that the big bang could not explain the clumping of galaxies in time scales under a trillion years.[15] He therefore suggested that the big bang model be dumped in favor of a plasma model. But the COBE satellite discovery of temperature fluctuations in the cosmic background radiation, confirmations by balloon-borne and ground-based measurements (see chapter 4), and positive detections of exotic matter (see chapter 5) now establish that Lerner's application is unwarranted. Both galaxies and galaxy clusters can easily form in the relatively brief time scale permitted by the big bang model without any need for plasma at all.

A guiding principle in astronomy research is to develop explanations with the simplest possible theories. All astronomers acknowledge that magnetic fields are present in galaxies and quasars and that these fields play a significant role in the production of non-thermal radiation (the explosive processes at work in the centers of a small class of galaxies called "active galaxies"). However, the magnetic field strengths here are a thousand times less than for the solar system. For larger systems—clusters of galaxies and clusters of clusters of galaxies—the magnetic field strengths are much weaker still. Nowhere has the need yet arisen to introduce electromagnetic effects to help explain cosmic dynamics.

I believe, however, that the need to consider electromagnetic effects will arise someday. When our observations become sufficiently detailed, electromagnetic refinements to our gravitational theories should provide a closer fit to the real universe. Let me emphasize that what I am predicting is an eventual electromagnetic *refinement* of our best gravitational big bang models. Plasma without some kind of big bang meets with the same failure to predict observable phenomena as does the steady state model.

What is encouraging to theists about these challenges from

atheists is how feeble each argument is. The remaining attempts by non-theists to escape theistic implications of general relativity and the big bang all fall under the category of quantum gravity speculations. These are dealt with in the next two chapters.

CHAPTER ELEVEN

A BRIEF LOOK AT
A BRIEF HISTORY OF TIME

Several years ago I was invited to speak to a gathering of movie and TV writers, directors, and producers. My idea was to present scientific evidences for the God of the Bible, but the group implored me to critique Stephen Hawking's book *A Brief History of Time*. A review of a science text for Hollywood media people? It seemed bizarre. But, come the night of the event, the place was packed with twice the number of people expected, and nearly everyone present had read the book.

What I learned that night is that British physicist Stephen Hawking has become a folk hero for many Americans and a cult figure for new agers. The folk hero status is easy to understand. Who can help but be stirred by the valor of a man who must force the communication of his brilliant mind through the constricting barriers of amyotrophic lateral sclerosis (Lou Gehrig's disease)? His status as a cult figure comes from his reputation for suggesting that theoretical physics renders God impersonal and unnecessary for our existence.

A Brief History of Time is Hawking's fourth book, but his first aimed at a popular audience. It has sold very well. In fact, it is the best selling science book of all time with more than seven million copies sold. More recently it has been made into a feature length film and distributed to theaters around the world.

Most of the book relates the history of the universe to the latest discoveries about the theories of gravity. It is engaging if for no other reason than that one of the key history-makers is telling the story. The chapters on black holes are perhaps the most lucid ever written. Its few technical flaws seem minor. Anyone desiring to learn about research on the application of gravitational theories to the origin and development of the universe will not be disappointed.

Controversial Theology

A Brief History of Time is more than a popular-level text on gravitational theories. What makes Hawking's book unique and controversial are its philosophical and theological pronouncements.

In his final chapter, Hawking declares the goal of his life and work. He bends all his efforts toward answering these fundamental questions: "What is the nature of the universe? What is our place in it and where did it and we come from? Why is it the way it is?"[1] Hawking's dream is to answer these questions through physics alone. Thus far he gives no reason for his refusal to acknowledge, or accept, answers already given elsewhere, specifically in the pages of the Bible. From his close contact with Christians—including his ex-wife, Jane, and physics colleague Don Page—we can assume he is aware, at least, that the Bible addresses these issues. Yet, he chooses to ignore its answers. In an interview for the *Sunday Times Magazine* (London), Jane Hawking said,

> There doesn't seem to be room in the minds of people who are working out these things for other sources of inspiration. You can't actually get an answer out of Stephen regarding philosophy beyond the realms of science. . . . I can never get an answer, I find it very upsetting.[2]

An Absent God

The thrust of Hawking's philosophizing in *A Brief History of Time* is to demean God's role in the affairs of the universe and to elevate the role of the human race. Spearheading this thrust is Carl Sagan, who foreshadows the theme in his introduction to the book. According to Sagan, *A Brief History of Time* speaks "about God, or perhaps about the absence of God." It represents an effort to posit "a universe with no edge in space, no beginning or end in time, and *nothing for a Creator to do*" (emphasis added).[3] Ironically, this message contradicts the conclusions from Hawking's remarkable work on singularity theorems, which in Hawking's own words establishes that "time has a beginning."[4]

Through the principle of cause and effect, this theorem pointed obviously, perhaps too obviously for Hawking, to the existence of some entity beyond the dimensions of the universe who created the universe and its dimensions of space and time. Hawking's only hope, then, for escaping the beginning, hence the Beginner, lay in finding some possible point in the universe's history where the equations of general relativity (on which his space-time theorem was based) might break down.

Even before writing that book, Hawking began to reveal his membership in the ranks of the loophole seekers. In 1983 Stephen Hawking and James Hartle advanced the notion that since we cannot determine conditions in the universe before 10^{-43} seconds (or, 0.0000000000000000000000000000000000000000001) after its origin, perhaps some unknown phenomenon in that speck of time might have disturbed the governance of general relativity.[5] (Note: This notion was advanced before string theorists had demonstrated that a ten-dimensional creation calculation established the validity of all the physical laws back to the actual cosmic creation event.) If so, space, time, matter, and energy might not have originated from a true singularity (beginning from an infinitely small volume). They went on to propose that just as the behavior of a hydrogen atom can be described by a quantum mechanical wave function, so might the behavior of the universe. If that is the case, they claimed, the universe could have just popped into existence out of absolutely nothing at what most would call the beginning of time.

This fanciful hypothesis provides the basis for Hawking's widely quoted statement, "The universe would not be created, not be destroyed; it would simply be. What place, then, for a Creator?"[6] It is the basis, too, for new agers' and atheists' claims that according to science a personal Creator-God need not be the agency for the origin of the universe. To Hawking's credit, he later admitted in *A Brief History of Time* that the whole idea is "just a proposal: it cannot be deduced from some other principle."[7]

Flaw in the Proposal

Even if Hawking's hypothesis were true, there would still be no escaping the need for a Creator-God. As Heinz Pagels, a theoretical physicist, explains:

> This unthinkable void converts itself into the plenum of existence—a necessary consequence of physical laws. Where are these laws written into that void? What "tells" the void that it is pregnant with a possible universe? It would seem that even the void is subject to law, a logic that exists prior to space and time.[8]

Hawking has not gotten around the need for a Creator. Neither has he escaped the singularity. Frank Tipler, another theoretical physicist, has pointed out that Hawking may simply be substituting, unawares, one kind of singularity for another, more specifically a classical singularity of general relativity for a quantum singularity:

> A quantum universe [such as Hawking proposes] . . . necessarily consists of not just one four-dimensional sphere, but rather the infinity of spheres of all possible radii. However, since it is meaningless for the radius of a sphere to be less than or equal to zero, a four-dimensional sphere of zero radius forms a boundary to Hawking's universe. . . . He [Hawking] has eliminated the classical singularity—the beginning of time—only to have it re-appear as the "beginning" to the space of all possible four-spheres.[9]

The God Beyond Boundaries
Hawking himself has argued the case against any real escape for the universe from the singularity and the boundary conditions:

> If the universe really is in such a quantum state, there would be no singularities in the history of the universe in imaginary time. . . . The universe could be finite in imaginary time but without boundaries or singularities. When one goes back to the real time in which we live, however, there will still appear to be singularities. . . . Only if [we] lived in imaginary time would [we] encounter no singularities. . . . In real time, the universe has a beginning and an end at singularities that form a boundary to space-time and at which the laws of science break down.[10]

If we substitute biblical terminology here, we can say that God transcends "real time"[11]—that is, the single time dimension of the physical universe. Thus He is not confined to boundaries and singularities. Both human beings and the physical universe, however, are limited to real time. Hence, they would be confined by boundaries and singularities.

Though Hawking undoubtedly seeks to put some limits on the role of the Creator or, more precisely, to eliminate the *need* of a Creator's involvement in the existence and development of the universe, he is not trying to eliminate Him altogether. He emphatically rejects the label "atheist." He comes closer, perhaps, to fitting the description of a deist. In *A Brief History of Time* he says, "These laws [of physics] may have originally been decreed by God, but it appears that he has since left the universe to evolve according to them and does not now intervene in it."[12] He goes on to conclude that "with the success of scientific theories in describing events, most people have come to believe that God allows the universe to evolve according to a set of laws and does not intervene in the universe to break these laws."[13]

Hawking's reasons for taking a deistic position lie beyond his perception that it is the majority view. He made clear from the outset that he believes there exists a complete set of physical laws that yields "a complete description of the universe we live in,"[14] and further, that these laws "would also presumably determine our actions."[15] Accordingly, "If there were a complete set of laws, that would infringe [on] God's freedom to change his mind and intervene in the world."[16]

Can We Know All?

The most fundamental clash between Hawking's philosophy and biblical Christianity (not to mention physical reality) is Hawking's belief that human beings can discover that "complete set of laws." By this, he means not just a complete and consistent unified field theory (a theory explaining how a single primal force splits into the strong and weak nuclear forces and the electromagnetic and gravitational forces) but "a complete understanding of the events around us, and of our own existence."[17] Elsewhere he has said that he wants to "know the mind of God."[18] Since the existence of the God of the Bible or the existence of singularities would guarantee that his goal could never be reached, it is understandable that he seeks to deny both.

Ironically, his goal is not just biblically impossible but was proven mathematically impossible by Kurt Gödel in 1930. According to Gödel's incompleteness theorem, "no non-trivial set of arithmetical propositions can have its proof of consistency within itself." When applied to the cosmos, this means it is intrinsically impossible to know from the universe that the universe can only be what it is.[19] Normal experience is sufficient to show most of us that our human limitations will never allow us to learn everything about ourselves and the universe. The nature quiz that God posed to Job some four thousand years ago would still stump even so brilliant and educated a man as Stephen Hawking (see Job 38–41). More ironically, Hawking's own words prove his goal impossible. He acknowledges two unavoidable limitations on our quest for more scientific knowledge:

1. The limitation of the Heisenberg uncertainty principle of quantum mechanics (the impossibility for the human observer to measure exactly both the position and the momentum of any quantum entity).
2. The impossibility of exact solutions to all but the very simplest of physical equations.[20]

As Romans 1:19-22 affirms, even a brilliant research scientist can waste his or her efforts, in this case on theoretically impossible lines of research, if he or she rejects clear evidence pointing to God.

All This for Us

Hawking also rejects the anthropic principle, which is the observation that the universe has all the necessary and narrowly defined characteristics to make human life possible. Hawking apparently finds it impossible to believe that "this whole vast construction [the universe] exists simply for our sake."[21] As support for his incredulity, he says that "there does not seem to be any need for all those other galaxies, nor for the universe to be so uniform and similar in every direction on the large scale."[21] But, he ignores a growing body of research. The uniformity, homogeneity, and mass density of the universe all must be precisely as they are for human life to be possible at any time in the universe's history[22] (details of this are discussed in chapters 5 and 14).

At the close of his book, Hawking suggests that a unified field theory might be "so compelling that it brings about its own [and the universe's] existence." Even if a unified field theory did not create us, Hawking claims, the God of the Bible is not a candidate since we would be stuck with the question of "Who created him?"[23]

Like so many others before and after him, the great historian of time falls into the trap of assuming that God is confined to the same time limitations as we human beings. As explained in chapter 10, Hawking's own theorem answers his objection, an answer that New Testament Scripture had given more than nineteen centuries earlier (see table 10.1, page 110).

Attacks by physicists and other scientists on the God of the Bible are not new. The Bible seems an affront to their intellectual prowess. This ancient "religious" document makes many pointed and challenging statements about cosmic origins, all of them provable.

What an affront to pride. I know I felt it. The call to humility and submission in view of the awesomeness of what God created and wrote is more than some are willing to handle.

No society has seen as much proof for God as ours. But neither has any other society had access to so much learning, research, and technology. These are all things human beings tend to take credit for, especially those who consider themselves the masters of learning, research, and technology. This is what the apostle Paul meant when he commented that not many who are wise by the world's standards are counted as true believers (1 Corinthians 1:20-26).

CHAPTER TWELVE

A MODERN-DAY GOLIATH

Several years ago an alarm sounded like the one that echoed through Israel's camp in the days of King Saul. The Goliath, this time, was quantum mechanics (a theory defining the energy relationships of particle-sized physical phenomena in terms of discrete levels). Many prominent theologians heralded this giant as "the greatest contemporary threat to Christianity."[1] Besides Stephen Hawking, several famous physicists and many new-age proponents have proliferated popular books exploiting the difficult and mysterious nature of quantum mechanics to undermine the Christian view of origins.

These attacks seem to express again the defiant reaction to mounting evidence from physics and astronomy that the universe — all matter, energy, space, and time—began in a creation event, and that the universe was strategically designed for life, as the following chapters describe. This evidence is now sufficient to rule out all theological options but one—the Bible's. Obviously, this unexpected turn of research proves discomfiting to those who reject the narrowness of the message of salvation in Jesus Christ.

In their insistence that the inescapable creator-designer cannot be the God of the Bible, researchers grope for a replacement, any replacement. Three quantum possibilities in addition to Stephen Hawking's "universe as a wave function" (discussed in the previous chapter) have been proposed:

1. Quantum Tunneling

British astrophysicist Paul Davies, in his book *God and the New Physics*, written in 1983, locked all cause-and-effect phenomena into the time dimension of the universe. Because the act of creating represents cause and effect, and thus a time-bound activity, the evidence for time's origin, said Davies, argued against God's agency in the creation of the cosmos.[2]

Apparently, Davies is (or was) unaware that the Bible speaks of God's causing effects even before the beginning of the time dimension of our universe. As indicated in table 10.1 (see page 110), the Bible also speaks of the existence of dimensions beyond our time and space, extra dimensions in which God exists and operates.

Davies began by pointing out that virtual particles can pop into existence from nothingness through quantum tunneling (see figure 12.1). Such particles can be produced out of absolutely nothing, providing they are converted back into nothingness before the human observer can possibly detect their appearance. This typically means that the particles so produced must disappear in less than a quintillionth of a second.

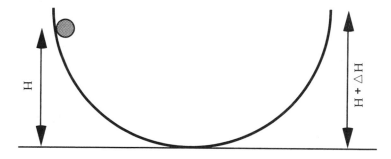

Figure 12.1: Quantum Tunneling
In classical physics a marble released from height H will roll down the side of a bowl and up the other side to the same height H, assuming the absence of friction. Since the lip of the bowl is at a height of H + ᴧH, the marble will remain forever trapped inside the bowl. But the uncertainty principle of quantum mechanics states that for a quantum particle there must always exist a minimum uncertainty in the energy of the particle. This uncertainty implies that a quantum particle released from height H has a finite possibility of exceeding H + ᴧH on the other side. The smaller ᴧH is relative to H, the greater the possibility. Also, the faster the particle can travel from one side to the other (the less shallow the bowl), the greater the possibility. So quantum tunneling implies that a quantum mechanical particle can escape from the bowl, whereas a typical marble could not.

Davies next appealed to the grand unified theories of particle physics to suggest that by the same means the entire cosmos could have popped into existence. However, he forgot to acknowledge that for a system as massive as the universe, the time for it to disappear back into nothingness must be less than 10^{-103} seconds (102 zeros between the decimal point and the one), a moment a bit briefer than the age of the universe.

Ironically, Davies' argument against God's creating can be turned against his hypothesis. Quantum mechanics is founded on the concept that quantum events occur according to finite probabilities within finite intervals of time. The larger the time interval, the greater the probability that a specific quantum event will occur. This means that if the time interval is zero, the probability for that quantum event occurring is also zero. Because time began when the universe was created, the time interval is zero, eliminating quantum tunneling as a possible candidate to be the creator of the cosmos.

Of course, some will argue that since we may not know exactly what occurred before the universe was 10^{-43} seconds old, the possibility may exist that the relationship between time and the probability for certain quantum events in that tiny time interval could break down. However, this argument is based on pure speculation, actually multiple speculations. First one must speculate that a specific breakdown occurred. Then one must speculate that the breakdown occurred at precisely the needed moment of time and location of space. Finally, one must speculate that this breakdown occurred in a such a fashion that the quantum tunneling of the entire universe took place.

String theory blocks this attempted loophole outright. As mentioned in chapter 4 (see page 43) and described fully in my book, *Beyond the Cosmos*,[3] solving the creation problem (the perceived incompatibility of quantum mechanics and gravity) in ten space-time dimensions not only permits gravity and quantum mechanics everywhere and every time to coexist and operate, not only predicts both special and general relativity as natural outcomes of the solution, but demonstrates that the laws of physics hold back to the creation event itself. While it is true that not all of the fundamental particles predicted by the solution have been discovered yet, many have. Also, all six of the experimental tests designed to critique the solution during the past three years have shown its validity.

As every student of philosophy knows, anything can be speculated in the realm of human ignorance, including even the nonexistence of the theorist engaged in the speculation. In his book Davies acknowledged the necessity of avoiding such philosophical conundrums by repeatedly appealing to Ockham's razor.[4] Ockham's razor is a guiding principle of Western science that the most plausible explanation is that which contains the simplest ideas and fewest assumptions. The possibility of quantum tunneling as creator of the universe fails to meet the criteria of Ockham's razor.

WHAT IS NOTHING?

Physicists, unlike philosophers, use five different definitions of *nothing* in their models on creation. The accuracy of the declaration that God created the cosmos out of "nothing" depends on which definition of *nothing* the statement implies. These are the five: (1) lack of matter, (2) lack of matter and energy, (3) lack of matter, energy, and the four large expanding space-time dimensions of the universe, (4) lack of matter, energy, and all ten space-time dimensions of the universe, and (5) lack of any entity, being, existence, dimensionality, activity, or substance whatever. The Bible says God created the universe we detect and measure from that which no human can detect and measure.[5] In other words, the universe came from *nothing* as defined in #4 above.

Davies deserves credit for ongoing reconsiderations and revisions of his position. In a book published in 1984 (*Superforce*), he argued that the laws of physics "seem themselves to be the product of exceedingly ingenious design."[6] In a more recent book (*The Cosmic Blueprint*, 1988) he posed this question: "If new organizational levels just pop into existence for no reason, why do we see such an orderly progression in the universe from featureless origin to rich diversity?"[7] He concluded that we have "powerful evidence that there is something going on behind it all" and the "impression of design is overwhelming."[8] In his latest book, *The Fifth Miracle*, Davies concludes that "the origin of life is virtually impossible" and that "you could be forgiven for concluding that a genome really is a miraculous object."[9] Davies seems to be moving toward some form of theism.

2. Infinite Changes

In spite of the spectacular successes by string theorists in demonstrating that their ten-dimensional creation solution (see box in chapter 4, page 43) is valid from the beginning of time (the creation event), several theoretical physicists, nonetheless, have speculated that quantum mechanics behaves in some fundamentally different way in that extremely early instant of the universe's history (previous to 10^{-43} seconds after the creation event) when all four of the fundamental forces (electromagnetism, weak nuclear force, strong nuclear force, and gravity) are unified. While successfully predicting special and general relativity and solving some outstanding problems in the physics of black holes, these theoreticians counter that the full panoply of fundamental particles predicted by string theory has yet to be discovered. Until knowledge of all these particles are in hand, they claim, we *might* not be able to close the door on alternate quantum physics.

Seizing the opportunity to speculate, these physicists hypothesize that sometime before the universe was 10^{-43} seconds old, different quantum physics allowed a vast seething space-time foam to form. This foam, they suggest, somehow split off or budded an infinite number of baby universes. They further hypothesize that each of these baby universes would take on characteristics distinct from all the others.

An infinite number of universes, all with different physical characteristics, these physicists state, could explain, without invoking a divine Creator, why one universe possesses so many properties that are so highly fine-tuned for the existence of physical life (see chapter 14). Their argument is that with an infinite number of universes, all with different physical characteristics, anything would be possible, even a universe as exquisitely fine-tuned or "apparently designed," as ours is for physical life. Where did the space-time foam come from? Andre Lindé boldly declares that "nothing is unstable." In other words, he claims that absolute nothingness will spontaneously generate something. I have six responses to this line of analysis and speculation:

1. There is no escape from a transcendent creation act. The speculation of these physicists all depend on something beyond physics as we observe it. This is no different from the creation statements in Hebrews 11:3 and Genesis 1:1 where the universe that we humans can detect is said to have been made from that which we humans have no possibility of detecting and that one universe at its beginning is created brand new.

2. If absolute nothingness spontaneously generates space, time, matter, and/or energy, then the principle of cause-and-effect has been violated. This would undermine the entire foundation of all the sciences, mathematics, and logic. Overwhelming evidence supports that foundation. Not one shred of evidence negates it. If absolute nothingness were truly unstable, as Lindé suggests, then even our own realm would be disturbed. That

is, we should be observing spontaneous creations within our universe. We do not.

3. Absolute nothingness implies a zero information state. How did a zero information system acquire its subsequent high information condition without the input of an intelligent, personal Creator? How else but through a personal Creator did a primeval radiation field come into existence and give birth to such high information systems as human beings?

4. The appeal to an infinite number of universes is a flagrant abuse of probability theory. It assumes the benefits of an infinite sample size without any evidence that the sample size exceeds one. Consider the following example. If a person spins 10^{1567} (the number one followed by 1,567 zeros) roulette wheels a thousand times each, by random chance, one of these roulette wheels would be likely to produce a thousand consecutive zeros. But, if a person had only one roulette wheel to spin, then regardless how many other spinning roulette wheels might conceivably exist, should that single roulette wheel produce a thousand consecutive zeros, one must rationally conclude the wheel had been manufactured to produce nothing but zeros.

5. What we see here is another case of the "no-God of the gaps." It seems that many non-theistic scientists (and others) are relying on gaps in our knowledge, in this case a very minute one, to provide a way around the theistic implications of scientifically established facts. Surely, the burden of proof lies with those who suggest that more than one universe exists or that physical conditions or physical laws were totally different before 10^{-43} seconds.

6. The evidence for more than one universe will never be forthcoming. The theory of general relativity implies that once physical observers exist in universe A, the space-time fabric of that universe can never overlap the space-time fabric of any other possibly existing universe.[10] Travel or contact between one universe and another that might possibly exist would be prohibited even in principle.[11] Therefore, even if God did create twenty different universes, philosophically and mathematically, the sample size of universes for us humans is just one, and as long as we reside in this universe it will always be just one.

3. Observer-Created Reality

In popular-level books on quantum mechanics a clear distinction is seldom made between the physics, the philosophy, and the religion of quantum mechanics. Therefore, let me briefly explain the differences:

- The *physics* of quantum mechanics tells us there are certain inviolable principles operating on quantum entities. These principles allow the human observer to predict accurately the probability for the outcome of any particular quantum event (for example, an electron moving from one energy level to another).
- The *philosophy* of quantum mechanics is the attempt to describe the nature of cause and effect in quantum phenomena and, in particular, the role of human observers in such cause and effect.
- The *religion* of quantum mechanics is the attempt to discern who or what is ultimately behind cause and effect in quantum events.

In the '20s and '30s, the physics of quantum mechanics was questioned, most notably by Einstein.[11] But not anymore. The experimental evidence puts the physical principles of quantum mechanics beyond dispute.

A remaining problem, however, lies in the wedding of one philosophical interpretation of quantum mechanics to the physics. Danish physicist Niels Bohr cast such a large shadow over the early history of quantum mechanics research that his "Copenhagen interpretation" has been assumed by many to be one of its basic physics principles. But that isn't the case.

Niels Bohr, who operated from presuppositions equivalent to those found in Hinduism, declared that, in the micro-world of quantum phenomena, reality in the absence of an observer does not exist. More to the point, he claimed the act of observing creates the reality. Thus he not only believed a quantum event could not take place without an observer, but that the observer, through his or her observations, actually brought about the quantum event.

Bohr arrived at his conclusions by noting a difference in a quantum particle before and after its detection by an observer. Before a specific quantum particle is detected, only a probability of where it might be located or of how energetic it is can be known. But after detection, the precise location or energy level is determined. This movement from imprecision to precision led Bohr and his associates at the Bohr Institute for Atomic Studies in Copenhagen to believe that the observer actually gives reality to the quantum particle.

ALTERNATIVE PHILOSOPHIES OF QUANTUM MECHANICS

Of late, the flaws in the philosophical aspects of the Copenhagen interpretation of quantum mechanics have proliferated a variety of alternatives. At last count, ten independent philosophical models have been developed and seriously proposed:[12]
1. A coherent reality exists independent of human thinking.
2. A common fundamental cause lies behind the cause-and-effect phenomena humans observe.
3. All possible outcomes will actually occur.
4. The act of observation dissolves the boundary between the observer and the observed.
5. The world obeys a nonhuman kind of reasoning.
6. The world is composed of objects that possess attributes whether or not the objects are observed.
7. The only observer who counts is the conscious observer.
8. The world is twofold, consisting of potentials and actualities.
9. The real essence of substances is beyond our knowledge.
10. The physical realm is the materialization of pure thought.

Since the founding of the Copenhagen interpretation of quantum mechanics, others, mainly non-physicists, have applied Bohr's conclusions about a quantum particle to the entire universe. If an observer can give reality to a quantum particle, they say, why not to the whole of the cosmos itself? Of course, these people assume that the observer in question is a human observer. From this assumption, it seems logical to conclude that human beings, not God, created the universe.

Some of the logical flaws in this line of reasoning are obvious; others are more subtle:

- There is no movement from imprecision to precision in quantum phenomena. All that happens is that the observer can choose where to put the imprecision. If the observer chooses to measure the position of the quantum particle accurately, he or she loses the potential for any precision in measuring the particle's momentum. Conversely, if the observer chooses to measure the momentum of the quantum particle accurately, the potential for any precision on the position of the particle will be irretrievably lost.

- While pure quantum events do exhibit effects that are significant and important, they result in no permanent change to any part of the universe.
- The observer does not give reality to the quantum entity. The observer can only choose what aspect of the reality he wants to discern. Though in quantum entities, indefinite properties become definite to the observer through measurements, the observer cannot determine how and when the indefinite property becomes definite. That is, at some point in the measurement sequence, the pure quantum mechanical description becomes invalid and the physical system assumes a specific physical state. However, exactly where and when this transition occurs cannot be determined by human observers.
- Rather than telling us that we human beings are more powerful than we otherwise thought, quantum mechanics tells us that we are weaker. In classical physics, no apparent limit exists on our ability to make accurate measurements. In quantum mechanics, a fundamental and easily determinable limit exists. In classical physics, we can see all aspects of causality. But in quantum mechanics, some aspect of causality always remains hidden from human investigation.
- Experiments in particle physics and relativity consistently reveal that nature is described correctly by the condition that the human observer is irrelevant.[13]
- The time duration between a quantum event and its observed result is always very brief, briefer by many orders of magnitude than the time period separating the beginning of the universe from the beginning of humans.
- For both the universe and human beings time is not reversible. Thus, no amount of human activity can ever affect events that occurred billions of years ago.
- There is nothing particularly special about human observers. Inanimate objects, like photoelectric detectors, are just as capable of detecting quantum mechanical events.

All these flaws punctuate what should be obvious to us all—the human race is neither powerful nor wise enough to create a universe.

To say that we created our own universe would imply that we can control time and restructure the past.

As time advances, the quantum mechanical alternatives to God become more and more absurd. Today, there are scientists and philosophers and mystics who are willing to claim that we humans are the creator.

The progression toward absurdity underscores these two observations:

1. The persistence of rejection of God's existence and creative work despite the build-up of evidence for both suggests that the source of rejection is not intellectual. This was brought home to me while reading an article in one of the humanist magazines to which I subscribe. The article noted that "atheists, agnostics, humanists, freethinkers—call them what you will—are almost all former Christians."[14] It seems the issue for these atheists, agnostics, humanists, and freethinkers is not so much the deficiency of evidence for the Christian faith but rather the deficiencies of Christians. They seem to be reacting to their past, holding bitterness over the wrongs or abuses they incurred in their experiences with Christians or with people who call themselves Christians.

2. The appeal to increasing absurdities in response to the evidences for the God of the Bible demonstrates again how secure these evidences must be. Nothing in our human experience can be proven absolutely. Our limitations in the space-time continuum of the cosmos guarantee this. But when a conclusion is opposed by increasingly absurd alternative explanations, that indicates something about the strength of the conclusion. For example, the Flat-Earth Society still has "reasons" for rejecting the conclusion that planet Earth is spherical. But the reasons presented today are much more absurd than those presented thirty years ago and far more absurd than those presented a hundred years ago. Thus, the history of their appeals for a flat-Earth interpretation reflect the growing certainty about Earth's roughly spherical shape. Likewise, the history of appeals for a non-theistic interpretation for the physical realm reflect the growing certainty about the existence of the God of the Bible.

CHAPTER THIRTEEN

THE DIVINE WATCHMAKER

The evidence for design in the natural realm has always been a favorite argument for God's existence. Though in the past it has been criticized for its lack of rigor and thoroughness, the design argument has consistently proved the most compelling argument for God. That's because the design evidence is simple, concrete, and tangible.

Paley's Watchmaker Argument

A classic historical example of such tangible simplicity comes from the eighteenth-century British theologian-naturalist William Paley and is called "the Watchmaker argument."

> In crossing a heath, suppose I pitched my foot against a stone, and were asked how the *stone* came to be there; I might possibly answer, that, for anything I knew to the contrary, it lain there for ever: nor would it perhaps be very easy to show the absurdity of this answer. But suppose I had found a *watch* upon the ground, and it should be inquired how the watch happened to be in that place; I should hardly think of the answer which I had before given, that for anything I knew, the watch might have always been there. . . . The watch must have had a maker: that there must have existed, at some time, and at some place or other, an artificer or artificers, who formed it for the purpose which we find it actually to answer; who comprehended its construction, and designed its use. . . . Every indication of contrivance, every manifestation of design, which existed in the watch, exists in

137

the works of nature; with the difference, on the side of nature, of being greater or more, and that in a degree which exceeds all computation.[1]

No one of sound mind, Paley explains, would ever conclude that a watch was the product of bits of dust, dirt, and rock being shuffled together under natural processes. Even if the natural processes were allowed to operate for a very long time, there would still be no rational hope for a watch to be assembled. Yet, as all the naturalists of Paley's day admitted and all the biologists of today emphatically concur, the complexity and capability of living organisms far transcends anything we see in a watch. If a watch's complexity and capability demand an intelligent and creative maker, surely, Paley reasoned, the living organisms on our planet demand a Maker of far greater intelligence and creative ability.

Rebuttals by Hume, Darwin, and Gould

As persuasive as Paley's Watchmaker argument may seem, it has been largely rejected by secular scholars. The basis for the rejection stems from three rebuttals: one by philosopher David Hume, one by biologist Charles Darwin, and one by paleontologist Stephen Jay Gould.

Hume argued that the analogy between the watch and a living organism was not close enough. He claimed that a living organism only has the *appearance* of an engine, and that, therefore, the complexity and capability of living organisms were only evidences for *apparent* design. As to where the apparent design of organisms came from, Hume hypothesized a universe composed of a finite number of particles all in perpetual random motion for infinite time. In such a universe, Hume declared, the random shuffling of matter eventually would produce complex bioforms well adapted to their environment. Such complexity and adaptation would bear to the casual observer the appearance of design.[2]

Darwin argued that observations within Earth's biosphere established three self-evident truths: (1) tremendous variations existed among populations of organisms, (2) these variations could be inherited, and (3) all organisms were involved in an intense competition for survival that would favor the preservation by natural selection of superior variations. To these three can now be added a fourth: New variations to replace those extinguished through natural selection are generated by random changes, or mutations, in the genetic codes within organisms that are responsible for the inheritable characteristics. Many modern Darwinists therefore conclude that random mutations and natural selection are capable of explaining all of the changes in life forms that have occurred during the history of our planet.

In summarizing the claims of such radical Darwinists, biochemist Jacques Monod says, "Chance *alone* is at the source of every innovation, of all creation in the biosphere. Pure chance, absolutely free but blind, at the very root of the stupendous edifice of evolution."[3]

In his best-selling book *The Blind Watchmaker: Why the Evidence of Evolution Reveals a Universe Without Design*, biologist and self-professed atheist Richard Dawkins declares,

> Natural selection, the blind, unconscious, automatic process which Darwin discovered, and which we now know is the explanation for the existence and apparently purposeful form of all life, has no purpose in mind. It has no mind and no mind's eye. It does not plan for the future. It has no vision, no foresight, no sight at all. If it can be said to play the role of watchmaker in nature, it is the *blind* watchmaker.[4]

This is the heart of the materialists' reply to Paley, the claim that the apparent design and purpose seen in Earth's life forms is not real but rather the product of strictly natural processes.

Gould attempts to buttress the Darwinists' attack on Paley by pointing out a number of "bad designs" in nature.[5] He argues from his examples that living organisms developed by random tinkering, not as the result of any real design. Specifically, he gives the credit to opportunistic utilization of previously existing parts. In his most famous example, he claims that the panda's thumb is a clumsy adaptation of a wrist bone, not the work of a divine designer.

A Reply to Hume

Hume's attack on Paley's watch analogy is unfounded for the following reason: While no mechanical engine is an organism, all organisms are engines. An engine is any system capable of processing energy to perform work. All organisms do this. But they do a lot more. Thus, since no one would rationally argue that a working engine designed by another human could be chance-assembled by purely natural processes, it is far more ludicrous to suggest that strictly natural processes could assemble living organisms.

Hume made his argument before astronomers could measure the cosmos. He did not know his necessary condition for the natural assembly of bioforms, namely infinite time, was false. Neither did he know that suitable conditions for life chemistry have existed for only a brief portion of the universe's duration.

Hume also wrote before biologists were capable of appreciating the incredible complexity and functionality of living organisms. Statistical mechanics tells us that if the means to preserve the initial and intermediate stages of assembly are absent, the greater the complexity and functionality of a system, the less advantageous additional time becomes for assembly by random processes (the parts wear out too soon). Moreover, assembly is not enough. Just as the assembled watch must first be wound up and the time set before it is able to function, so also something or Someone must set the assembled organism into operation.

Thanks to the invention of a new kind of microscope, Hume's claim that no strict analogy exists between a machine and an organism has been proven incorrect. For the last four years biochemists have possessed X-ray scanning electron microscopes so powerful they can map complex biological molecules down to the level of the individual atoms that make up the molecules.

Design that has been hidden from view now has been exposed. One of the earliest molecules so mapped was the crystal structure of the F1-ATPase enzyme. The Japanese team that produced the map discovered nature's own rotary engine—no bigger than ten billionths by ten billionths by eight billionths of a meter.[6] This tiny motor includes the equivalent of an engine block, a drive shaft, and three pistons. It is a variable speed motor that runs at speeds between 0.5 and 4.0 revolutions per second.

Near the other end of the size spectrum is a map produced by a German research team of the yeast 26S proteasome molecule.[7] This molecule contains over two million protons and neutrons. Its map reveals that it serves as an intracellular waste-disposal and recycling system. Smaller molecules within the cell attach protein markers (called ubiquitin) to other protein molecules deemed waste material. (Apparently the cell's command center informs the marker molecules which proteins are ready for disposal.) Since these ready-for-disposal proteins resemble tangled balls of yarn, the first job of the 26S proteasome, after identifying a tagged protein, is to unfold, untwist, and unravel it. This function is performed by an apparatus at one end of the proteasome.

Once the targeted protein is straightened out, the proteasome slowly drags it into its core and cuts the protein into segments. These segments are precisely measured by a "ruler" inside the proteasome. The cut-up pieces are then ejected from the proteasome, and a "sanitation" fleet (other proteins) drives by to pick them up and sort them, separating the stuff that can be reused from the stuff that cannot.

To date, several dozen different biological molecules have been so mapped. Not only do biochemists now see strict analogies in these molecules to humanly designed machines, they are observing designs that are actually superior to our best human efforts. Nanomotors (motors that are just several billionths of a meter in diameter) designed and built by human engineers, for example, are more than ten times less efficient than the equivalently sized motors biochemists find in biological molecules.

The molecular biological machines biochemists have so far mapped do not work in isolation. They are strict analogies to factories. The biological machines cooperatively support one another in their tasks. Thus, not only have all of Hume's rebuttals been refuted, Paley's design argument is now acknowledged as being far too conservative.

The Origins Question

A major flaw in the attack by radical Darwinists on the Watchmaker argument is their failure to address the origin of life. The Darwinist mechanisms of natural selection and mutations are useless *until the first life form is assembled.* In spite of decades of intense research, origin-of-life scientists have yet to demonstrate the feasibility of any mechanism(s) for the assembly of a living organism from inorganic materials by strictly natural processes (see chapter 16). Here the analogy with Paley's watch remains quite close. Both have a high degree of complexity, and both move from zero functionality to complete functionality.

Another flaw is that, just like Hume, Darwin failed to understand that the geologic eras do not provide even remotely sufficient time for living organisms to change significantly by natural processes. While it is beyond dispute that life forms have changed very significantly over the course of the history of planet Earth, only micro-evolutionary changes have been determined to occur by strictly natural processes.

Natural selection can move a species only a limited distance from the species' norm, and the greater the distance, the lower the probability for survival. A good example of these limitations is demonstrated in dog breeding. One cannot possibly breed a dog significantly smaller than a teacup poodle. Moreover, such a poodle requires an intense level of care just to survive. More tellingly, if all the dog breeds were allowed to interact sexually, they would quickly revert back to their wild dog ancestries.

For macro-evolution to occur by strictly natural processes, multiple favorable mutations must take place simultaneously at a rate sufficient to overcome the natural extinction rate. This leads to an insurmountable problem, a problem I address more fully in my book, *The Genesis Question*.[8]

Evolution Reversal

According to the fossil record, more and more species of life came into existence through the millennia before the appearance of modern humans. Through time, the number of species extinctions nearly balanced the number of introductions, but introductions remained slightly more numerous.

Everything changed, however, with the arrival of the human species. Since the first human being, the number of species going extinct has remained high while the number of new species appearing measures a virtual zero. Estimates of the current rate of extinction vary, from a low of one species per day to a high of five species per hour.[9] Though many believe that the influence of the human race on that rate predominates, environmental experts are willing to say that even if no humans existed, at least one species per year would still go extinct.[10] Meanwhile, as biologists Paul and Anne Ehrlich disclose, "The production of a new animal species in nature has yet to be documented." Furthermore, "in the vast majority of cases, the rate of change is so slow that it has not even been possible to detect an increase in the amount of differentiation."[11] Obviously, a tremendous imbalance between extinctions and speciation now exists.

The imbalance between speciation today and speciation in the fossil record era cannot be explained by radically different natural conditions. The conditions are known, and they are not significantly different. What is different is God's activity. The Bible declares that since God created Eve He has ceased from His work of creating new life forms. But in the fossil record era (God's six days of creation), God was active in creating millions of species of life, introducing new species and replacing and upgrading all those going extinct by natural processes.

What the materialists fail to address in their Darwinist musings is the reversal in the direction of biological evolution. Before the appearance of the human race, life on Earth was becoming progressively complex and diverse (during God's days of creation). Since the appearance of human beings, life on Earth has become less complex and diverse (during God's seventh day of rest).

Much more could be added to the argument against the materialistic interpretation of life, such as the problems of mass extinctions, similarities in chemistry and form among Earth's species, the origin of sex, non-random mutations, missing horizontal branches in the fossil record tree, genetic decay, etc. But space does not permit. Modern research in astronomy, biology, and paleontology, far from discrediting Paley, fully exonerate him.

A Bad Design?

As for Gould's examples of bad design, three responses come to mind. The first is that his judging of certain biological components as bad is largely subjective. Others have disagreed with his evaluations. In particular, Peter Gordon takes issue with Gould's best-known example of the panda's thumb. Gordon argues that rather than the thumb being clumsy and jury-rigged, it is a functional, original design.[12] Gordon's conclusion has been established in a recent study by six Japanese biologists who used three-dimensional computed tomography and magnetic resonance imaging to demonstrate that certain bones of the giant panda's hand form a double pincer-like apparatus that allows the panda to "manipulate objects with great dexerity."[13]

Organisms are so complex that no biologist can claim to understand them completely. Thus, even biologists are in a poor position to judge the quality of the Creator's work.

A second response is that to believe in creation by God is not to claim that all the development in organisms is strictly divine. In addition to divine intervention, natural processes are obviously at work to change, at least to some degree, the form and function of organisms. Thus the second law of thermodynamics, for example, would guarantee increasing degradation of the divine designs.

A third response is that Gould provides no new explanation for the design in the "previously existing parts." All he can muster are the already discredited Darwinist explanations.

A Better Argument

Far from being shattered, Paley's Watchmaker argument stands firm. But an obvious way to strengthen Paley's argument is to look at the whole in addition to the part. Paley did the only thing he could do: examine a tiny part of God's creation in search of evidence for Him. That left unanswered, however, the relationship of the whole to the part. But this is a relationship that can now be explored. The universe now has been measured and new understandings of the whole help us to comprehend more about the Creator.

CHAPTER FOURTEEN

A "JUST RIGHT" UNIVERSE

No other generation has witnessed so many discoveries about the universe. No other generation has seen the measuring of the cosmos. For previous generations the universe remained a profound mystery. But we are alive to see several of its mysteries solved.

Not only can we measure certain aspects of the universe, but in these measurements we are discovering some of the characteristics of the One who fashioned it all. Astronomy has provided us with new tools to probe the Creator's personality.

Building Blocks Problem

Before the measuring of the cosmos, non-theists assumed the availability of the appropriate building blocks for life. They posited that, with enough time, the right natural processes, and enough building blocks, even systems as complex as organisms could be assembled without the help of a supreme being. In chapters 4, 5, 7, 8, and 9, we have seen there is not sufficient time. In this chapter we'll consider just how amazing it is that the universe provides the right building blocks and the right natural processes for life.

To put this situation in perspective, imagine the possibility of a Boeing 747 aircraft being completely assembled as a result of a tornado striking a junkyard. Now imagine how much more unlikely that possibility would be if bauxite (aluminum ore) is substituted for the junk parts. Finally, imagine the possibility if instead of bauxite, river silt is substituted. So, too, as one examines the building blocks necessary for life to come into existence, the possibility of that happening without someone or something designing them stretches the imagination beyond the breaking point. Four major building blocks must be designed "just right" for life.

1. Getting the Right Molecules

For life to be possible, more than forty different elements must be able to bond together to form molecules. Molecular bonding depends on two factors, the strength of the force of electromagnetism and the ratio of the mass of the electron to the mass of the proton.

If the electromagnetic force were significantly larger, atoms would hang on to electrons so tightly no sharing of electrons with other atoms would be possible. But if the electromagnetic force were significantly weaker, atoms would not hang on to electrons at all, and again, the sharing of electrons among atoms, which makes molecules possible, would not take place. If more than just a few kinds of molecules are to exist, the electromagnetic force must be more delicately balanced yet.

The size and stability of electron orbits about the nuclei of atoms depends on the ratio of the electron mass to the proton mass. Unless this ratio is delicately balanced, the chemical bondings essential for life chemistry could never take place.

2. Getting the Right Atoms

Life molecules cannot result unless sufficient quantities of the elements essential for life are available, which means atoms of various sizes must be able to form. For that to happen, a delicate balance must exist among the constants of physics which govern the strong and weak nuclear forces, gravity, and the nuclear ground state energies (quantum energy levels important for the forming of elements from protons and neutrons) for several key elements.

In the case of the strong nuclear force—the force governing the degree to which protons and neutrons stick together in atomic nuclei—the balance is easy to see. If this force were too weak, protons and neutrons would not stick together. In that case, only one element would exist in the universe, hydrogen, because the hydrogen atom has only one proton and no neutrons in its nucleus. On the other hand, if the strong nuclear force were of slightly greater strength than what we observe in the cosmos, protons and neutrons would have such an affinity for one another that not one would remain alone. They would all find themselves attached to many other protons and neutrons. In such a universe there would be no hydrogen, only heavy elements. Life chemistry is impossible without hydrogen; it is also impossible if hydrogen is the only element.

How delicate is the balance for the strong nuclear force? If it were just 2% weaker or 0.3% stronger than it actually is, life would be impossible at any time and any place within the universe.[1]

Are we just considering life as we know it? No, we're talking about any conceivable kind of life chemistry throughout the cosmos. This delicate condition must be met universally.

In the case of the weak nuclear force—the force that governs, among other things, the rates of radioactive decay—if it were much stronger than what we observe, the matter in the universe would quickly be converted into heavy elements. But if it were much weaker, the matter in the universe would remain in the form of just the lightest elements. Either way, the elements essential for life chemistry (such as carbon, oxygen, nitrogen, phosphorus) either would not exist at all or would exist in amounts far too small for all the life-essential chemicals to be built. Further, unless the weak nuclear force were delicately balanced, those life-essential elements that are produced only in the cores of supergiant stars would never escape the boundaries of those cores (supernova explosions would become impossible).[2]

The strength of the force of gravity determines how hot the nuclear furnaces in the cores of stars will burn. If the gravitational force were any stronger, stars would be so hot they would burn up relatively quickly, too quickly and too erratically for life. Additionally, a planet capable of sustaining life must be supported by a star that is both stable and long burning. However, if the gravitational force were any weaker, stars never would become hot enough to ignite nuclear fusion. In such a universe no elements heavier than hydrogen and helium would be produced.

In the late 1970s and early 1980s, Fred Hoyle discovered that an incredible fine-tuning of the nuclear ground state energies for helium, beryllium, carbon, and oxygen was necessary for any kind of life to exist. The ground state energies for these elements cannot be higher or lower with respect to each other by more than 4% without yielding a universe with insufficient oxygen or carbon for life.[3] Hoyle, who has written extensively against theism[4] and Christianity in particular,[5] nevertheless concluded on the basis of this quadruple fine-tuning that "a superintellect has monkeyed with physics, as well as with chemistry and biology."[6]

In 2000, a team of astrophysicists from Austria, Germany, and Hungary demonstrated that the level of design for electromagnetism and the strong nuclear force is much greater than what physicists previously had determined.[7] The team began by noting that for any kind of conceivable physical life to be possible in the universe certain minimum abundances of both the elements carbon and oxygen must exist. Next, they pointed out that the only astrophysical sources of significant quantities of carbon and oxygen are red giant stars. (Red giant stars are large stars that through nuclear fusion have consumed all of their hydrogen fuel and subsequently engage in the fusion of helium into heavier elements.)

What the astrophysical team did was to mathematically construct models of red giant stars that adopted slightly different values of the strong nuclear force and electromagnetic force constants. They discovered that tiny adjustments in the values of either of these constants imply that red giant stars would produce too little carbon, too little oxygen, or too little of both oxygen and carbon. Specifically, they determined that if the value of the coupling constant for electromagnetism were 4% smaller or 4% larger than what we observe, then life would be impossible. In the case of the coupling constant for the strong nuclear force, if it were 0.5% smaller or larger, life would be impossible.

These new limits on the strengths of the electromagnetic and strong nuclear forces provide much tighter constraints on quark masses and on the Higgs vacuum expectation value.[8] Without getting into the details of what the Higgs vacuum expectation value and quarks are all about, the new limits not only demonstrate an enhanced design for the physics of stars and planets but also an enhanced mathematical design of fundamental particle physics.

3. Getting the Right Nucleons

One must monkey with the physics of the universe to get enough of the right elements for life, and further to get those elements to join together to form life molecules. One must also fine-tune the universe to get enough nucleons (protons and neutrons) to form the elements.

In the first moments after creation, the universe contained about 10 billion and 1 nucleons for every 10 billion anti-nucleons. The 10 billion anti-nucleons annihilated the 10 billion nucleons, generating an enormous amount of energy. All the galaxies and stars that make up the universe today were formed from the leftover nucleons. If the initial excess of nucleons over anti-nucleons were any smaller, there would not be enough matter for galaxies, stars, and heavy elements to form. If the excess were any greater, galaxies would form, but they would so efficiently condense and trap radiation that none of them would fragment to form stars and planets.

The neutron is 0.138% more massive than a proton. Because of this extra mass, neutrons require slightly more energy to make than protons. So as the universe cooled from the hot big bang creation event, it produced more protons than neutrons—in fact, about seven times as many.

If the neutron were just another 0.1% more massive, so few neutrons would remain from the cooling off of the big bang that there would not be enough of them to make the nuclei of all the heavy elements essential for life. The extra mass of the neutron relative to the proton also determines the rate at which neutrons decay into protons and protons build into neutrons (one neutron = one proton + one electron + one neutrino). If the neutron were 0.1% less massive, so many protons would be built up to make neutrons that all the stars in the universe would have rapidly collapsed into either neutron stars or black holes.[9] Thus for life to be possible in the universe, the neutron mass must be fine-tuned to better than 0.1%.

Another decay process involving protons must also be fine-tuned for life to exist. Protons are believed to decay into mesons (a type of fundamental particle). I say "believed to" because the decay rate is so slow experimenters have yet to record a single decay event (average decay time for a single proton exceeds 4×10^{32} years). Nevertheless, theoreticians are convinced that protons must decay into mesons, and at a rate fairly close to the current experimental limits. If protons decay any slower into mesons, the universe of today would not have enough nucleons to make the necessary galaxies, stars, and planets.[10] This is because the factors that determine this decay rate also determine the ratio of nucleons to antinucleons at the time of the creation event. Thus, if the decay rate were slower, the number of nucleons would have been too closely balanced by the number of antinucleons, which after annihilation would have left too few nucleons.

If, however, the decay rate of protons into mesons were faster, in addition to the problem of a too large ratio of nucleons to antinucleons, there would also be an additional problem from the standpoint of maintaining life. Because a tremendous amount of energy is released in this particular decay process, the rate of decay would destroy or harm life. Thus the decay rate cannot be any greater than it is.

4. Getting the Right Electrons

Not only must the universe be fine-tuned to get enough nucleons, but also a precise number of electrons must exist. Unless the number of electrons is equivalent to the number of protons to an accuracy of one part in 10^{37} or better, electromagnetic forces in the universe would have so overcome gravitational forces that galaxies, stars, and planets never would have formed.

One part in 10^{37} is such an incredibly sensitive balance that it is hard to visualize. The following analogy might help: Cover the entire North American continent in dimes all the way up to the moon, a height of about 239,000 miles. (In comparison, the money to pay for the U.S. federal government debt would cover one square mile less than two feet deep with dimes.) Next, pile dimes from here to the moon on a million other continents the same size as North America. Paint one dime red and mix it into the billion piles of dimes. Blindfold a friend and ask him to pick out one dime. The odds that he will pick the red dime are one in 10^{37}. And this is only one of the parameters that is so delicately balanced to allow life to form.

At whatever level we examine the building blocks of life—electrons, nucleons, atoms, or molecules—the physics of the universe must be very meticulously fine-tuned. The universe must be exactingly constructed to create the necessary electrons. It must be exquisitely crafted to produce the protons and neutrons required. It must be carefully fabricated to obtain the needed atoms. Unless it is skillfully fashioned, the atoms will not be able to assemble into complex enough molecules. Such precise balancing of all these factors is truly beyond our ability to comprehend. Yet with the measuring of the universe, even more astounding facts become apparent.

Cosmos' Expansion

The first parameter of the universe to be measured was the universe's expansion rate. In comparing this rate to the physics of galaxy and star formation, astrophysicists found something amazing. If the universe expanded too rapidly, matter would disperse so efficiently that none of it would clump enough to form galaxies. If no galaxies form, no stars will form. If no stars form, no planets will form. If no planets form, there's no place for life. On the other hand, if the universe expanded too slowly, matter would clump so effectively that all of it, the whole universe in fact, would collapse into a super-dense lump before any solar-type stars could form.

The creation event itself imbues the universe with a certain rate of expansion. Subsequent to the creation event, the cosmic mass density and cosmic space energy density modify in different ways the universe's expansion velocity. As described in chapter 5 (see pages 51-53), for the universe to produce all the stars and planets necessary to explain the possibility of Earth sustaining physical life, the value of the cosmic mass density must be fine-tuned to better than one part in 10^{60} and the value of the space energy density to better than one part in 10^{120}.

In the words of Lawrence Krauss and many other astrophysicists, this one part in 10^{60} and 10^{120} is by far the most extreme fine-tuning yet discovered in physics.[11] An analogy that does not even come close to describing the precarious nature of this cosmic balance would be a billion pencils all simultaneously positioned upright on their sharpened points on a smooth glass surface with no vertical supports.

Relativity, Quantum Uncertainty, and Dimensionality

In addition to requiring exquisite fine-tuning of the forces and constants of physics, the existence of life demands still more. It demands that the fundamental particles, the energy, and the space-time dimensions of the universe enable the principles of quantum tunneling and special relativity to operate exactly as they do. Quantum tunneling must function no more or less efficiently than what we observe for hemoglobin to transport the right amount of oxygen to the cells of all vertebrate and most invertebrate species.[12] Likewise, relativistic corrections, not too great and not too small, are essential in order for copper and vanadium to fulfill their critical roles in the functioning of the nervous system and bone development of all the higher animals.[13]

For quantum tunneling to operate so that hemoglobin functions properly, the uncertainty in the Heisenberg uncertainty principle must be fine-tuned. The uncertainty we observe is quite large. If the observer chooses to measure the momentum of a particle with precision, he or she discovers that the position of the particle is now known to only about ± half a mile. However, if the uncertainty in the position becomes much greater or smaller than half a mile, hemoglobin will not function as it does and advanced life becomes impossible. (There are other life-essential proteins like hemoglobin that depend on fine-tuned quantum tunneling.[14]) Counter to Einstein's famous quote that "God does not play dice," this evidence demonstrates that, given God's goals, God must play dice, but He has exquisitely designed the dice for the benefit of physical life.

For relativity to operate so that certain proteins containing copper and vanadium will adequately support life means that the value of the velocity of light must be fine-tuned. This proves not to be the only reason why the velocity of light must be held constant and fixed at the value of 299,792.458 kilometers per second. Because of Einstein's equation, $E = mc^2$, even small changes in c, the velocity of light, lead to huge changes in E, the energy, or m, the mass. Thus, a slight change in light's velocity implies that starlight will either be too strong or too feeble for life or that stars will produce the wrong elements for life.

As explained in chapter 4, stable orbits of planets about stars and of electrons about the nuclei of atoms are only possible in a universe described by three large and rapidly expanding dimensions of space. In addition, six extremely tiny dimensions that are presently dormant but actively expanded during the first 10^{-43} seconds of the universe's history are critical for quantum mechanics and gravity to coexist. Therefore, physical life requires a different fine-tuning of the number of effective dimensions both in the present, namely four (three space plus one time), and in the earliest moment of the universe's existence, namely ten (nine space plus one time).

Measuring the Universe's Age
The second parameter of the universe to be measured was its age. For many decades astronomers and others have wondered why, given God exists, He would wait so many billions of years to make life. Why did He not do it right away? The answer is that, given the laws and constants of physics God chose to create, it takes about ten to twelve billion years just to fuse enough heavy elements in the nuclear furnaces of several generations of giant stars to make life chemistry possible.

Life could not happen any earlier in the universe than it did on Earth. Nor could it happen much later. As the universe ages, stars like the sun—located in the right part of the galaxy for life (see chapter 16) and in a stable nuclear burning phase—become increasingly rare. If the universe were just a few billion years older, such stars would no longer exist.

A third parameter that I already discussed to some extent is entropy, or energy degradation. In chapter 4, I explained the evidence for the universe possessing an extreme amount of specific entropy. This high level of entropy is essential for life. Without it, systems as small as stars and planets would never form. But as extremely high as the entropy of the universe is, it could not be much higher. If it were higher, systems as large as galaxies would never form. Stars and planets cannot form without galaxies.

Star Masses

A fourth parameter, another very sensitive one, is the ratio of the electromagnetic force constant to the gravitational force constant. If the electromagnetic force relative to gravity were increased by just one part in 10^{40}, only large stars would form. And, if it were decreased by just one part in 10^{40}, only small stars would form. But for life to be possible in the universe, both large and small stars must exist. The large stars must exist because only in their thermonuclear furnaces are most of the life-essential elements produced. The small stars like the sun must exist because only small stars burn long enough and stably enough to sustain a planet with life.[15]

Considering again the piles of dimes, one part in 10^{40} looks like this: a blindfolded person rummages through a brillion piles of dimes, each pile the size of North America, and reaching as high as the moon, and picks out, on the first try, the one red dime.

In the late '80s and early '90s, several other characteristics of the universe were measured successfully. Each of these, too, indicated a careful fine-tuning for the support of life. Currently, researchers have uncovered thirty-five characteristics that must take on narrowly defined values for life of any kind to possibly exist. A list of these characteristics and the reasons they must be so narrowly defined is given in table 14.1 (see page 154).

The list of finely tuned characteristics for the universe continues to grow. The more accurately and extensively astronomers measure the universe, the more finely tuned they discover it to be.[16] Also, as we have seen for many of the already measured characteristics, the degree of fine-tuning is utterly amazing—far beyond what human endeavors can accomplish.

For example, arguably the best machine built by man is a brand new gravity wave detector engineered by California and Massachusetts Institutes of Technology physicists. It makes measurements accurate to one part in 10^{23}. By comparison, four different characteristics of the universe must be fine-tuned to better than one part in 10^{37} for life of any kind to exist (for comment on why life must be carbon-based, see section entitled "Another Kind of Life" on page 178). My point is that the Entity who brought the universe into existence must be a personal Being, for only a person can design with anywhere near this degree of precision. Consider, too, that this personal Entity must be at least a hundred trillion times more "capable" than are we human beings with all our resources.

Table 14.1: Evidence for the Fine-Tuning of the Universe[17]
More than two dozen parameters for the universe must have values falling within narrowly defined ranges for physical life of any conceivable kind to exist.

1. strong nuclear force constant
   if larger: no hydrogen; nuclei essential for
      life would be unstable
   if smaller: no elements other than hydrogen
2. weak nuclear force constant
   if larger: too much hydrogen converted to helium in big bang, hence too
      much heavy element material made by star burning; no expulsion
      of heavy elements from stars
   if smaller: too little helium produced from big bang, hence too little
      heavy element material made by star burning; no expulsion of
      heavy elements from stars
3. gravitational force constant
   if larger: stars would be too hot and would burn up too quickly and too
      unevenly
   if smaller: stars would remain so cool that nuclear fusion would never
      ignite, hence no heavy element production
4. electromagnetic force constant
   if larger: insufficient chemical bonding; elements more massive than
      boron would be too unstable for fission
   if smaller: insufficient chemical bonding; inadequate quantities of
      either carbon or oxygen
5. ratio of electromagnetic force constant to gravitational force constant
   if larger: no stars less than 1.4 solar masses, hence short stellar life spans
      and uneven stellar luminosities
   if smaller: no stars more than 0.8 solar masses, hence no heavy
      element production
6. ratio of electron to proton mass
   if larger: insufficient chemical bonding
   if smaller: insufficient chemical bonding
7. ratio of numbers of protons to electrons
   if larger: electromagnetism would dominate gravity, preventing galaxy,
      star, and planet formation

if smaller: electromagnetism would dominate gravity, preventing galaxy, star, and planet formation

8. expansion rate of the universe

    if larger: no galaxy formation

    if smaller: universe would collapse prior to star formation

9. entropy level of the universe

    if smaller: no proto-galaxy formation

    if larger: no star condensation within the proto-galaxies

10. baryon or nucleon density of the universe

    if larger: too much deuterium from big bang, hence stars burn too rapidly

    if smaller: insufficient helium from big bang, hence too few heavy elements forming

11. velocity of light

    if faster: stars would be too luminous

    if slower: stars would not be luminous enough

12. age of the universe

    if older: no solar-type stars in a stable burning phase in the right part of the galaxy

    if younger: solar-type stars in a stable burning phase would not yet have formed

13. initial uniformity of radiation

    if smoother: stars, star clusters, and galaxies would not have formed

    if coarser: universe by now would be mostly black holes and empty space

14. fine structure constant (a number used to describe the fine structure splitting of spectral lines)

    if larger: DNA would be unable to function; no stars more than 0.7 solar masses

    if larger than 0.06: matter would be unstable in large magnetic fields

    if smaller: DNA would be unable to function; no stars less than 1.8 solar masses

15. average distance between galaxies

    if larger: insufficient gas would be infused into our galaxy to sustain star formation over an adequate time span

    if smaller: the sun's orbit would be too radically disturbed

16. average distance between stars

    if larger: heavy element density too thin for rocky planets to form

    if smaller: planetary orbits would become destabilized

17. decay rate of the proton

    if greater: life would be exterminated by the release of radiation

    if smaller: insufficient matter in the universe for life

18. ^{12}Carbon (^{12}C) to ^{16}Oxygen (^{16}O) energy level ratio

    if larger: insufficient oxygen

    if smaller: insufficient carbon

19. ground state energy level for ^{4}Helium (^{4}He)

    if larger: insufficient carbon and oxygen

    if smaller: insufficient carbon and oxygen

20. decay rate of ^{8}Beryllium (^{8}Be)

   if slower: heavy element fusion would generate catastrophic explosions
   in all the stars

   if faster: no element production beyond beryllium and, hence,
   no life chemistry possible

21. mass excess of the neutron over the proton

   if greater: neutron decay would leave too few neutrons to form
   the heavy elements essential for life

   if smaller: neutron decay would produce so many neutrons as to cause
   all stars to collapse rapidly into neutron stars or black holes

22. initial excess of nucleons over anti-nucleons

   if greater: too much radiation for planets to form

   if smaller: not enough matter for galaxies or stars to form

23. polarity of the water molecule

   if greater: heat of fusion and vaporization would be too great for life to
   exist

   if smaller: heat of fusion and vaporization would be too small for life's
   existence; liquid water would become too inferior a solvent for life
   chemistry to proceed; ice would not float, leading to a runaway
   freeze-up

24. supernovae eruptions

   if too close: radiation would exterminate life on the planet

   if too far: not enough heavy element ashes for the formation of rocky
   planets

   if too frequent: life on the planet would be exterminated

   if too infrequent: not enough heavy element ashes for the formation of
   rocky planets

   if too late: life on the planet would be exterminated by radiation

   if too soon: not enough heavy element ashes for the formation of rocky
   planets

25. white dwarf binaries

   if too few: insufficient fluorine produced for life chemistry to proceed

   if too many: disruption of planetary orbits from stellar density;
   life on the planet would be exterminated

   if too soon: not enough heavy elements made for efficient fluorine
   production

   if too late: fluorine made too late for incorporation in proto-planet

26. ratio of exotic to ordinary matter

   if smaller: galaxies would not form

   if larger: universe would collapse before solar type stars could form

27. galaxy clusters

   if too dense: galaxy collisions and mergers would disrupt star and planet
   orbits; too much radiation

   if too sparse: insufficient infusion of gas into galaxies to sustain star
   formation for a long enough time period

28. number of effective dimensions in the early universe

   if smaller: quantum mechanics, gravity, and relativity could not coexist
   and life would be impossible

if larger: quantum mechanics, gravity, and relativity could not coexist and life would be impossible

29. number of effective dimensions in the present universe
    if smaller: electron, planet, and star orbits would become unstable
    if larger: electron, planet, and star orbits would become unstable
30. mass of the neutrino
    if smaller: galaxy clusters, galaxies, and stars would not form
    if larger: galaxy clusters and galaxies would be too dense
31. big bang ripples
    if smaller: galaxies would not form; universe expands too rapidly
    if larger: galaxy clusters and galaxies would be too dense; black holes would dominate; universe collapses too quickly
32. total mass density
    if smaller: universe would expand too quickly for solar type stars to form
    if larger: universe would expand too slowly, resulting in unstable orbits and too much radiation
33. space energy density
    if smaller: universe would expand too slowly, resulting in unstable orbits and too much radiation
    if larger: universe would expand too quickly for solar type stars to form
34. size of the relativistic dilation factor
    if smaller: certain life-essential chemical reactions would not function properly
    if larger: certain life-essential chemical reactions would not function properly
35. uncertainty magnitude in the Heisenberg uncertainty principle
    if smaller: oxygen transport to body cells would be too small; certain life-essential elements would be unstable; certain life-essential chemical reactions would not function properly
    if larger: certain life-essential elements would be unstable; certain life-essential chemical reactions would not function properly

God and the Astronomers

The discovery of this degree of design in the universe is having a profound theological impact on astronomers. As we noted already, Hoyle concludes that "a superintellect has monkeyed with physics, as well as with chemistry and biology,"[18] and Davies has moved from promoting atheism[19] to conceding that "the laws [of physics] . . . seem themselves to be the product of exceedingly ingenious design."[20] He further testifies:

> [There] is for me powerful evidence that there is something going on behind it all. . . . It seems as though somebody has fine-tuned nature's numbers to make the Universe. . . . The impression of design is overwhelming.[21]

Astronomer George Greenstein, in his book *The Symbiotic Universe,* expressed these thoughts:

> As we survey all the evidence, the thought insistently arises that some supernatural agency—or, rather, Agency—must be involved. Is it possible that suddenly, without intending to, we have stumbled upon scientific proof of the existence of a Supreme Being? Was it God who stepped in and so providentially crafted the cosmos for our benefit?[22]

Tony Rothman, a theoretical physicist, in a popular-level article on the anthropic principle (the idea that the universe possesses narrowly defined characteristics that permit the possibility of a habitat for humans) concluded his essay with these words:

> The medieval theologian who gazed at the night sky through the eyes of Aristotle and saw angels moving the spheres in harmony has become the modern cosmologist who gazes at the same sky through the eyes of Einstein and sees the hand of God not in angels but in the constants of nature. . . . When confronted with the order and beauty of the universe and the strange coincidences of nature, it's very tempting to take the leap of faith from science into religion. I am sure many physicists want to. I only wish they would admit it.[23]

In a review article on the anthropic principle published in the journal *Nature,* cosmologists Bernard Carr and Martin Rees state in their summary: "Nature does exhibit remarkable coincidences and these do warrant some explanation."[24] Carr in a more recent article on the anthropic principle continues:

> One would have to conclude either that the features of the universe invoked in support of the Anthropic Principle are only coincidences or that the universe was indeed tailor-made for life. I will leave it to the theologians to ascertain the identity of the tailor![25]

Physicist Freeman Dyson concluded his treatment of the anthropic principle with, "The problem here is to try to formulate some statement of the ultimate purpose of the universe. In other words, the problem is to read the mind of God."[26] Vera Kistiakowsky,

MIT physicist and past president of the Association of Women in Science, commented, "The exquisite order displayed by our scientific understanding of the physical world calls for the divine."[27] Arno Penzias, who shared the Nobel prize for physics for the discovery of the cosmic background radiation, remarked:

> Astronomy leads us to a unique event, a universe which was created out of nothing, one with the very delicate balance needed to provide exactly the conditions required to permit life, and one which has an underlying (one might say "supernatural") plan.[28]

Years before communism's fall, Alexander Polyakov, a theoretician and fellow at Moscow's Landau Institute, declared:

> We know that nature is described by the best of all possible mathematics because God created it. So there is a chance that the best of all possible mathematics will be created out of physicists' attempts to describe nature.[29]

China's famed astrophysicist Fang Li Zhi and his coauthor, physicist Li Shu Xian, recently wrote, "A question that has always been considered a topic of metaphysics or theology the creation of the universe has now become an area of active research in physics."[30]

In the 1992 film about Stephen Hawking, *A Brief History of Time*, Hawking's colleague, distinguished mathematician Roger Penrose, commented, "I would say the universe has a purpose. It's not there just somehow by chance."[31] Hawking and Penrose's colleague George Ellis made the following statement in a paper delivered at the Second Venice Conference on Cosmology and Philosophy:

> Amazing fine-tuning occurs in the laws that make this [complexity] possible. Realization of the complexity of what is accomplished makes it very difficult not to use the word "miraculous" without taking a stand as to the ontological status of that word.[32]

Stephen Hawking himself concedes:

> It would be very difficult to explain why the universe should have begun in just this way, except as the act of a God who intended to create beings like us.[33]

Cosmologist Edward Harrison makes this deduction:

> Here is the cosmological proof of the existence of God—the design argument of Paley—updated and refurbished. The fine-tuning of the universe provides prima facie evidence of deistic design. Take your choice: blind chance that requires multitudes of universes or design that requires only one. . . . Many scientists, when they admit their views, incline toward the teleological or design argument.[34]

Allan Sandage, winner of the Crafoord prize in astronomy (equivalent to the Nobel prize), remarked, "I find it quite improbable that such order came out of chaos. There has to be some organizing principle. God to me is a mystery but is the explanation for the miracle of existence, why there is something instead of nothing."[35] Robert Griffiths, who won the Heinemann prize in mathematical physics, observed, "If we need an atheist for a debate, I go to the philosophy department. The physics department isn't much use."[36] Perhaps astrophysicist Robert Jastrow, a self-proclaimed agnostic,[37] best described what has happened to his colleagues as they have measured the cosmos:

> For the scientist who has lived by his faith in the power of reason, the story ends like a bad dream. He has scaled the mountains of ignorance; he is about to conquer the highest peak; as he pulls himself over the final rock, he is greeted by a band of theologians who have been sitting there for centuries.[38]

In all my conversations with those who do research on the characteristics of the universe, and in all my readings of articles or books on the subject, not one person denies the conclusion that somehow the cosmos has been crafted to make it a fit habitat for life. Astronomers by nature tend to be independent and iconoclastic. If an opportunity for disagreement exists, they will seize it. But on the issue of the fine tuning or careful crafting of the cosmos, the evidence is so compelling that I have yet to hear of any dissent.

The Creator's Personality

Does the fine-tuning imply purposeful design? So many parameters must be fine-tuned and the degree of fine-tuning is so high, no other conclusion seems possible.

As Harrison pointed out, the evidence permits only two options:

divine design or blind chance. Blind chance, as we saw in chapter 12, is ruled out since conclusions based on chance must be derived from known, not hypothetical, sample sizes. The known sample size for the universe(s) is one and always will be only one since the space-time manifold for the universe is closed (meaning we humans cannot, even in principle, ever discover anything about others possibly existing).

Much more is going on, however, than mere talk by astronomers about the design of the cosmos for life support. Words such as *somebody fine-tuned nature, superintellect, monkeyed, overwhelming design, miraculous, hand of God, ultimate purpose, God's mind, exquisite order, very delicate balance, exceedingly ingenious, supernatural Agency, supernatural plan, tailor-made, Supreme Being, and providentially crafted* obviously apply to a Person. Beyond just establishing that the Creator is a Person, the findings about design provide some evidence of what that Person is like.

One characteristic that stands out dramatically is His interest in and care for living things, particularly the human race. We see this care in the vastness and quality of the resources devoted to life support.

For example, the baryon density (density of neutrons and protons) of the universe, as huge as it is, focuses on the needs of humans. How? The baryon density determines how efficiently nuclear fusion operates in the cosmos. The baryon density we measure translates into about a hundred-billion-trillion stars for the presently observable universe. As table 14.1 indicates (page 154), if the baryon density is too great, too much deuterium (an isotope of hydrogen with one proton and one neutron in the nucleus) is made in the first few minutes of the universe's existence. This extra deuterium will cause the stars to burn much too quickly and erratically for any of them to support a planet with life. On the other hand, if the baryon density is too small, so little deuterium and helium are made in the first few minutes that the heavier elements necessary for life will never form in stars. What this means is that the approximately hundred-billion-trillion stars we observe in the universe—no more and no less—are needed for life to be possible in the universe. God invested heavily in living creatures. He constructed all these stars and carefully crafted them throughout the age of the universe so that at this brief moment in the history of the cosmos humans could exist and have a pleasant place to live.

Non-Theistic Responses

When it comes to the finely-tuned characteristics of the universe, non-theists find themselves in a difficult spot. The evidence is too weighty and concrete to brush aside. The evidence is inanimate; so appeals to Darwinist hypotheses cannot be made. Appeals to near infinite time are thwarted by the proofs for time's creation only a few billion years ago. The following five arguments seem to cover the range of non-theistic replies to the evidence for cosmic design:

Argument 1: We would not be here to observe the universe unless the extremely unlikely did take place.
The evidence for design is merely coincidental. Our existence simply testifies that the extremely unlikely did, indeed, take place by chance. In other words, we would not be here to report on the characteristics of the universe unless chance produced these highly unlikely properties.

  Rebuttal: This argument is fundamentally an appeal to infinite chances, which already has been answered (see chapter 12). Another response has been developed by philosopher Richard Swinburne[39] and summarized by another philosopher, William Lane Craig:

> Suppose a hundred sharpshooters are sent to execute a prisoner by firing squad, and the prisoner survives. The prisoner should not be surprised that he does not observe that he is dead. After all, if he were dead, he could not observe his death. Nonetheless, he should be surprised that he observes that he is alive.[40]

To extend Craig and Swinburne's argument, the prisoner could conclude, since he is alive, that all the sharpshooters missed by some extremely unlikely chance. He may wish to attribute his survival to an incredible bit of good luck, but he would be far more rational to conclude that the guns were loaded with blanks or that the sharpshooters all deliberately missed. Someone must have purposed he should live. Likewise, the rational conclusion to draw from the incredible fine-tuning of the universe is that Someone purposed we should live.

Argument 2: The design of the universe is mere anthropomorphism.
American astrophysicist Joseph Silk in his latest effort to communicate the physics of big bang cosmology to lay people mocks the conclusion

that the universe has been fine-tuned for the support of life. He compares the "silliness" of the design idea with the folly of a flea's assumption that the dog on which it feeds has been designed precisely for its benefit. The flea's error, he suggests, becomes all too apparent once the dog is outfitted with a flea collar.[41]

Rebuttal: Silk's argument ignores some key issues. While the flea may be a little self-centered in assuming that the dog was designed exclusively for it, there's no reason to deny that the dog was designed for a purpose, or for several purposes. (The myth that life is strictly the product of accidental natural processes is addressed in chapter 17.) The flea collar analogy may argue more strongly for design (e.g., population control) than for lack of it. More importantly, while we can imagine a wide range of hosts suitable for the support of the flea, each of them requires elements of design to facilitate the flea's survival. Though suitable hosts for the flea are relatively abundant, suitable universes for life are not. Astrophysicists have been unable to invent hypothetical universes significantly different from ours that could support human beings or, for that matter, any conceivable kind of physical, intelligent life.

Argument 3: Design arguments are outside the realm of science and, therefore, must be ignored.

The publications of the National Center for Science Education, among other anti-creationist groups, repeatedly assert that science is "empirically based and necessarily materialist; miracles cannot be allowed," and that "any theory with a supernatural foundation is not scientific."[42] Since the design arguments imply supernatural intervention, they can be justifiably ignored because they "cannot be considered scientific."[43]

Rebuttal: To affirm that science and theology are mutually exclusive may be convenient for materialists unwilling to defend their philosophy, but it is untenable. Science is rarely religiously neutral. Similarly, religious faith is rarely scientifically neutral. Both science and theology frequently address cause and effect and processes of development in the natural realm. Both science and theology deal with the origin of the universe, the solar system, life, and humankind.

When it comes to causes, developmental processes, and origins, two possibilities always exist: natural or supernatural. To dogmatically insist that supernatural answers must never be considered is equivalent to demanding that all human beings follow only one religion, the religion of atheistic materialism. I find it ironic that in the name of religious freedom certain science education proponents insist on ridding our teaching and research institutions of any faith that dares to compete with their own.

Argument 4: Order can come out of chaos.

The idea that under strictly natural conditions order can and will arise out of chaos was first proposed by David Hume nearly two hundred years ago. Recently it has been revived by chemist and Nobel Laureate Ilya Prigogine in his book *Order Out of Chaos*,[44] and popularized by the blockbuster movie *Jurassic Park*. Hume made the claim without any evidential support. Prigogine pointed to several chemical reactions in which order appears to arise from chaotic systems. *Jurassic Park* actually addresses a different subject, namely chaos theory and fuzzy logic.

Rebuttal: The principle behind chaos theory and fuzzy logic is that in trying to predict the outcome or future state of exceptionally complex systems, the investigator is better off settling for approximate answers or conclusions at each step in the solution of a problem rather than exact answers or conclusions. The presumption of a natural self-ordering principle in chaotic systems arises from the fact that the more complex a system, the greater the opportunity for departures from thermodynamic equilibrium in small portions of the system (and the greater the difficulty in determining what the thermodynamic equilibrium states actually are). According to the second law of thermodynamics, entropy increases in all systems, but entropy can decrease (i.e., order can increase) in part of a system, providing an extra increase of entropy (i.e., disorder) occurs in a different part of the system. Because human investigators may be prone to underestimate the complexity of some systems, they occasionally are surprised by how far from thermodynamic equilibrium a small portion of a system can stray. However, the thermodynamic laws predict that these departures are temporary, and the greater the departure, the more rapidly the departures are corrected.

Without departures from thermodynamic equilibrium, raindrops and snowflakes, for example, would not form. But, raindrop and snowflake formation comes close to the self-ordering limits of natural process. Though snowflake patterns exhibit a high degree of order, their information content or level of design remains quite low. The distinction is roughly like the difference between the New Testament and a book containing the sentence "God is good" repeated

90,000 times. The latter shows considerable order but not much information. The former contains both a high degree of order and a high degree of information (or design). Prigogine's examples exhibit increases in order but without significant increases in information content. Natural processes cannot explain the exceptionally high level of design and information content in living organisms or in the structure of the universe that makes life possible.

*Argument 5: As we continue to evolve, we will become
the Creator-Designer.*

In their book *The Anthropic Cosmological Principle*, astrophysicists John Barrow and Frank Tipler review many new evidences for the design of the universe.[45] They go on to discuss versions of the anthropic principle like WAP (weak anthropic principle: conscious beings can only exist in an environment with characteristics that allow for their habitation), SAP (strong anthropic principle: nature must take on those characteristics to admit somewhere, sometime the existence of conscious beings), and more radical versions, including PAP (participatory anthropic principle: conscious observers are necessary to bring the universe into existence, and the universe is necessary to bring observers into existence). But what they favor is FAP (final anthropic principle).

With FAP, the life that exists (past, present, and future) will continue to evolve with the inanimate resources of the universe until it all reaches a state that Barrow and Tipler call the "Omega Point."[46] This Omega Point, they say, is an Entity that has the properties of omnipotence, omnipresence, and omniscience, with the capacity to create in the past.[47] In other words, the Creator-God does not exist yet, but we (all life and all inanimate structures in the universe) are gradually evolving into God. When God is thus finally constructed, His power will be such that He can create the entire universe with all of its characteristics of design billions of years ago.

In his latest book, *The Physics of Immortality*,[48] Tipler proposes that evolution toward the Omega Point will occur through advancing computer technology. By extrapolating computer capability doubling time (currently, about eighteen months) some millions of years into the future, Tipler predicts that a future generation of human beings will be able not only to alter the entire universe and all the laws of physics but also to create a God who does not yet exist. Furthermore, we will be able to resurrect every human being who has ever lived by recovering the memories that once resided in each person's brain.

Rebuttal: It is hard to treat these FAP and Omega Point hypotheses seriously. In *The New York Review of Books,* noted critic Martin Gardner offered this evaluation of Barrow and Tipler's work:

> What should we make of this quartet of WAP, SAP, PAP, and FAP? In my not so humble opinion I think the last principle is best called CRAP, the Completely Ridiculous Anthropic Principle.[49]

In *The Physics of Immortality* Tipler grossly overestimates the role of human memory and the future capability of computers. Just as computers cannot function with memory banks only, so, too, the human mind and human consciousness do not operate by memory alone. While remarkable advances in computer technology are taking place now, the laws of physics impose predictable finite limits on future computer hardware. As Roger Penrose has documented rigorously in *The Emperor's New Mind* and *Shadows of the Mind*, these limits do not even permit the duplication of human consciousness let alone the fantastic capabilities Tipler suggests.[50]

Tipler's cosmic model on which his whole premise rests is now out of date. It depends on the universe possessing enough matter to force the universe into a future stage of collapse. But, as we noted in chapter 5, measurements made in 1999 and 2000 establish that only three-tenths of the mass necessary to force a future collapse of the universe exists. Moreover, the measured value for the space energy density term guarantees that the universe not only will expand forever, it will expand at an exponentially increasing rate.

But Tipler apparently wants to alter much more than just the universe and the laws of physics. He believes, for example, that future computers will be able to expose people to game theory principles so effectively that all destructive thoughts and actions will be purged and villainy no longer occur, even for the likes of Adolf Hitler and Mata Hari.[51] In Tipler's religion, the redemptive work of a Savior becomes unnecessary. Consider, however, that if Tipler's proposal were true, the better people comprehend game theory, the less propensity they would exhibit to commit evil. Unfortunately for Tipler, no such correlation is in evidence.

Tipler not only banishes hell but also redesigns heaven. Tipler's "heaven" brings relational (more accurately, sexual) bliss to every man and woman. He produces an equation to "prove" that this computer generated cosmic utopia will bring a woman to every man and a man to every woman capable of delivering 100,000 times the impact and satisfaction of the most fulfilling partner each can imagine in life as we know it.[52] The popular appeal of such a notion documents the spiritual bankruptcy of our times. Evidently, many people have never tasted any greater delight than what sexual experience can bring.

In an article for the *Skeptical Inquirer,* Gardner again brandished his satiric knives:

> I leave it to the reader to decide whether they should opt for OPT (Omega Point Theology) as a new scientific religion superior to Scientology—one destined to elevate Tipler to the rank of a prophet greater than L. Ron Hubbard—or opt for the view that OPT is a wild fantasy generated by too much reading of science fiction.[53]

In their persistent rejection of an eternal, transcendent Creator, some cosmologists (and others) are resorting to increasingly irrational options. There is a certain logic to it, however. If for personal or moral reasons the God of the Bible is unacceptable, then given all the evidence for transcendence and design, the alternatives are limited to flights of fancy.

Through time, as we unlock more of the secrets of the vast cosmos, men and women will be even more awed about how exquisitely designed the universe is. But where will that awe be aimed—at the created thing, or at the Creator? That is each person's choice.

CHAPTER FIFTEEN

A LAYPERSON'S GUIDE TO ALTERNATE COSMOLOGIES

The layperson must first understand that, no matter how tightly observations constrain the properties of the universe, there always will exist some alternate cosmologies. There always will be some people, who for nonscientific reasons, reject the big bang. As I pointed out in my book, *The Fingerprint of God*, atheistic and agnostic biases for several decades drove astrophysicists to do all they could to dream up some alternative to the big bang.[1] There comes a point, however, where such attempts cease to be rational.

An example of loss of rationality can be found in the Flat-Earth Society. That society still points to "scientific" evidences for their view of the earth's shape. However, one of the reasons scientists and laypeople give no credibility to these evidences is simply because advancing knowledge about the shape of the earth has forced flat-earth proponents to appeal to progressively more absurd evidences for their position, and to ignore or "explain away" progressively stronger evidences against their position.

Asking Probing Questions

A similar track record found among some cosmologists suggests a question that may be helpful for laypeople to ask about any particular cosmological model: As astronomers have learned more about the universe, has the evidence for that model relative to others become stronger or weaker? A follow-up question would be how much stronger or weaker? If one suspects bias on the part of the expert, one can ask how many astronomers actively advocate for the model today compared to a year ago, five years ago, and twenty years ago.

Laypeople often assume that every cosmic model is undergirded by a provable or, at least, a testable mechanism. In fact, this is rarely the case. For example, there is no evidence whatsoever for the creation field of the steady state models. Astronomers and physicists never have witnessed protons, neutrons, or any other real mass particles spontaneously popping into existence. Neither steady state proponents nor any one else has ever been able to conceive of a possible experiment or an observation that could affirm the existence of a creation field. Therefore, at least for now, all creation field hypotheses must be classified as metaphysics, not physics.

What would help lay discussions on cosmology are questions that distinguish between physics and metaphysics. In terms of God's role or lack thereof in cosmology, audiences would be wise to draw their conclusions based primarily on what is known, secondarily on what might become knowable through future scientific advances, and not at all on what has little or no likelihood of ever being discovered.

Finally, audiences should always beware of any cosmology based on a breakdown of known physical laws, where the physical evidence gives no warrant for such a breakdown. For example, the appeal to a quantum mechanical space-time foam as a source of an infinite or near infinite number of universes radically violates the laws of quantum mechanics. One law of quantum mechanics states that the smaller the time interval, the smaller the probability for a quantum event. The singularity theorems establish that at the cosmic creation event for our universe the time interval is zero (time is created at the creation event). With a zero time interval the probability for a baby universe to pop into existence through a quantum event would be zero. Another quantum mechanical law stipulates that the bigger the mass brought into existence through a quantum fluctuation in the space-time fabric, the faster that mass must be returned to the space-time continuum. For something as massive as our observable universe, the return time must be briefer than 10^{-103} seconds (less than a trillionth of a trillionth of a trillionth of a trillionth of a trillionth of a trillionth of a trillionth of a trillionth of a second). Clearly, our universe is a wee bit older.

Could not there still be different quantum mechanical laws when the universe is younger than 10^{-34} seconds than when it is older that might overcome these difficulties? While the answer to this question is yes (it is possible), astrophysicists can point to no evidence for any different quantum mechanical laws during the first trillionth of a trillionth of a trillionth of a second of the universe's history. Given that we know the quantum mechanical laws hold for 99.999999999999999999999999999999999999999999999999% of the universe's history, we should demand at least some physical evidence before conceding that different quantum mechanical laws operated during the first 10^{-49}th of a percent of its history. Also, no longer can it be said that the incompatibility of gravity and quantum mechanics during the first split second of cosmic history demands alternate physical laws. The ten-dimensional string theory I discuss in *Beyond the Cosmos* demonstrates how gravity and quantum mechanics can successfully coexist all the way back to the cosmic creation event, to that moment when time begins.[2]

An Infinity of Universes?
The weight of evidence for a divinely designed universe is now so overwhelming that it has forced astronomers and philosophers who reject the God of the Bible as the Author of the cosmos to propose the existence of an infinite number of universes. These scholars readily concede that dozens of different characteristics of the universe must be exquisitely fine-tuned for any kind of conceivable physical life to be possible. They also concede that the degree of fine-tuning observed is many, many orders of magnitude greater than any degree of fine-tuning that we humans can manifest when we attempt to create. However, rather than conceding that a God who is trillions of trillions of trillions of times more intelligent, knowledgeable, powerful, caring, and loving than us humans must have designed the universe for our benefit, they instead choose to speculate that an infinite number of universes must exist where each universe is different in its characteristics from all the others. An infinite number of different universes would imply that no matter how unlikely or fine-tuned a set of cosmic characteristics might be, in at least one of the infinity of universes those characteristics would be found. Thus, the God of the Bible is replaced by Chance, or, in the language of nonChristian cosmologists, by an infinite number of random fluctuations in some kind of primeval field.

The first thing to note in the above commentary is that I purposely capitalized chance. Where do the infinite number of universes come from? If one says, from some kind of primeval field, then where does the primeval field come from? If one says that "nothing" is unstable and, therefore, that "nothing" must produce something, then how is it that we never observe anything arising from "nothing"? My point is that, if you ask enough questions, ultimately you will be confronted with an all-powerful, transcendent, uncaused Creator.

The second thing to note is why is it necessary that the infinite number of universes all be different. If there is no MIND behind the birthing process, could not all the universes be identical, or most or at least some of them be the same? And, why an infinite number? No process we observe delivers an infinity of products. What if only a quintillion of universes are spawned? All of these possibilities, of course, reduce the probability of having one like ours appear.

The third thing to note is that in spite of what many astrophysicists try to suggest, the inflationary hot big bang models are not necessarily linked to multi-universe models. It is true that growing evidence points to a universe where an extremely brief period of hyper expansion (at many times light's velocity) takes place during the first 10^{-33} seconds of cosmic history, and that many of the models proposed to explain this history are multi-universe in nature. However, there is no inflationary big bang multi-verse that cannot be reconfigured as an inflationary big bang uni-verse.

The most important thing to note is that all appeals to an infinite number of different universes as an escape from the conclusion of a divinely designed universe are forms of the gambler's fallacy. To illustrate, consider the circumstance of a person who flips a single coin in front of a large audience ten thousand consecutive times, where that coin comes up heads all ten thousand times. The rational people in the audience will conclude that the coin has been designed to come up heads on every flip. One committing the gambler's fallacy will speculate that outside the auditorium there possibly could exist $2^{10,000}$ coins (2 x 2 x 2 x . . . 10,000 such multiplications equals ~$10^{3,000}$ coins). If $2^{10,000}$ people flip those $2^{10,000}$ coins 10,000 consecutive times each, that gambler would conclude that the laws of probability would predict that one of those $2^{10,000}$ succession of flips would produce one example of ten thousand consecutive heads. On this basis, that gambler concludes that the coin in the auditorium is fair and decides to bet on tails for the 10,001st flip.

The gambler here commits three major errors. He has no evidence that $2^{10,000}$ coins must exist outside the auditorium. He has no evidence that all the coins outside the auditorium are flipped ten thousand consecutive times each. And, he especially has no evidence that all the coin flipping results outside the auditorium are different from those he has observed inside the auditorium.

Where the coin sample size is only one, a rational conclusion to draw from 10,000 consecutive coin flips yielding nothing but heads is that the coin has been purposed or designed to always produce a heads result. The reason one might conclude otherwise is if one has a nonrational conviction that no coins can possibly be designed to always come up heads. Where the universe sample size is only one, a rational conclusion to draw from cosmic fine-tuning that is many orders of magnitude greater than anything we humans can manifest in our creations, is that a BEING must have purposed or designed the universe in such a manner that it can support physical life. To do otherwise only can be based on the nonrational conviction that no universe can possibly be designed.

In the case of the universe we can draw a stronger conclusion than we can for the coin. Whereas we know that more than one coin exists, we do not know whether more than one universe exists. Moreover, we will never gain the technological capacity to scientifically discover the existence of another universe. Once observers exist in universe A, the theory of general relativity tells us that the space-time manifold or envelope of that universe can never overlap the space-time manifold of any other possibly existing universe. In other words, if God made ten universes, we would forever lack the scientific means to detect any universe but our own. Thus, the sample size of universes for us humans is one and it always will be just one. Speculating that there are an infinite number of universes "out there" is a perfectly acceptable option for those who choose to do so, but it is in the arena of metaphysics, not physics. The only rational option for us right now and at any time in the future, regardless of the speculations of theoretical physicists, philosophers, and others, is that God exquisitely designed the universe for the benefit of humanity.

Returning to the gambler, one could argue that his greatest error upon witnessing 10,000 consecutive flips producing 10,000 consecutive heads was his failure to more carefully investigate the properties of the coin before placing his bet on the 10,001st flip. If he had done so, he would have seen additional evidence for purposeful coin design. For example, he might have discovered that the coin had heads imprinted on both sides, or he might have noted that it had been weighted so that the heads side would always land face up.

Just like the gambler, astronomers and others can continue to make measurements on the universe. Such additional measurements will confirm the purposefulness of the universe for the support of physical life. Indeed, this already has been done. For the past forty years, the more astronomers have learned about the universe, the stronger has become the conclusion that it is exquisitely designed for the support of physical life and especially for the support of human beings. For any remaining skeptic all she or he need do is wait two or three weeks. In that time period additional measurements will reveal whether the evidence for cosmic design has become weaker or stronger.

CHAPTER SIXTEEN

EARTH: THE PLACE FOR LIFE

The mind boggles in trying to grasp the minute detail the Designer wove together to make the universe suitable for life. That same beautiful intricacy is apparent as one looks closer to home—at our galaxy, our sun, our neighboring planets, our earth, our moon, and more.

The first astronomers to provide evidence of these intricacies were Frank Drake, Carl Sagan, and Iosef Shklovskii. They developed the evidence out of their desire to estimate the number of planets in the universe with favorable environments for the support of life. By 1966 Shklovskii and Sagan had determined it takes a certain kind of star with a planet located at just the right distance from that star to provide the minimal conditions for life.[1] Working with just these two parameters, they estimated that 0.001% of all stars could have a planet capable of supporting advanced life.[2]

Much subsequent evidence has shown that Shklovskii and Sagan overestimated the range of permissible star types and the range of permissible planetary distances, and they also ignored dozens of other significant parameters. But their estimate of a million-plus possible life sites for our galaxy persisted. It is this optimistic estimate that has fueled the search for extraterrestrial intelligent life.

In addition to much private money, more than $100 million in U.S. taxpayer support has been devoted to the search for radio signals from extraterrestrial intelligent life.[3] With all the evidence for divine design (and against a naturalistic explanation) in the universe, one would think some caution (and some theology) would be in order before committing this much money. As we will see, the evidence for divine design mounts dramatically as we move from a large system, like the universe as a whole, to smaller systems such as our galaxy, our star, our planet, and life itself.

The Right Galaxy Cluster

Our Milky Way Galaxy resides in a loose grouping of galaxies called The Local Group. The Local Group is located on the far outer edge of the Virgo supercluster of galaxies.

This location makes our galaxy exceptional. The vast majority of galaxies in the universe find themselves in rich clusters of galaxies. As such, they are subject to frequent collisions and mergers with other galaxies.[4] These mergers and collisions can be devastating for physical life since they disturb a star with a life-sustainable planet into a different orbit about the galaxy. That different orbit either exposes the planet to deadly radiation or to encounters with other stars that pull the planet out of its safe orbital path about its star.

On the other hand, our galaxy cannot maintain its spiral structure without absorbing large amounts of gas and dust from dwarf galaxies in its immediate neighborhood. It's that spiral structure that allowed our sun to form at the right time for life and to remain in a safe path in its orbit about the center of the Milky Way.

Our galaxy has just the right number and kind of neighboring galaxies to make life possible on a special star within it. Those neighboring galaxies are at just the right distances at just the right time. Recent studies demonstrate that only during the time window when life is possible in our universe is our galaxy protected from life-destroying encounters with its neighbors.[5] In fact, astronomers recently have determined that a life-destroying merger may be in the offing. Four billion years hence the galaxy known as the Large Magellanic Cloud will merge with the Milky Way.[6]

The Right Galaxy

Not all galaxies are created equal in terms of their capacity to support life. Popular media often give the impression that all galaxies are spirals like our Milky Way. Actually only 5% of the galaxies in the universe are spirals.[7] The other 95% are either elliptical or irregular.

In elliptical galaxies star formation ceases before the interstellar medium becomes enriched enough with heavy elements. For life, stellar systems need to form late enough that they can incorporate this heavy-element-enriched material.

The problem with large irregular galaxies is they have active nuclei. These nuclei spew out life-destroying radiation and material. Meanwhile most small irregular galaxies have insufficient quantities of the heavy elements essential for life.

Physicists R. E. Davies and R. H. Koch recently published a paper on the necessary cosmic conditions for the solar system to contain the elements essential for life.[8] Since the 1960s astronomers have realized the emerging solar system would need contact with exploded supernovae remains to possess sufficient heavy elements for rocky planets and life chemistry.

Davies and Koch estimate how many supernovae must erupt in our galaxy to produce the needed quantity of elements heavier than helium. The answer: an average of one every three years from the time our galaxy originated (about 10 billion years ago). Since the present rate is less than one supernova every 50 years, the rate must have been extremely high in the early history of our galaxy.

This conclusion matches the results from the best astrophysical models and observations of star formation in our galaxy. It also matches the requirements for life. Supernovae must occur in great abundance early in the history of a galaxy to supply enough heavy element enrichment to allow a planet like Earth to form as early as it did.

It also is essential that the supernova event rate be relatively low in the present era. If it were not, the radiation from supernova eruptions would frequently exterminate life on Earth.

The frequency of supernova eruptions (per unit volume) is strongly dependent on location. The solar system must be positioned in the right part of the galaxy. It must be at a just right distance from a spiral arm. It must also be at a just right distance from the center of our galaxy.

But there is one life-essential heavy element that is not made by supernovae: fluorine. It is made in sufficient quantities only on relatively rare objects: the surfaces of white dwarf stars bound into binary systems with larger stellar companions. The larger star must orbit closely enough to the white dwarf that it loses significant material to the white dwarf. At the surface of the white dwarf, some of this material is converted to fluorine. Then the white dwarf must lose this fluoridated material to interstellar space for it to be incorporated into a future solar system. This sequence means that the universe, our galaxy, and the sun's position in our galaxy must assume narrowly specified characteristics if Earth is to obtain the fluorine it needs for the support of life.

The location, types, rates, and timings of both supernova events and white dwarf binaries severely constrains the possibility of finding a life support site. The vast majority of galaxies are eliminated from contention, and the vast majority of stars in the few remaining galaxies also are eliminated.

Another Kind of Life?

The significance of these findings is underscored by John Maddox, a former member of the editorial board of *Nature* and a staunch opponent of theism, who attempted to find a way around Davies and Koch's implications for creation.[9] He suggested life need not be at all like terrestrial life as we know it. What support did he offer? None.

As physicist Robert Dicke observed thirty-two years ago, if you want physicists (or any other life forms), you must have carbon.[10] Boron and silicon are the only other elements on which complex molecules can be based, but boron is rare and, where concentrated, is poisonous to life, and silicon can hold together no more than about a hundred amino acids. Given the constraints of physics and chemistry, we can reasonably assume that physical life must be carbon-based.

Live Here or Nowhere

What makes life possible on Earth is that the sun is located in between two spiral arms at the "corotation distance" relative to the center of our galaxy. Almost all the stars in our galaxy reside either in the central bulge, the spiral arms, or in the globular star clusters. In all three of these locations the star densities are high enough to disrupt the orbits of planets like Earth. Moreover, the presence there of supergiant stars, neutron stars, black holes, and/or supernova remnants would expose Earth-like planets to radiation intense enough to damage the planets' ionospheric and atmospheric layers.

A new piece of research by two Russian astronomers establishes that the sun is special in another respect.[11] It *stays* between spiral arms. This is because the sun is one of those especially rare stars that are at the "galactic corotation radius." Typically, the stars in our galaxy orbit about the center of our galaxy at a rate different from that of the spiral arm pattern. If such stars are located between spiral arms, they will not remain there for very long. With a star revolving around the galaxy's center at a rate different from the spiral arm structure, it is just a matter of time before that star is swept inside a spiral arm. Only at the corotation radius could a star remain between two spiral arms.

Another way our sun is special is that it does not deviate much from its Newtonian (that is, nearly circular) orbit about the center of our galaxy.[12] Most stars exhibit rather large up-and-down, back-and-forth, and side-to-side random motions away from their normal Newtonian orbital paths. The sun's tiny up-and-down motions keep us from getting too exposed to deadly radiation from the galactic nucleus and from supernovae remnants.[12] Now, we understand that the sun's tiny back-and-forth and side-to-side motions also play a crucial role in keeping our solar system from getting too close to a spiral arm.

Window to God's Glory

The sun's unique location benefits us in yet another way. We get a clear view of the heavens. If we were in a spiral arm, 80 to 85% of the light from other galaxies would be absorbed by intervening dust.[13] If we were near the galactic bulge, in a globular cluster, or even in an open star cluster, the light of other stars would make the night sky too bright. If it were not for our unique location, we would not have had the capacity to discover that we dwell in a spiral galaxy, that over a hundred billion other galaxies exist, that the universe is continually expanding, that there is a cosmic background radiation, and that our universe is traceable back to an exquisitely designed, transcendent creation event.

Situated where we are, however, we have what can be described as a window seat to the splendors of the universe. We are granted an unobstructed view, in a language understandable to all, of God's glory, power, and righteousness written in the heavens.[14]

The Right Star

Not only is a particular kind of galaxy essential for life, the star around which a life-bearing planet revolves must be just right. As we have seen, it must be located in the right part of the galaxy. It must also be a single star system. Zero or two-plus star systems will fail.

A planet ripped away from its star will be too cold for life. But if a planet is orbiting a binary or multiple star system, the extra star(s) frequently will pull the orbit of a planet small enough for life support out of the temperature zone essential for that life support.

As Shklovskii and Sagan first pointed out, a life support planet must be maintained by a star of very specific mass. A star more massive than the sun will burn too quickly and too erratically for life on the planet to be sustained. But the star cannot be any less massive either. Smaller mass stars have more frequent and violent flares. Also, the smaller the mass of the star, the closer the planet must be to that star to maintain a temperature suitable for life chemistry. This causes a problem because the tidal interaction between a star and its planet increases dramatically as the distance separating them shrinks: Bringing the planet just the slightest bit closer causes such a tremendous increase in tidal interaction that the planet's rotation period quickly lengthens from hours to months. This is the fate, for example, of both Mercury and Venus.

The star must form at just the right time in the history of the galaxy. If it forms too soon or too late, the mix of heavy elements suitable for life chemistry will not exist. It is also essential that the star be middle-aged. Only middle-aged stars are in a sufficiently stable burning phase. Only stars in the very middle part of their middle-aged phase manifest subdued enough flaring to make advanced life sustainable.

Even stars that are the most stable and in the most stable parts of their burning cycles experience changes in luminosity that can be detrimental for life. The sun's luminosity, for example, has increased by more than 35% since life was first introduced on Earth. Such a change is more than enough to exterminate life. But life survived on Earth because the increase in solar luminosity was exactly cancelled out each step of the way by a decrease in the efficiency of the greenhouse effect in Earth's atmosphere. This decrease in greenhouse efficiency arose through the careful introduction of just the right species of life in just the right quantities at just the right times. The slightest "evolutionary accident" would have caused either a runaway freeze-up or runaway boiling (see box on page 181).

Here, the materialists offer no explanation. How could strictly natural Darwinist processes possibly have anticipated the physics of solar burning?

The Right Planet

As biochemists now concede, for life molecules to operate so that organisms can live requires an environment where water vapor, liquid water, and frozen water are all stable and abundant. This means that a planet cannot be too close to its star or too far away. In the case of planet Earth, given a particular atmosphere, a change in the distance from the sun as small as 2% would rid the planet of all life.[15]

The temperature of a planet and its surface gravity determine the escape velocity, a measure of which atmospheric gases dissipate to outer space and which are retained. For a planet to support life, it is essential for water vapor (molecular weight 18) to be retained while molecules as heavy as methane (molecular weight 16) and ammonia (molecular weight 17) dissipate. Therefore, a change in surface gravity or temperature of just a few percent will make the difference.

While planet Earth has just the right surface gravity and temperature,[16] ammonia and methane, in fact, disappear much faster than their escape velocities would indicate. The reason is that chemical conditions in Earth's upper atmosphere—also indicative of fine-tuning—work efficiently to break down both molecules.[17]

CLIMATIC RUNAWAYS

Earth's biosphere is poised between a runaway freeze-up and a runaway evaporation. If the mean temperature of the earth's surface cools by even a few degrees, more snow and ice than normal will form. Snow and ice reflect solar energy much more efficiently than other surface materials. The reflection of more solar energy translates into lower surface temperatures, which in turn cause more snow and ice to form and subsequently still lower temperatures.

If the mean temperature of the earth's surface warms just a few degrees, more water vapor and carbon dioxide collect in the atmosphere. This extra water vapor and carbon dioxide create a better greenhouse effect in the atmosphere. This in turn causes the surface temperature to rise again, which releases even more water vapor and carbon dioxide into the atmosphere resulting in still higher surface temperatures.

Rotation and Life

The rotation period of a life-supporting planet cannot be changed by more than a few percent. If the planet takes too long to rotate, temperature differences between day and night will be too great. On the other hand, if the planet rotates too rapidly, wind velocities will rise to catastrophic levels. A quiet day on Jupiter (rotation period of ten hours), for example, generates thousand mph winds. Though our hurricanes and tornadoes are tough to endure, we are better off with their occasional blasts than we would be with more extreme differences between day and night temperatures.

Our present-day hurricanes provide some notable benefits. Recent studies done off Australia, Bermuda, and Nicaragua establish that hurricanes help us in five ways:

1. They significantly increase the diversity of species in the habitats they affect.[18]
2. They counterbalance the oceans' tendency to leach carbon dioxide from the atmosphere. This leaching, if unchecked, would result in catastrophic cooling of the planet.[19]
3. They help disperse greenhouse gases globally.[19]
4. They prevent heat buildup by shading local areas of the oceans that normally trap the sun's heat. Such shading saves some sea creatures from extinction.[19]
5. They help regulate the salinity of the oceans, the salt cycle, and the water cycle.[20]

Rotation periods of life-supportable planets, however, are not constant. Though Earth does not suffer catastrophic tidal interaction with the sun as Venus does, it still experiences enough that its rotation period is gradually braked. Every year, Earth's rotation period is slowed by the sun and moon by a small fraction of a second. If Earth was much younger than its 4.6 billion years, it would be rotating too quickly for life. If it were much older, it would be rotating too slowly. Since primitive life can tolerate more rapid rotation than advanced life, life can and did survive being placed on Earth when Earth was only 0.7 billion years old.

In addition to the length of the rotation period, the rate of change in that period is also sensitive for life support. Each species that has existed throughout the earth's history has had a range of tolerable rotation periods and a range of tolerable change in that period. As it turns out, most of the species that have ever existed throughout the earth's history could not have survived if the earth's rotational slowing had been greater or lesser than a certain narrow range (roughly between two and four hours per day per billion years).

Two additional factors have been identified. One is that the more rapid rotation of Earth in the past decreased the size of weather systems (relative to the surface area they covered) and concentrated them along the equator.[21] The net result was that extra light and heat from the sun necessary at that time for life support did indeed reach the earth's surface. The other is that the percentage of the earth's surface area covered by water was greater in the past.[22] Volcanic activity and plate tectonics caused continents to rise and increase in area until the rate of erosion balanced the increase. Since water bodies absorb and retain heat far more effectively than land masses, the larger ocean area of the past contributed significantly to the warmth of the early Earth's climate.

Even tectonic plate activity (often expressed as earthquakes) is a sensitive parameter for life. Without earthquakes, nutrients essential for life on the continents would erode and accumulate in the oceans. However, if earthquake activity were too great, it would be impossible for humans to reside in cities. On Earth, the number and intensity of earthquakes is large enough to recycle life-essential nutrients back to the continents but not so intense that dwelling in cities is impossible.

The Right Planetary Companions
Late in 1993, planetary scientist George Wetherill, of the Carnegie Institution of Washington, D.C., made an exciting discovery about our solar system. In observing computer simulations of our solar system, he found that without a Jupiter-sized planet positioned just where it is, Earth would be struck about a thousand times more frequently than it is already by comets and comet debris.[23] In other words, without Jupiter, impacts such as the one that wiped out the dinosaurs would be common.[24]

Here is how the protection system works. Jupiter is two and a half times more massive than all the other planets combined. Because of its huge mass, thus huge gravity, and its location between the earth and the cloud of comets surrounding the solar system, Jupiter either draws comets (by gravity) to collide with itself, as it did in July 1994,[25] or, more commonly, it deflects comets (again by gravity) right out of the solar system. In Wetherill's words, if it were not for Jupiter, "we wouldn't be around to study the origin of the solar system."[26]

Neither would we be around if it were not for the very high regularity in the orbits of both Jupiter and Saturn. Also in July 1994, French astrophysicist Jacques Laskar determined that if the outer planets were less [orbitally] regular, then the inner planets' motions would be chaotic, and Earth would suffer orbital changes so extreme as to disrupt its climatic stability.[27] In other words, Earth's climate would be unsuitable for life. (As it is, the tiny variations in Jupiter and Saturn's orbits may someday, but not soon, bounce lightweight Mercury right out of the solar system.) Thus, even the characteristics of Jupiter and Saturn's orbits must fit within certain narrowly defined ranges for life on Earth to be possible.

The Right Collider

The rule of thumb in planetary formation is that the greater a planet's surface gravity and the greater a planet's distance from its star, the heavier and thicker its atmosphere. And yet Earth departs dramatically from that rule. Theoretically, Earth should have an atmosphere much heavier and thicker than that of Venus, but in fact it has one about forty times lighter and thinner.

The solution to this mystery apparently lies with Earth's moon. Most moons in our solar system form out of the same solar disk material that generates the planets. As such, they are relatively small compared to their planets. A few moons orbiting the outer planets are foreign bodies that have been captured. Earth's moon, however, is the exception. It orbits a planet that is close to the sun and it is huge compared to its planet.

The moon is younger than Earth. According to Apollo lunar rock samples, it is only 4.25 billion years old compared to Earth's 4.57 billion years. The same rocks gathered by Apollo astronauts tell us the moon's crust is chemically distinct from Earth's. Astronomers have seen and measured the moon's slow, steady spiraling away from Earth. Their calculations suggest that the moon was in contact, or near contact, with Earth a little over 4.25 billion years ago.

The moon's distinct chemical make-up and its younger age establish that it and Earth did *not* form together. The moon's movement away from Earth[28] and the measured slowing of Earth's rotation[29] imply some kind of collision or near collision more than 4 billion years ago.

Only one collision scenario fits all the observed Earth-moon parameters and dynamics: a body at least the size of Mars (nine times the mass of the moon and one-ninth the mass of Earth) and possibly twice as large made a nearly head-on hit and was absorbed, for the most part, into Earth's core.[30] Such a collision would have blasted almost all of Earth's original atmosphere into outer space. The shell or cloud of debris arising from the collision would orbit Earth and eventually coalesce to form our moon.

This remarkable event delivered Earth from a life-suffocating atmosphere and produced a replacement atmosphere thin enough and of the right chemical composition to permit the passage of light to Earth's surface. It boosted the mass and density of Earth high enough to retain (by gravity) a large quantity of water vapor (molecular weight 18) for billions of years, but not so high as to keep life-threatening quantities of ammonia (molecular weight 17) and methane (molecular weight 16). This event so boosted the iron content of Earth's crust as to permit a huge abundance of ocean life (the quantity of iron, a critical nutrient, determines the abundance and diversity of marine algae, which form the base of the food chain for all ocean life), which in turn permitted advanced land life.[31] It played a major role in salting Earth's crust with a huge abundance of radioisotopes—the heat from which drives most of Earth's exceptionally high rates of tectonics and vulcanism.[32] (Heavy elements from the body colliding with Earth were largely transferred to Earth whereas the light elements were either dissipated to the interplanetary medium or transferred to a cloud that would eventually form the moon.) This collision gradually slowed Earth's rotation rate so that a wide variety of lower life forms could survive long enough to sustain the existence of advanced life forms.

Because the moon is so large relative to our planet, it exerts a significant gravitational pull on Earth. Thanks to this pull, coastal seawaters are cleansed and their nutrients replenished. The moon, again because of its great size and proximity to Earth, stabilized the tilt of Earth's rotation axis, protecting the planet from life-extinguishing climatic extremes[33] (see box "Climatic Runaways," page 181).

In summary, this amazing collision, for which we have an abundance of circumstantial evidence, appears to have been perfectly timed and designed to transform Earth from a "formless and empty" place into a site where life could survive and thrive. In fact, the degree of fine-tuning favorable to life manifested in this single event argues powerfully on its own for a divine Creator. Even if the universe contains as many as 10 billion trillion planets (10^{22}), we would not expect even one, by natural processes alone, to end up with the surface gravity, surface temperature, atmospheric composition, atmospheric pressure, crustal iron abundance, tectonics, vulcanism, rotation rate, rate of decline in rotation rate, and stable rotation axis tilt necessary for the support of life.[34] To those who express the desire to see a miracle, we can assure them they are looking at one whenever they gaze up at the moon.

Vital Poisons

The Food and Drug Administration recently issued warnings about overdoing dietary supplements of chromium, molybdenum, selenium, and vanadium. Each of these elements, in sufficient quantity, becomes a deadly poison. On the other hand, a lack of any one of these elements will kill us. Each of them is essential for building proteins that are vital for our existence. There is a fine line, for example, between too little vanadium in the diet and too much. Molybdenum also plays a crucial and unique role in nitrogen fixation, the process by which nitrogen from the atmosphere gets fixed into chemicals that can be assimilated by plants. In fact, the nitrogen fixation necessary for life on the land would be impossible unless just the right amount of molybdenum exists in the soil.

These four elements are not the only elements whose quantities must be fine-tuned for life's possible existence. We all know the devastating effects of iron deficiency. However, too much iron in the diet can prove just as damaging. Other elements whose abundances must be carefully controlled are arsenic, boron, chlorine, cobalt, copper, fluorine, iodine, manganese, nickel, phosphorus, potassium, sulfur, tin, and zinc. All these elements are essential for advanced life but too much of any one of them proves lethal.[35]

The relative abundance of elements measured in the earth's crust is very different from that of any other solar system body. The earth's crust manifests the precise quantities of all the life-essential elements necessary to permit the existence of advanced land life.

Extrasolar Planets

At the time this book went to press, astronomers had discovered 52 confirmed planets outside of our solar system orbiting normal stars (stars burning through the nuclear fusion of hydrogen into helium).[36] One is as small as a few times the mass of Earth.[37] Six are in the mass range of Saturn (Saturn = 95 Earth masses).[38] The rest range from half a Jupiter mass to about a dozen Jupiter masses (Jupiter = 317 Earth masses).

The sample of discovered extrasolar planets is biased toward the largest planets. They are much easier to observe. Also, the predominant observing technique biases the sample toward planets that are closest to their stars. Nevertheless, in spite of these present biases, it is becoming clear to astronomers that our solar system is exceptional. The age-old myths that extrasolar planetary systems would be common and would resemble our own are proving incorrect.

Astronomers are finding planets around only the most metal-rich stars. (To astronomers, anything that is not hydrogen or helium is a metal.) This makes sense since it takes a minimum quantity of metals just to make planet formation possible. The metallicity cutoff astronomers observe for planetary systems eliminates 98% of the stars in our galaxy as candidates for planetary companions.[39]

The 2% of the stars that are metal-rich enough to form planets are, with very few exceptions, younger than the sun. This makes sense, too. The older our galaxy becomes, the more metal-rich the gas clouds that form new stars become as a consequence of older stars exploding their ashes to the interstellar medium. Our sun is one of those very few stars both metal-rich and relatively old. While the present age of our sun is not essential for the simplest life forms, it is critical for advanced life.

Stars that are overly metal-rich present the problem that they will make too many planets, moons, asteroids, and comets. These extra bodies introduce chaos into the planetary system, which leads to either too many collisions or the disruption of planetary orbits.

The planets seen orbiting other stars, at least so far, are nothing like the planets in our solar system. The planet that is a few times the mass of Earth is in a system with no gas giants (that is, no planets the mass of Saturn or greater). The extrasolar gas giants astronomers observe either orbit too close to their stars or orbit their stars with eccentric orbits (that is, orbits where the distance between the planet and the star vary greatly). Either way, hypothesized planets like Earth in such systems would lose their capacity to support life. Therefore, not only are planetary systems relatively rare, of the systems that do exist, few, if any, are like our solar system.

Many Fine-Tuned Characteristics

We see here that Earth is prepared for physical life through a variety of finely-tuned characteristics of our galaxy group, galaxy, star, planet, collider, and moon. This discussion by no means exhausts the list of characteristics that must be fine-tuned for physical life to exist. The astronomical and geophysical literature now includes discussions on more than a hundred different characteristics that must take on narrowly defined values.

The list of design characteristics for our solar system grows longer with every year of new research. What were 2 parameters in 1966 grew to 8 by the end of the 1960s, to 23 by the end of the 1970s, to 30 by the end of the 1980s, to the current list of 123. A sampling of the parameters that must be fine-tuned for the support of physical life is presented in table 16.1 (see page 188).

Table 16.1: Evidence for the Fine-Tuning of the Galaxy-Sun-Earth-Moon System for Life Support[40]
The following parameters of a planet, its moon, its star, and its galaxy must have values falling within narrowly defined ranges for life of any kind to exist. Characteristics #5 and #6 are repeated from table 14.1 since they apply to both the universe and the galaxy.

1. galaxy cluster type
    if too rich: galaxy collisions and mergers would disrupt solar orbit
    if too sparse: insufficient infusion of gas to sustain star formation for a
        long enough time
2. galaxy size
    if too large: infusion of gas and stars would disturb sun's orbit and ignite
        too many galactic eruptions
    if too small: insufficient infusion of gas to sustain star formation for a
        long enough time
3. galaxy type
    if too elliptical: star formation would cease before sufficient heavy
        element build-up for life chemistry
    if too irregular: radiation exposure on occasion would be too severe and
        heavy elements for life chemistry would not be available
4. galaxy location
    if too close to a rich galaxy cluster: galaxy would be gravitationally disrupted
    if too close to very large galaxy(ies): galaxy would be gravitationally
        disrupted
5. supernovae eruptions
    if too close: life on the planet would be exterminated by radiation
    if too far: not enough heavy element ashes would exist for the formation
        of rocky planets
    if too infrequent: not enough heavy element ashes present for the
        formation of rocky planets
    if too frequent: life on the planet would be exterminated
    if too soon: not enough heavy element ashes would exist for the
        formation of rocky planets
    if too late: life on the planet would be exterminated by radiation
6. white dwarf binaries
    if too few: insufficient fluorine would be produced for life chemistry to
        proceed
    if too many: planetary orbits disrupted by stellar density; life on planet
        would be exterminated
    if too soon: not enough heavy elements would be made for efficient
        fluorine production
    if too late: fluorine would be made too late for incorporation in
        protoplanet
7. proximity of solar nebula to a supernova eruption
    if farther: insufficient heavy elements for life would be absorbed
    if closer: nebula would be blown apart

8. timing of solar nebula formation relative to supernova eruption
   if earlier: nebula would be blown apart
   if later: nebula would not absorb enough heavy elements
9. parent star distance from center of galaxy
   if farther: quantity of heavy elements would be insufficient to make
      rocky planets
   if closer: galactic radiation would be too great; stellar density would
      disturb planetary orbits
10. parent star distance from closest spiral arm
   if too large: exposure to harmful radiation from galactic core would be
      too great
11. z-axis heights of star's orbit
   if more than one: tidal interactions would disrupt planetary orbit of life
      support planet
   if less than one: heat produced would be insufficient for life
12. number of stars in the planetary system
   if more than one: tidal interactions would disrupt planetary orbit of life
      support planet
   if less than one: heat produced would be insufficient for life
13. parent star birth date
   if more recent: star would not yet have reached stable burning phase;
      stellar system would contain too many heavy elements
   if less recent: stellar system would not contain enough heavy
      elements
14. parent star age
   if older: luminosity of star would change too quickly
   if younger: luminosity of star would change too quickly
15. parent star mass
   if greater: luminosity of star would change too quickly; star would burn
      too rapidly
   if less: range of planet distances for life would be too narrow; tidal forces
      would disrupt the life planet's rotational period; uv radiation
      would be inadequate for plants to make sugars and oxygen
16. parent star metallicity
   if too small: insufficient heavy elements for life chemistry would exist
   if too large: radioactivity would be too intense for life; life would be
      poisoned by heavy element concentrations
17. parent star color
   if redder: photosynthetic response would be insufficient
   if bluer: photosynthetic response would be insufficient
18. H_3+ production
   if too small: simple molecules essential to planet formation and life
      chemistry would not form
   if too large: planets would form at wrong time and place for life
19. parent star luminosity relative to speciation
   if increases too soon: runaway green house effect would develop
   if increases too late: runaway glaciation would develop

20. surface gravity (escape velocity)
    if stronger: planet's atmosphere would retain too much ammonia and
        methane
    if weaker: planet's atmosphere would lose too much water
21. distance from parent star
    if farther: planet would be too cool for a stable water cycle
    if closer: planet would be too warm for a stable water cycle
22. inclination of orbit
    if too great: temperature differences on the planet would be too extreme
23. orbital eccentricity
    if too great: seasonal temperature differences would be too extreme
24. axial tilt
    if greater: surface temperature differences would be too great
    if less: surface temperature differences would be too great
25. rate of change of axial tilt
    if greater: climatic changes would be too extreme; surface temperature
        differences would become too extreme
26. rotation period
    if longer: diurnal temperature differences would be too great
    if shorter: atmospheric wind velocities would be too great
27. rate of change in rotation period
    if longer: surface temperature range necessary for life would not be
        sustained
    if shorter: surface temperature range necessary for life would not be
        sustained
28. planet age
    if too young: planet would rotate too rapidly
    if too old: planet would rotate too slowly
29. magnetic field
    if stronger: electromagnetic storms would be too severe
    if weaker: ozone shield would be inadequately protected from hard
        stellar and solar radiation
30. thickness of crust
    if thicker: too much oxygen would be transferred from the atmosphere to
        the crust
    if thinner: volcanic and tectonic activity would be too great
31. albedo (ratio of reflected light to total amount falling on surface)
    if greater: runaway glaciation would develop
    if less: runaway greenhouse effect would develop
32. asteroidal and cometary collision rate
    if greater: too many species would become extinct
    if less: crust would be too depleted of materials essential for life
33. mass of body colliding with primordial Earth
    if smaller: Earth's atmosphere would be too thick; moon would be too
        small
    if greater: Earth's orbit and form would be too greatly disturbed

34. timing of body colliding with primordial Earth
    if earlier: Earth's atmosphere would be too thick; moon would be too small
    if later: sun would be too luminous at epoch for advanced life
35. collision location of body colliding with primordial Earth
    if too close to grazing: insufficient debris to form large moon; inadequate annihilation of Earth's primordial atmosphere; inadequate transfer of heavy elements to Earth
    if too close to dead center: damage from collision would be too destructive for future life to exsist
36. oxygen to nitrogen ratio in atmosphere
    if larger: advanced life functions would proceed too quickly
    if smaller: advanced life functions would proceed too slowly
37. carbon dioxide level in atmosphere
    if greater: runaway greenhouse effect would develop
    if less: plants would be unable to maintain efficient photosynthesis
38. water vapor level in atmosphere
    if greater: runaway greenhouse effect would develop
    if less: rainfall would be too meager for advanced life on the land
39. atmospheric electric discharge rate
    if greater: too much fire destruction would occur
    if less: too little nitrogen would be fixed in the atmosphere
40. ozone level in atmosphere
    if greater: surface temperatures would be too low
    if less: surface temperatures would be too high; there would be too much uv radiation at the surface
41. oxygen quantity in atmosphere
    if greater: plants and hydrocarbons would burn up too easily
    if less: advanced animals would have too little to breathe
42. seismic activity
    if greater: too many life-forms would be destroyed
    if less: nutrients on ocean floors from river runoff would not be recycled to continents through tectonics; not enough carbon dioxide would be released from carbonates
43. volcanic activity
    if lower: insufficient amounts of carbon dioxide and water vapor would be returned to the atmosphere; soil mineralization would become too degraded for life
    if higher: advanced life, at least, would be destroyed
44. rate of decline in tectonic activity
    if slower: advanced life could never survive on the planet
    if faster: advanced life could never survive on the planet
45. rate of decline in volcanic activity
    if slower: advanced life could never survive on the planet
    if faster: advanced life could never survive on the planet
46. oceans-to-continents ratio
    if greater: diversity and complexity of life-forms would be limited
    if smaller: diversity and complexity of life-forms would be limited

47. rate of change in oceans-to-continents ratio
    if smaller: advanced life would lack the needed land mass area
    if greater: advanced life would be destroyed by the radical changes
48. global distribution of continents (for Earth)
    if too much in the southern hemisphere: seasonal differences would be too
        severe for advanced life
49. frequency and extent of ice ages
    if smaller: insufficient fertile, wide, and well-watered valleys produced
        for diverse and advanced life forms; insufficient mineral
        concentrations occur for diverse and advanced life
    if greater: planet inevitably experiences runaway freezing
50. soil mineralization
    if too nutrient poor: diversity and complexity of life-forms would be limited
    if too nutrient rich: diversity and complexity of life-forms would be limited
51. gravitational interaction with a moon
    if greater: tidal effects on the oceans, atmosphere, and rotational period
        would be too severe
    if less: orbital obliquity changes would cause climatic instabilities;
        movement of nutrients and life from the oceans to the continents
        and vice versa would be insufficient; magnetic field would be too
        weak
52. Jupiter distance
    if greater: too many asteroid and comet collisions would occur on Earth
    if less: Earth's orbit would become unstable
53. Jupiter mass
    if greater: Earth's orbit would become unstable
    if less: too many asteroid and comet collisions would occur on Earth
54. drift in major planet distances
    if greater: Earth's orbit would become unstable
    if less: too many asteroid and comet collisions would occur on Earth
55. major planet eccentricities
    if greater: orbit of life supportable planet would be pulled out of life
        support zone
56. major planet orbital instabilities
    if greater: orbit of life supportable planet would be pulled out of life
        support zone
57. atmospheric pressure
    if too small: liquid water would evaporate too easily and condense too
        infrequently
    if too large: liquid water would not evaporate easily enough for land life;
        insufficient sunlight would reach planetary surface; insufficient uv
        radiation would reach planetary surface
58. atmospheric transparency
    if smaller: insufficient range of wavelengths of solar radiation would
        reach planetary surface
    if greater: too broad a range of wavelengths of solar radiation would
        reach planetary surface

59. chlorine quantity in atmosphere
   if smaller: erosion rates, acidity of rivers, lakes, and soils, and certain
      metabolic rates would be insufficient for most life forms
   if greater: erosion rates, acidity of rivers, lakes, and soils, and certain
      metabolic rates would be too high for most life forms
60. iron quantity in oceans and soils
   if smaller: quantity and diversity of life would be too limited for support
      of advanced life; if very small, no life would be possible
   if larger: iron poisoning of at least advanced life would result
61. tropospheric ozone quantity
   if smaller: insufficient cleansing of biochemical smogs would result
   if larger: respiratory failure of advanced animals, reduced crop yields,
      and destruction of ozone-sensitive species would result
62. stratospheric ozone quantity
   if smaller: too much uv radiation would reach planet's surface causing
      skin cancers and reduced plant growth
   if larger: too little uv radiation would reach planet's surface causing reduced
      plant growth and insufficient vitamin production for animals
63. mesospheric ozone quantity
   if smaller: circulation and chemistry of mesospheric gases so disturbed
      as to upset relative abundances of life essential gases in lower
      atmosphere
   if greater: circulation and chemistry of mesospheric gases so disturbed as
      to upset relative abundances of life essential gases in lower
      atmosphere
64. quantity and extent of forest and grass fires
   if smaller: growth inhibitors in the soils would accumulate; soil
      nitrification would be insufficient; insufficient charcoal production
      for adequate soil water retention and absorption of certain growth
      inhibitors.
   if greater: too many plant and animal life forms would be destroyed
65. quantity of soil sulfur
   if smaller: plants would become deficient in certain proteins and die
   if larger: plants would die from sulfur toxins; acidity of water and soil
      would become too great for life; nitrogen cycles would be disturbed
66. biomass to comet infall ratio
   if smaller: greenhouse gases accumulate, triggering runaway surface
      temperature increase
   if larger: greenhouse gases decline, triggering a runaway freezing

Chances for Finding a Life Support Planet

Each of these 66 parameters must be within certain limits to avoid
disturbing a planet's capacity to support life. For some, including
many of the stellar parameters, the limits have been measured quite
precisely. For others, including many of the planetary parameters, the
limits are less precisely known. Trillions of stars are available for

study, and star formation is quite well understood and observed. On the other hand, only 61 planets have been studied, and though astrophysicists have developed a good theory of planetary formation with significant observational confirmation, not all the details have yet been worked out.

Let's look at how confining these limits can be. Among the least confining would be the number of stars in the planetary system and the distribution of a planet's continents. The limits here are loose, eliminating perhaps only 20% of all candidates. More confining would be parameters such as the planet's rotation period and its albedo (reflectivity), which eliminate about 90% of all candidates from contention. Most confining of all would be parameters such as the parent star's mass and the planet's distance from its parent star, which eliminate 99.9% of all candidates.

Of course, not all the listed parameters are strictly independent of the others. Dependency factors could reduce the degree of confinement. On the other hand, all these parameters must be kept within specific limits for the total time span needed to support life on a candidate planet. This increases the degree of confinement.

An attempt at calculating the possibility that a randomly selected planet in our universe will possess the capacity to support physical life is presented in table 16.2 (see page 195). Although I have tried to be optimistic (that is, conservative) in assigning the probabilities, I readily admit many of the estimates may need to be modified.

Future research should provide us with much more accurate probabilities. If past research is any indication, however, the number of parameters should increase and the probabilities decrease. Indeed, the parameter list has grown from 41 to 128 between the second edition of this book and the present third edition, while the probability for finding a planet anywhere in the universe with the capacity to support physical life has shrunk from 10^{-53} to 10^{-144}.

With considerable security, therefore, we can draw the conclusion that even with a hundred billion trillion stars in the observable universe, the probability of finding, without divine intervention, a single planet capable of supporting physical life is much less than one in a trillion, trillion, trillion, trillion, trillion, trillion, trillion, trillion, trillion, trillion, trillion. The odds actually are higher that the reader will be killed by a sudden reversal in the second law of thermodynamics.[41]

HABITABLE ZONES

The environmental requirements for life to exist depend quite strongly on the life form in question. The conditions for primitive life to exist, for example, are not nearly as demanding as they are for advanced life. Also, it makes a big difference how active the life form is and how long it remains in its environment. On this basis there are six distinct zones or regions in which life can exist. In order of the broadest to the narrowest they are as follows:

1. for unicellular, low metabolism life that persists for only a brief time period
2. for unicellular, low metabolism life that persists for a long time period
3. for unicellular, high metabolism life that persists for a brief time period
4. for unicellular, high metabolism life that persists for a long time period
5. for advanced life that survives for just a brief time period
6. for advanced life that survives for a long time period

Complicating factors, however, are that unicellular, low metabolism life is more easily subject to radiation damage and has a very low molecular repair rate. The origin of life problem (see chapter 17) also is much more difficult for low metabolism life. Given how little we still know about the complexities of organisms and their interdependent relations with one another and their environment, no attempt is made in table 16.2 to distinguish between possibly different habitable zones. Future research, however, may make such distinctions possible.

Table 16.2: An Estimate of the Probability for Attaining the Necessary Parameters for Life Support[42]

Parameter	Probability that feature will fall in the required range for life
local abundance and distribution of dark matter	.1
galaxy cluster size	.1
galaxy cluster location	.1
galaxy size	.1
galaxy type	.1
galaxy location	.1
variability of local dwarf galaxy absorption rate	.1
star location relative to galactic center	.2
star distance from corotation circle of galaxy	.005
star distance from closest spiral arm	.1
z-axis extremes of star's orbit	.02

proximity of solar nebula to a supernova eruption	.01
timing of solar nebula formation relative to supernova eruption	.01
number of stars in system	.7
number and timing of close encounters by nearby stars	.01
proximity of close stellar encounters	.1
masses of close stellar encounters	.1
star birth date	.2
star age	.4
star metallicity	.05
star orbital eccentricity	.1
star mass	.001
star luminosity change relative to speciation types & rates	.00001
star color	.4
star's carbon to oxygen ratio	.01
star's space velocity relative to Local Standard of Rest	.05
star's short term luminosity variability	.05
star's long term luminosity variability	.05
number & timing of solar system encounters with interstellar gas clouds	.1
H_3+ production	.1
supernovae rates & locations	.01
white dwarf binary types, rates, & locations	.01
planetary distance from star	.001
inclination of planetary orbit	.5
axis tilt of planet	.3
rate of change of axial tilt	.01
period and size of axis tilt variation	.1
planetary rotation period	.1
rate of change in planetary rotation period	.05
planetary orbit eccentricity	.3
rate of change of planetary orbital eccentricity	.1
rate of change of planetary inclination	.5
period and size of eccentricity variation	.1
period and size of inclination variation	.1
number of moons	.2
mass and distance of moon	.01
surface gravity (escape velocity)	.001
tidal force from sun and moon	.1
magnetic field	.01
rate of change & character of change in magnetic field	.1
albedo (planet reflectivity)	.1
density	.1
thickness of crust	.01
oceans-to-continents ratio	.2
rate of change in oceans-to-continents ratio	.1
global distribution of continents	.3
frequency, timing, & extent of ice ages	.1

frequency, timing, & extent of global snowball events	.1
asteroidal & cometary collision rate	.1
change in asteroidal & cometary collision rates	.1
rate of change in asteroidal & cometary collision rates	.1
mass of body colliding with primordial Earth	.002
timing of body colliding with primordial Earth	.05
location of body's collision with primordial Earth	.05
position & mass of Jupiter relative to Earth	.01
major planet eccentricities	.1
major planet orbital instabilities	.05
drift and rate of drift in major planet distances	.05
number & distribution of planets	.01
atmospheric transparency	.01
atmospheric pressure	.01
atmospheric viscosity	.1
atmospheric electric discharge rate	.01
atmospheric temperature gradient	.01
carbon dioxide level in atmosphere	.01
rate of change in carbon dioxide level in atmosphere	.1
rate of change in water vapor level in atmosphere	.01
rate of change in methane level in early atmosphere	.01
oxygen quantity in atmosphere	.01
chlorine quantity in atmosphere	.1
cobalt quantity in crust	.1
arsenic quantity in crust	.1
copper quantity in crust	.1
boron quantity in crust	.1
fluorine quantity in crust	.1
iodine quantity in crust	.1
manganese quantity in crust	.1
nickel quantity in crust	.1
phosphorus quantity in crust	.1
tin quantity in crust	.1
zinc quantity in crust	.1
molybdenum quantity in crust	.05
vanadium quantity in crust	.1
chromium quantity in crust	.1
selenium quantity in crust	.1
iron quantity in oceans	.1
tropospheric ozone quantity	.01
stratospheric ozone quantity	.01
mesospheric ozone quantity	.01
water vapor level in atmosphere	.01
oxygen to nitrogen ratio in atmosphere	.1
quantity of greenhouse gases in atmosphere	.01
rate of change in greenhouse gases in atmosphere	.01
quantity of forest & grass fires	.01

quantity of sea salt aerosols	.1
soil mineralization	.1
quantity of anaerobic bacteria in the oceans	.01
quantity of aerobic bacteria in the oceans	.01
quantity of decomposer bacteria in soil	.01
quantity of mycorrhizal fungi in soil	.01
quantity of nitrifying microbes in soil	.01
quantity & timing of vascular plant introductions	.001
quantity, timing, & placement of carbonate-producing animals	.00001
quantity, timing, & placement of methanogens	.00001
quantity of soil sulfur	.1
quantity of sulfur in the planet's core	.1
quantity of silicon in the planet's core	.1
quantity of water at subduction zones in the crust	.01
hydration rate of subducted minerals	.1
tectonic activity	.05
rate of decline in tectonic activity	.1
volcanic activity	.1
rate of decline in volcanic activity	.1
viscosity at Earth core boundaries	.01
viscosity of lithosphere	.2
biomass to comet infall ratio	.01
regularity of cometary infall	.1
number, intensity, & location of hurricanes	.02

dependency factors estimate	1,000,000,000,000,000,000,000.
longevity requirements estimate	.0000001

Probability for occurrence of all 128 parameters $\approx 10^{-166}$
Maximum possible number of planets in universe $\approx 10^{22}$

Thus, less than 1 chance in 10^{144} (trillion trillion trillion trillion trillion trillion trillion trillion trillion trillion trillion trillion) exists that even one such planet would occur anywhere in the universe.

These factors would seem to indicate that the local group of galaxies, the Milky Way galaxy, the sun, Jupiter, Saturn, the collider with the primordial earth, the earth, and the moon, in addition to the universe, have undergone divine design. It seems apparent that personal intervention on the part of the Creator takes place not just at the origin of the universe but also much more recently. In other words, Earth seems more than simply "the pick of the litter," the planet selected from the Creator's searching through the vastness of the cosmos for life's best home. Rather, the remoteness of the probability of finding a planet fit for life suggests that the Creator personally and specially designed and constructed our galaxy group, our galaxy, our sun, Jupiter, Saturn, Earth's collider, the moon, and Earth for life.

If divine design is essential to explain the properties of simpler systems such as the universe, our galaxy, and the solar system, then God's involvement is even more essential to explain systems as complex as organisms, including human beings. As for the millions of dollars spent in the past by the U. S. government on the search for extraterrestrial intelligence, former Senator William Proxmire may have said it best. We would be far wiser to have spent the money looking for intelligent life in Washington.

HOW MANY PLANETS DID GOD CREATE FOR LIFE?

While there is not the remotest chance that the natural conditions and physical laws of the universe will spawn a planet capable of sustaining physical life, there is nothing to stop the Creator of the universe from miraculously designing several planets, rather than just one planet, with the capacity to support life. The question of how many planets God created for physical life is open to speculation.

Some theologians and scientists argue that since God so obviously enjoys creating He would not limit Himself to just planet Earth. Other scholars point out that the Bible reveals God as a Being who conserves His miracles. In other words, the God of the Bible appears to perform only those miracles necessary to achieve His purposes. The only possibility the Bible definitively rules out is another planet in the universe with physical intelligent life that has fallen into a state of spiritual rebellion against God's authority. The book of Hebrews, chapters 9 and 10, states that Jesus Christ died one time at one place for all sinners.

CHAPTER SEVENTEEN

BUILDING LIFE

In previous chapters we looked at some of the burgeoning evidence for divine design in the universe, our galaxy, our sun, our planet, and our moon. This glowing testimony to the work of the Designer pales, however, in comparison to the evidence that resides in living organisms.

For the universe and the solar system, some characteristics must be fine-tuned to better than one part in 10^{37} for life to be possible. But, the fine-tunings necessary to build an independent, functioning organism require precision crafting beyond what people have ever imagined possible, precision to one part in a number so big that it would fill thousands of books to write out.

The Time Scale

When it comes to the origin of life, many biologists (and others) have typically assumed that plenty of time is available for natural processes to perform the necessary assembly. But discoveries about the universe and the solar system have shattered that assumption. What we see now is that life must have originated on Earth quickly.

In early 1992, Christopher Chyba and Carl Sagan published a review paper on the origins of life.[1] *Origins* is plural for a good reason. Research indicates that life began, was destroyed, and began again many times during that era before it finally took hold.

Fully formed cells show up in the fossil record as far back as 3.5 billion years, and limestone, formed from the remains of organisms, dates back 3.8 billion years. The ratio of ^{12}carbon to ^{13}carbon found in ancient sediments[2] also indicates a plenitude of life on Earth for the era between 3.5 and 3.86 billion years ago.

Now, the earth's crust remained molten until 3.9 billion years ago. Life obviously could not survive on or in a molten crust. That leaves just 40 million years between the earth's molten state and the first definitive evidence of life.

But the era between 3.86 and 3.5 billion years ago also had its grave dangers for life. Though the research is recent, it leaves no room for doubt (based on dating of lunar craters and on comparisons of craters on the moon, Mars, and Mercury) that Earth and other bodies close to the sun experienced heavy bombardment by meteors, comets, asteroids, and dust in their early history.[3] From about 4.3 until 3.9 billion years ago, the bombardment of Earth was so intense that no life could have survived it and the earth's crust was kept in a molten state. From 3.9 until 3.5 billion years ago, the bombardment gradually decreased to its present comparatively low level. But during those 400 million years at least thirty life-exterminating impacts must have occurred. These findings have enormous significance to our theories about the origin of life. They show that life sprang up on Earth (and re-sprang) in what could be called geologic instants, periods of 10-million years or less (between devastating impacts).[4]

From the perspective of our life span, a 40-million-year (for the first origin of life) or a 10-million-year (for the subsequent origins of life) window may seem long, but it is impossibly short to those seeking to explain life's origins without divine input.

Laboratory Prebiotic Soups

Attempts to show that life can and does come together on its own have resulted in experiments with prebiotic soups (warm ponds enriched with life-building molecules). Even under the highly favorable conditions of a laboratory, these soups have failed to produce anything remotely resembling life. One problem is that they produce only a random distribution of left- and right-handed prebiotic molecules. (Many prebiotic molecules, notably all but one of the bioactive amino acids, occur in two mirror-image forms that are arbitrarily termed left- and right-handed.) Life chemistry demands that all the nucleotide sugars be right-handed and all the bioactive amino acids that have mirror-image forms (19 out of 20) be left-handed. With all our learning and technology we cannot even come close in the lab to lining up molecules with the correct handedness and assembling them together in the correct sequence to make life. How can we expect life to bring itself together in just a few million years in the chaotic world of nature?

Amazingly, Chyba and Sagan find hope in the extraterrestrial bombardment. Glossing over the destructive effects of the collisions, they hypothesize a possibly beneficial effect. They suggest that this extraterrestrial bombardment may have assisted life formation by delivering concentrated doses of prebiotic molecules. How reasonable is this suggestion? Though comets, meteorites partly composed of carbon, and interplanetary dust particles may carry some prebiotics, they carry only the simplest ones and far too few of them to make a difference. In fact, with every helpful molecule they may bring, come several more that would get in the way—useless molecules that would substitute for the needed ones. And again, the left- or right-handedness problem persists. (The discovery of a slight excess of left-handed over right-handed amino acids in a few meteorites has proved to be the result of terrestrial contamination.[5])

Atmosphere Problem
Chyba, Sagan, and others cling to yet another slim chance. They suggest that the atmospheric conditions 3.9 to 3.5 billion years ago might not have been too unfavorable for life. Perhaps the conditions were just neutral. Unfavorable in the context of life assembly is an "oxidizing" atmosphere, one in which atoms and molecules bond with oxygen atoms. Favorable would be a "reducing" atmosphere, one in which atoms and molecules bond with hydrogen rather than with oxygen atoms. Neutral, as Chyba and Sagan define it, would be an atmosphere that allows at least some hydrogen bonding. But this idea, too, reflects wishful thinking.

Atmospheric physicists established more than ten years ago that Earth's atmosphere has been fully oxidizing (enough free oxygen exists to oxidize all organic substances) for the last 4 billion years.[6] Recently, a Romanian physicist discovered why. The radiation released from the decay of uranium, thorium, and potassium-40 in the earth's crust will dissociate some of the water molecules in the primordial ocean into hydrogen and oxygen.[7] Thus, at the moment the earth's crust cools enough to permit an ocean to form, a continuous production of oxygen into both the ocean and the atmosphere begins.

Under oxidizing conditions, processes producing amino acids (protein building blocks) and nucleotides (DNA and RNA building blocks) operate 30 million times less efficiently than they would under reducing conditions.[8] Natural primordial soups would contain far too few prebiotic molecules to overcome this inefficiency, not to mention the destructive chemical processes. Worse yet, the minute amino acid production would almost entirely be composed of the simple acid, glycine.[9] The more complex acids that are also needed would be virtually missing.

Missing Soup

The ^{12}carbon to ^{13}carbon isotope ratio studies referred to earlier in this chapter (see page 201) distinguish between inorganic carbonaceous molecules that form some of the critical building blocks of life and the same molecules that result from the decay of once living organisms. Such studies reveal that all of these carbonaceous molecules are post-biotic. None are prebiotic. In other words, there never existed at any point in Earth's history either a prebiotic soup or a prebiotic mineral substrate. Lacking a prebiotic soup or a prebiotic mineral substrate, there is no possibility of a naturalistic explanation for the origins of life.

Something called the oxygen-ultraviolet paradox explains why no evidence for a prebiotic soup or a prebiotic mineral substrate has ever been found on Earth. As already noted, the existence of oxygen in the atmosphere and the ocean guarantees the shutdown of prebiotic chemistry. The absence of oxygen, however, means that intense ultraviolet radiation will penetrate Earth's atmosphere and upper ocean layer. Such ultraviolet radiation also guarantees the shutdown of prebiotic chemistry. So, either way, a naturalistic explanation for the origins of life on Earth is doomed.

The Odds

The problems of primordial soups are big, but bigger yet is the infeasibility of generating, without supernatural input, an enormous increase in complexity. A wide gulf separates an aqueous solution containing a few amino acids from the simplest living cell.

Years ago, molecular biophysicist Harold Morowitz calculated the size of this gulf. If one were to take the simplest living cell and break every chemical bond within it, the odds that the cell would reassemble under ideal natural conditions (the best possible chemical environment) would be one chance in $10^{100,000,000,000}$.[10] Most of us cannot even begin to picture a speck of chance so remote. Another way of depicting the assembly problem is schematically outlined in figure 17.1 (see page 205).

With odds as remote as 1 in $10^{100,000,000,000}$, the time scale issue becomes completely irrelevant. What does it matter if the earth has been around for 10 seconds, 10 thousand years, or 10 billion years? The size of the universe is of no consequence either. If all the matter in the visible universe were converted into the building blocks of life, and if assembly of these building blocks were attempted once a microsecond for the entire age of the universe, then instead of the odds being 1 in $10^{100,000,000,000}$, they would be 1 in $10^{99,999,999,916}$.

A.

B.   ≤ p◀ % ♣ Σ £ ✦ r Ω α ✄ y□ ◆ $

C.   y e s R g o l m v u E B f q z d r

D.   ye sRm vuB gol mEf qd zr Ctp al til

E.   yevuaBgol SrnymEfa saxpqadCtpgo alznrtihIo

F.   I love mango and papaya yoghurt.

Figure 17.1: An Analogy for Some of the Steps Needed in the Assembly of Life Molecules

Life molecules are composed of proteins and nucleic acids. The proteins, for example, are built from 20 distinct amino acids, 19 of which must be oriented in a left-handed configuration. Moreover, most of these amino acids must be sequenced in a specific manner and to a specific length. In the natural world over 80 distinct amino acids exist, 50% right-handed and 50% left-handed. The problem for life assembly is to select from the randomly oriented amino acids only those that are correctly oriented (step A to B), then to select out only the life-specific amino acids (step B to C), then to bond the amino acids together into short chains (step C to D), then to bond the short chains together to make chains of the necessary lengths, typically, several hundred amino acids long (step D to E), and finally to select out those chains in the right order that have the amino acids in the proper sequences (step E to F). Meanwhile, the whole process must be protected so that the rate of formation remains sufficiently above the rate of destruction.

Non-Theists' Responses

Non-theists typically counter Morowitz' odds by pointing out that not every amino acid and nucleotide must be strictly sequenced for life molecules to function. They are right, and thus the probability for reassembly improves. But Morowitz also assumed that all the amino acids were bioactive. In fact, only twenty of the more than eighty naturally occurring amino acids are bioactive, and only those that are left-handed can be used. So the probability declines again. Furthermore, Morowitz assumed totally favorable conditions, only constructive chemical processes operating. Under natural circumstances, destructive chemical processes operate at least as frequently as constructive chemical processes. The bottom line is the odds for the assembly of the simplest living entity actually grow worse as more details are figured into the calculation.

Another attempt to wiggle out is to suggest that the simplest living entity 3.5 billion years ago was far simpler than what exists today. The difficulty here is that conditions on Earth 3.5 billion years ago were not enough different from conditions today to warrant such an idea. In fact, conditions were so similar that if life were spontaneously generating 3.5 billion years ago, we could expect to see it doing so today. Minimum complexity presents another problem. Organisms below a certain level of complexity cannot survive independently. As Morowitz demonstrated, this minimum complexity is not much below what we see in organisms today. Complete genome sequences of the simplest life forms capable of independent survival, life forms whose fossils are identical to the most ancient fossils known, circa 3.5 billion years old, reveal between 1,400 and 1,900 gene products.[11]

Finally, as astronomer Michael Hart demonstrated in 1982, even if you grant non-theists their wildest scenario concerning the origin of life, it still fails:

> Let us suppose (very optimistically) that in a strand of genesis DNA there are no fewer than 400 positions where any one of the four nucleotide residues will do, and at each of 100 other positions either of two different nucleotides will be equally effective, leaving only 100 positions which must be filled by exactly the right nucleotides. This appears to be an unrealistically optimistic set of assumptions; but even so, the probability that an arbitrarily chosen strand of nucleic acid could function as genesis DNA is only one in 10^{90}. Even in 10 billion

years, the chance of forming such a strand spontaneously would be only 10^{-90} times 10^{60}, or 10^{-30}. . . . For each of 100 different specific genes [the minimum needed] to be formed spontaneously (in ten billion years) the probability is $(10^{-30})^{100}$ = 10^{-3000}. For them to be formed at the same time, and in close proximity, the probability is very much lower.[12]

For those who want the most realistic calculation of the odds of life assembly under natural conditions, the papers[13] and book[14] by information theorist Hubert Yockey are excellent.

New Hope in RNA?
A smattering of papers published recently in *Science* momentarily lifted non-theistic biologists' mood of despair. Those papers discussed what seemed a possible way around some of the complexities of life.[15] Here's the background.

Molecules responsible for life chemistry cannot function by themselves. DNA (molecules that hold the blueprints for the construction of life molecules), proteins (molecules that follow portions of the blueprints in building and repairing life molecules), and RNA (molecules that carry the blueprints from the DNA to specific proteins) are all interdependent.

Thus, for life to originate mechanistically, all three kinds of molecules would need to emerge spontaneously and simultaneously from inorganic compounds. Even the most optimistic of researchers agreed that the chance appearance of these incredibly complex molecules at exactly the same time and place was beyond the realm of natural possibility.

However, in 1987 an experiment demonstrated that one kind of RNA can act as an enzyme or catalyst (an agent to facilitate a chemical process). It can function like a protein, at least to a limited degree.[16] This finding led to some leaps of faith. Since it was assumed already that RNA could be more easily constructed under prebiotic conditions than DNA or proteins, the suggestion arose that a primitive RNA molecule—capable of functioning as a protein and as DNA—evolved by natural means out of a primordial soup. In time, this "primitive" RNA was said to specialize, evolving into the three kinds of molecules we now recognize as RNA, DNA, and proteins.

The discoveries reported a few years ago showed yet more

protein-like capabilities of RNA molecules. A research group presented evidence that a certain RNA molecule could stimulate two amino acids to join together with a peptide bond (the kind of chemical bond formed in proteins).[17] A second research team observed another RNA molecule both making and breaking the bonds that join amino acids to RNA.[18] Though these capabilities plus the ones observed earlier add up to only a tiny fraction of all the functions proteins perform, several origin-of-life theorists have proposed that no proteins were necessary for the first life forms.

These findings may seem to make "easier" the origin of life by strictly natural processes, but that is not necessarily the case. Even if a single primordial molecule could perform all the functions of modern DNA, RNA, and proteins, such a molecule would have to be no less complex in its information content (i.e., its built-in "knowledge" of what to do) than the sum of modern DNA, RNA, and proteins. In other words, the task of assembling such an incredibly versatile molecule is no easier than assembling the three different kinds of molecules. The information content of the three is simply concentrated into one enormously complex molecule. Even Leslie Orgel, a leading proponent of an RNA origin of life, admitted, "You have to get an awful lot of things right and nothing wrong."[19]

Another catch in these arguments is the false notion that RNA is easier to assemble than proteins or DNA. For 20 years researchers and texts taught that RNA had been synthesized in a lab under prebiotic conditions. This myth was exploded by Robert Shapiro at a meeting of the International Society for the Study of the Origin of Life held at Berkeley in 1986. Some 300 of the top origin-of-life researchers from around the world were present.

Shapiro traced all the references to RNA synthesis back to one ambiguous paper published in 1967. At the same meeting he went on to demonstrate that the synthesis of RNA under prebiotic conditions is essentially impossible. No one at the meeting challenged the soundness of his conclusion. Shapiro then published his case against RNA synthesis in the journal *Origin of Life and Evolution of the Biosphere*,[20] a case that remains unchallenged to this day.[21]

Finally, RNA molecules and the nucleotides that comprise them are unstable outside of cells. At the time of life's origin Earth's surface was relatively hot, probably between 80 and 90°C (176-194°F), with little temperature variation.[22] That is, Earth's surface was without any cold spots. At these warm temperatures RNA nucleotide sequences decouple. Moreover, new experimental results demonstrate that all of the RNA nucleotides themselves degrade at warm temperatures. They can last only from 19 days to 12 years.[23] The most optimistic naturalist hypotheses demand that they hold together for many millions of years. Even at water's freezing point, cytosine (one of the RNA nucleotides) decomposes in less than 17,000 years.[24] Outside the cell there is no environment providing sufficient stability and protection for RNA molecules and their nucleotide bases. This means RNA molecules cannot survive without cells while cells cannot survive without RNA. Both must be constructed simultaneously.

Error-Handling Capability

Proteins and nucleic acids demonstrate a considerable tolerance for substitutions of alternative amino acids and nucleotides at certain sites. This has led to some questioning of their divine design. But as we saw in chapter 14, life cannot possibly exist in the universe unless several sources of radiation exist at highly specified levels. These radiation sources inevitably will cause some breakdown or changes in the structures of life molecules. Therefore, it is essential for life molecules to be so designed that they can still function even after suffering some limited destruction.

One useful analogy for visualizing the error-handling capability of proteins and nucleic acids would be computer programs. Consider a computer program with a million lines of code which, in spite of the random destruction of ten thousand lines of code, still performs its intended function. No one has written such an error-tolerant program. It could be done, but the task would be orders of magnitude more difficult than writing a program where the programer need not worry about random destruction of his code. Likewise, the tolerance for substitutions in life molecules should drive us toward, not away from, the conclusion of divine design.

Life on Mars?

Though I'm convinced that the origin of life defies a naturalistic explanation, I am expecting that life, or the remains of life, will eventually be discovered on Mars and possibly other solar system bodies. My reason has nothing to do with spontaneous generation. It has everything to do with Mars' proximity to Earth.

In 1989, on ABC's "Nightline" with Ted Koppel, two astronomers and a science journalist declared that the discovery of life on Mars would provide virtual proof that life does indeed originate and evolve, and quite easily, by natural processes. Here is their line of reasoning: So far, we know of life's existence on only one planet orbiting one star out of 10-billion-trillion stars in the cosmos. If life is found on Mars, we would know it exists on two planets, but not just any two planets, two planets orbiting the same star. Instead of just one life site out of 10-billion-trillion candidates, we would have two life sites out of nine (the nine planets of our solar system). Such a finding would suggest that life is abundant throughout our universe, abundant by spontaneous generation.

By their faulty reasoning and failure to acknowledge relevant data, these influential men are setting their audience up for a deception. The remains, at least, of many micro-organisms are likely to be found on Mars for no other reason than that Mars is only 35 million miles away from Earth. In other words, these zealous evolutionists, bent on searching for life on Mars, seem to ignore important facts about the transportability and survivability of Earth life forms. Consider the following data:[19]

1. Meteorites large enough to make a crater greater than 60 miles across will cause Earth rocks to escape Earth's gravity. Out of 1,000 such rocks ejected, on the average, 291 will strike Venus, 20 go to Mercury, 17 hit Mars, 14 make it to Jupiter, and 1 would go all the way to Saturn.
2. Balloon missions and experiments done from high-flying aircraft have found a few floating diatoms (unicellular algae with siliceous cell walls) at altitudes ranging from 30,000 to 130,000 feet.
3. The sun's radiation exerts a pressure that is capable of wafting tiny life forms (sizes ranging from 0.2 microns to about 1 micron) outward through the solar system and perhaps beyond.
4. Many microorganisms can be kept at liquid air temperatures (about −200° Centigrade) for more than six months without losing their capacity to germinate.
5. Several microbial species exposed for five days to the vacuum conditions of outer space did not lose their viability.
6. Some microbes are capable of absorbing 600 kilorads of x-ray radiation without losing their viability.

7. Even very tiny amounts of graphite (of which there is more than an adequate supply in interplanetary space) will protect microorganisms from harmful ultraviolet radiation. The sun's radiation pressure can still push such tiny graphite grains through the inner part of the solar system.

Thus there are many reasons to believe that millions of Earth's minute creatures have been deposited on the surface of Mars and other solar system planets.

Admittedly, conditions on Mars are unfavorable for the germination of such life except for only the briefest of moments. A liquid drop of water on the Martian surface, for example, evaporates in less than a second. Thus, living "adult" organisms should be quite rare on Mars. But, we should not be surprised to find considerable quantities of spores and the remains of biological material.

The discovery of microbial life and creatures perhaps as large as nematodes on Mars—a discovery we can expect as technology continues to advance—will probably be touted as proof of naturalistic evolution, when in truth it proves nothing of the kind. It will prove something, however, about the amazing vitality of what God created.

For Further Study

Because outstanding work done by specialists is available on the origin of life, I have limited my discussion here to a brief review. For those who want more, I recommend *Origins* by Robert Shapiro (a nontheist),[26] *Information Theory and Molecular Biology* by Hubert Yockey (an agnostic),[27] and *The Mystery of Life's Origin* by Charles Thaxton, Walter Bradley, and Roger Olsen (all professing Christians).[28]

Universal Revelation

Wherever we look in the realm of nature, we see evidence for God's design and exquisite care for His creatures. Whether we examine the cosmos on its largest scale or its tiniest, His handiwork is evident. Whether we work in disciplines where simplicity and rigor predominate (for example, mathematics, astronomy, and physics) or in disciplines where complexity and information predominate (for example, biochemistry, botany, and zoology), God's fingerprints are visible.

Because of the quickening pace of technology and scientific research, the picture of God's attributes available to us through nature grows clearer. Further, since all the nations and cultures of the world are gaining scientific knowledge and technological competence, this testimony to God through nature is reaching out to all the peoples of the earth, paving the way for a surge of response to the gospel of Jesus Christ proclaimed by human messengers. Referring to God's revelation through the heavens, the apostle Paul stated:

> Their sound has gone out to all the earth, and their words to the ends of the world.[29]

CHAPTER EIGHTEEN

EXTRA-DIMENSIONAL POWER

As we have seen in previous chapters, the recent measurings of the cosmos have revealed not only the existence of God but also His transcendence, His personality, and even His care and love for human beings. These discoveries lead to some important conclusions about the awesome power available to God and consequently the extent of His ability to bless humankind.

Because human beings can visualize phenomena only in dimensions that they can experience, in their attempts to describe God, they characterize Him as a Being confined to a four-dimensional box. One reason we know the Bible comes from a supernatural source is that, just like the implications from the recent measurings of the cosmos, it claims that God is not so confined—He transcends the ten space-time dimensions of the universe. In its unique insistence that God moves and operates in dimensions independent of length, width, height, and time, the Bible not only insists on extra-dimensional capacities for God, but it also specifically describes how He functions in these extra dimensions (see table 10.1, page 110).

The Bible is unique, too, in describing certain attributes of God, such as the Trinity—in which God is depicted simultaneously as singular and plural, three Persons but one essence. It also portrays God as predetermining everything for us while simultaneously giving us freedom of choice. These concepts are provable contradictions if God is confined to just four dimensions, but each can be resolved by a God who both fills all ten cosmic space-time dimensions and transcends them. Let us examine the Trinity and the nearness of God as specific examples.

The Trinity: An Absurdity?

Ironically, adherents of nonChristian religions—like Islam and the Jehovah's Witnesses—often appeal to limited dimensionality as a proof against Christianity. Often I have encountered apologists from such faiths who state categorically Christianity is false since the Trinity is mathematically absurd.

My initial response is to agree. The Trinity is a mathematical absurdity in the context of a god limited in his operations to just the four dimensions of length, width, height, and time. Then I share with them the evidence from general relativity, the big bang, and string theory for the existence of six more dimensions besides the four we humans experience. Since God created and controls all these dimensions, He must be able to operate in them. The new physics proves, too, that He can create space-time dimensions at will and that He transcends all the space-time dimensions He has created or could create. A trinitarian nature is no problem for such a Being. Neither is His capacity to predetermine all of our actions, words, and thoughts from before He created the universe some 15 billion years ago while at the present moment granting us the freedom to choose those actions, words, and thoughts.

Given the time and the interest, I can demonstrate to those skeptical about the Trinity, the simultaneity of God's predetermination and human free choice, God's capacity to be both dead and alive, and several other paradoxical Christian doctrines of how the God who both fills and transcends ten space-time dimensions can manifest such characteristics and capabilities. Indeed, this was the theme of my book *Beyond the Cosmos.* The key point, however, is that we would expect man-invented theologies to be constrained by the limitations of human perspective while a theological message from a transcendent Being should at least in some ways transcend the limits of human perspective and visualization.

Nearness of God

The Bible declares forthrightly that God is very close to each and every one of us.[1] But, it just as forthrightly states that God is invisible.[2] The apostle Paul says that no one has ever seen God, nor can see Him.[3] Evidently, it is impossible for us humans to make physical contact with God. How, then, can God be so close and yet be beyond physical contact?

An analogy that might help was developed partly by Edwin

Abbott, a nineteenth-century schoolmaster and preacher who published the book *Flatland: A Romance of Many Dimensions* in 1884.[4] Imagine a universe where only two dimensions of space exist rather than three. In such a universe, flatlanders would be confined to a plane of length and width with no possibility of operating in the dimension of height. A three-dimensional being then could approach the plane of the flatlanders and place his hand just a tenth of a millimeter above the two-dimensional bodies of two flatlanders separated from one another by just one centimeter. Since the three-dimensional being is slightly above the plane of the flatlanders, there is no possibility that the flatlanders can see him. And yet, the three dimensional being is a hundred times closer to each of the flatlanders than they are to one another.

As with the flatlanders, so it is with human beings. God is closer to each of us than we ever can be to one another. But because God's proximity to us takes place in dimensions or realms we cannot tangibly experience, we cannot possibly see Him.

The only way we could see God is if He were to place a portion of His being into our space-time fabric. This would be analogous to the three-dimensional being poking his finger through the plane of the flatlanders. If one of the flatlanders were to investigate, he would draw the conclusion that this visitor to their realm is a small circle. But what if the three-dimensional being were to reveal separately to the friend of that flatlander three of his fingers? The friend then would draw the conclusion that the visitor to their realm was not one small circle but rather three small circles. We could then imagine a theological debate between the two flatlanders that would end up with the first flatlander founding the Church of the One Circle while the second would establish the Church of the Three Circles.

This analogy may appear amusing, but it fairly represents what nonChristians have done with the Trinity or Tri-Unity of God. Some have accepted God's singularity but rejected His plurality while others accept His plurality and reject His singularity. Only Christians accept that God is simultaneously singular and plural.

Good That He Goes Away?
Just hours before Jesus was arrested by His enemies to be crucified, He told His disciples that He would be leaving them.[5] He informed them that He would be returning to His Father. As He said these things, His disciples' hearts were filled with sorrow.[6] It's easy to

understand their feelings but not so easy to understand His words of reassurance: "It is for your good that I am going away."[7]

How could Jesus' going away be good? And how does this statement fit with His promise to be with them always? Paul's letter to the Philippians sheds some light:

> [Christ Jesus], being in very nature God, did not consider equality with God something to be grasped, but made himself nothing, taking the very nature of a servant, being made in human likeness. And being found in appearance as a man, he humbled himself and became obedient to death—even death on a cross! Therefore God exalted him to the highest place and gave him the name that is above every name.[8]

Jesus Christ was fully God, sharing in all the power, all the authority, and all the extra-dimensional capabilities God possesses. But for our sake, Christ lowered Himself and accepted the weakness and limitations of a human. He came into our dimensions to show us God, whom we could never otherwise picture, to give us an example of humility, and to pay the price for our redemption. After fulfilling His purpose in coming, Jesus once again took up all the power, authority, and extra-dimensional capacities that were rightfully His as God.

It is easy to empathize with the disciples' grief. Who would want to give up the tangible nearness of Jesus, seeing His face, hearing His words, feeling His touch, walking at His side? But as a human, Jesus could be in only one place at a time, holding one conversation at a time, performing one miracle at a time, etc. He needed rest, too.

Imagine all that He could gain by giving up His physical presence and regaining His extra-dimensional nearness. As He told His disciples, they would do greater miracles than the ones He had performed in front of them.[9] Further, He would never leave them, never fall asleep on them, never walk away to take care of someone else's need.[10] He could live in them, as well as beside them. The same powerful promise is made to every person who gives his or her life to Christ.

CHAPTER NINETEEN

THE POINT

Several years ago, I spoke at a prestigious American university to a group of about forty science professors. I presented much of the information that appears in the pages of this book. Afterward, I conversed with four physics professors and asked for their response.

One of the four said he could not deny the truth of my message. The others nodded in agreement. I asked if they could see, then, the rationality of turning over their lives to Jesus Christ. Another of the four spoke up, saying, yes, they could see it, but they weren't yet ready to be that rational.

This statement was not a brush-off. Each man went on to name his reasons for resistance. One confessed his unwillingness to give up sexual immorality. The others spoke of deep wounds inflicted long ago by people who called themselves Christians. What each of them needed and showed willingness to receive was compassion— not to mention further dialogue.

Other professors expressed their need for more time to assimilate the information, to check references, and to investigate the Bible for themselves. I could empathize. After all, it took me two years of study to become willing to entrust my life to God's care and keeping (see chapter 2).

The beauty of the scientific (and other) evidences God has allowed us to discover about Him is that these meet the needs of two large segments of society: (1) those whose barriers to personal faith in Christ are intellectual, barriers of misinformation and misunderstanding, and (2) those whose barriers to faith come from personal pain or stubborn rebellion lurking under the cover of intellectual objections.

Drawing Near to God

It is awesome and wonderful to behold the character of the Creator in what He has made, but not everyone seems to see it. In the elegant architecture of the universe, a galaxy, the sun, the planets, the earth, the moon, a human being, or even the simplest living thing, some people are struck by the wisdom, power, and care of the Creator, while others see an amazing coincidence or the work of some unidentified extraterrestrials.

The book of Hebrews declares, "Anyone who comes to [God] must believe that he exists and that he rewards those who earnestly seek him."[1] In a sense, this verse sets forth a test of the heart. The person who wants to draw near to God must be (and will be) humble-hearted enough not only to see and accept His existence but also to see and trust His goodness, His love.

Israel's King David said, "The LORD is close to the broken-hearted," and "The LORD is near to all who call on him, to all who call on him in truth."[2]

Drawing near to God, calling on Him "in truth," begins with humbly acknowledging *who we are*—His creation and no one else's, foolishly inclined to place ourselves or others in God's place of authority over our lives—and *who He is*—the Divine Maker and Provider of all things, including a way across the gulf that divides us from Him.

Nature itself shows us these truths. But the Bible brings us the details and clarifies specifically how God bridges that gulf to bring us to Himself in a personal, everlasting relationship.

His care for us and desire to draw us near are best demonstrated in Christ's coming to Earth to pay the death penalty for our rebellious nature. The Bible says that we "who once were far away have been brought near through the blood of Christ."[3]

The way has been made, it has been made clear, and it has been proven by the resurrection of Jesus Christ—a testable fact of history.[4] But knowing the way and knowing God are not one and the same thing.

The crucial difference lies in our moving beyond acceptance of facts to acceptance of Him. Acceptance of His life in exchange for ours, of His death in exchange for ours, of His goodness in exchange for ours, of His authority in exchange for ours, even of His faithfulness in exchange for ours—this will be our step toward Him. The Bible assures us that if we draw near to Him, He will draw near to us.[5]

Why Extra Evidence to This Generation?

One question I hear often is, "Why has our generation been singled out to receive such an abundance of evidences for God and His Word?" Why have we been given so much more proof than previous generations?

The answer I see from the Bible is that God measures out evidence in direct proportion to the level of resistance to His truth. Where the resistance is relatively low, less hard evidence for the God of the Bible is necessary to overcome it. But where resistance, namely arrogance, is high, so also is the quantity and quality of evidence He provides to overcome it.

Let's consider our world, especially the Western world. We have the most wealth, the most discretionary time, the most education, and the most technology of any previous generation. And how do we respond to these blessings? The loudest voices say that we humans deserve all the credit. The loudest voices say that humanity is deity. Given such arrogance, no wonder evidences are being flooded upon us.

Though the opposition seems great, God has equipped us to overcome it. He says, "See, I have placed before you an open door that no one can shut."[6] Let's make good use of these evidences to build our own faith and the faith of others while He is holding that door open.

SUMMARY OF SCIENTIFIC EVIDENCES FOR A BIG BANG CREATION EVENT

In this simple listing of 30 scientific evidences for a big bang creation event as described in the Bible (see chapter 3) I cite one or two primary sources and a secondary source that gives an extensive list of other primary sources. Many other sources can be found in the text of this book where many of these evidences are described in more detail.

1. **Existence and temperature of the cosmic background radiation.**[1]
   Ralph Alpher and Robert Herman calculated in 1948 that cooling from a big bang creation event would yield a faint cosmic background radiation with a current temperature of roughly 5° Kelvin (-455°F).[2] In 1965 Arno Penzias and Robert Wilson detected a cosmic background radiation and determined that its temperature was about 3° Kelvin (-457°F).[3]

2. **Black body character of the cosmic background radiation.**[4]
   Deviations between the spectrum of the cosmic background radiation and the spectrum expected from a perfect radiator measured to be less than 0.03% over the entire range of observed wavelengths.[5] The only possible explanation for such an extremely close fit is that the entire universe must have expanded from an infinitely or near infinitely hot and compact beginning.

3. **Cooling rate of the cosmic background radiation.**[6]
   According to the big bang, the older, and hence more expanded, the universe becomes, the cooler will be the cosmic background radiation. Measurements of the cosmic background radiation at distances so great that we are looking back to when the universe

was just a half, a quarter, or an eighth of its present age show temperature measures that are hotter than the present 2.726°K by exactly the amount that the big bang theory would predict.[7] That is, astronomers actually witness the universe getting hotter and hotter as they look back in time.

4. **Temperature uniformity of the cosmic background radiation.**[8]
The temperature of the cosmic background radiation varies by no more than one part in ten thousand from one direction in the heavens to any other.[9] Such high uniformity only can be explained if the background radiation arises from an extremely hot primordial creation event.

5. **Ratio of photons to baryons in the universe.**[10]
The ratio of photons to baryons (protons and neutrons) in the universe exceeds 100,000,000 to 1.[11] This proves the universe is so extremely entropic (efficient in radiating heat and light) the only possible explanation is that the entire universe must be rapidly exploding from an infinitely or near infinitely hot, dense state.

6. **Temperature fluctuations in the cosmic background radiation.**[12]
For galaxies and galaxy clusters to form out of a big bang creation event temperature fluctuations in maps of the cosmic background radiation should measure at a level of about one part in a hundred thousand. The predicted fluctuations were detected at the expected level.[13]

7. **Power spectrum of the temperature fluctuations in the cosmic background radiation.**[14]
For a big bang universe with a geometry suitable for the formation of stars and planets capable of supporting physical life, the temperature fluctuations in the cosmic background radiation will peak at an angular resolution close to one degree with a few much smaller spikes at other resolutions. In other words, the power spectrum graph will look like a bell curve with a few sub-peaks to the side of the main peak. The Boomerang balloon experiment in April 2000 confirmed this big bang prediction.[15] (See descriptions on deuterium and lithium abundances for another confirmation of this discovery.)

8. **Cosmic expansion rate.**[16]
A big bang creation event implies a universal expansion of the universe from a beginning several billion years ago. The most careful measurements of the velocities of galaxies establish that

such a cosmic expansion has been proceeding for the past 14.9 billion years,[17] a cosmic age measure that is consistent with all other cosmic age measurements.[18]

9. **Stable orbits of stars and planets.**[19]

Our universe manifests stable orbits of planets about stars and of stars about the nuclei of galaxies. Such stable orbits are physically impossible unless the universe is comprised of three very large and rapidly expanding dimensions of space.

10. **Existence of life and humans.**[20]

Life and humans require a stable solar-type star. However: If the universe cools down too slowly, galaxies would trap radiation so effectively as to prevent any fragmentation into stars. If the universe cools too rapidly, no galaxies or stars will ever condense out of the cosmic gas. If the universe expands too slowly, the universe will collapse before solar-type stars reach their stable burning phase. If it expands too rapidly, no galaxies or stars will ever condense from the general expansion.

11. **Abundance of helium in the universe.**[21]

According to the big bang, almost exactly one-fourth of the universe's hydrogen, by mass, was converted into helium within the first four minutes following the cosmic creation event. Stellar burning provides the only other possible source of helium. Therefore, astronomers can test the big bang by measuring the helium abundance in gas clouds and galaxies where little or no star burning has taken place. When they do this they determine a primordial helium abundance = 0.2489 ± 0.0015, a near perfect fit with what the big bang predicts.

12. **Abundance of deuterium (heavy hydrogen) in the universe.**[22]

Only the big bang can produce deuterium. Stars, on the other hand, destroy deuterium. By measuring the deuterium abundance in gas clouds and galaxies where little or no star burning has occurred, astronomers can not only prove that we live in a big bang universe but also determine what kind of big bang the universe manifests. The measured results are consistent with the same kind of big bang demonstrated by all the other big bang tests.

13. **Abundance of lithium in the universe.**[23]

Only the big bang can produce lithium. Stars destroy lithium. By measuring the lithium abundance in gas clouds and galaxies where little or no star burning has occurred, astronomers cannot only prove that we live in a big bang universe but also determine what kind of big bang the universe manifests. The measured results are consistent with the same kind of big bang demonstrated by all the other big bang tests.

14. Evidences for general relativity.[24]

Recent measurements now elevate the theory of general relativity to the most exhaustively tested and best proven principle in all of physics.[25] The solution to the equations of general relativity demonstrate that the universe must be expanding from a beginning in the finite past.

15. Space-time theorem of general relativity.[26]

A mathematical theorem proven by Stephen Hawking and Roger Penrose in 1970 establishes that if the universe contains mass, and if its dynamics are governed by general relativity, then time itself must be finite and must have been created when the universe was created.[27] Also, there must exist a CAUSE responsible for bringing the universe (which must be expanding) into existence independent of matter, energy, and all ten of the cosmic space-time dimensions.

16. Space energy density measurements.[28]

Albert Einstein and Arthur Eddington both developed cosmological models without a big bang by altering the theory of relativity to include a cosmic space energy density term (a.k.a. the cosmological constant) and assigning a particular value to that term. Recently, astronomers determined that indeed a cosmic space energy density term does exist.[29] Its value, however, proves that Einstein's and Eddington's models are incorrect. The measured value actually increases the evidence for the big bang in that it establishes the universe will continue to expand to an ever increasing rate.

17. Ten-dimensional creation calculation.[30]

A team led by Andrew Strominger demonstrated that only in a universe framed in ten space-time dimensions where six of the ten dimensions stop expanding when the universe is a 10 millionth of a trillionth of a trillionth of a trillionth of a second old is it possible to have gravity and quantum mechanics coexist.[31] This demonstration also successfully predicted both special and general relativity and solved a number of outstanding problems in both particle physics and black hole physics. It implies that the big bang and the laws of physics are valid all the way back to the creation event itself.

18. Stellar ages.[32]

According to the big bang theory, different types of stars will form at different epochs after creation. The colors and surface temperatures of stars tells astronomers how long they have been burning. These measured burning times are consistent with the big bang. They also are consistent with all other methods for measuring the time back to the cosmic creation event.

19. Galaxy ages.[33]

According to the big bang theory, nearly all the galaxies in the universe will form early in its history within about a 4-billion-year window of time. Indeed, astronomers measure the galaxies to have the predicted ages.[34]

20. Decrease in galaxy crowding.[35]

The big bang predicts that galaxies will spread farther and farther apart from one another as the universe expands. Hubble Space Telescope images show that the farther away in the cosmos one looks (and, because of light's finite velocity, the farther back in time) the more crowded together are the galaxies.[36] In fact, looking back to when the universe was but a third of its present age, the Space Telescope images reveal galaxies so tightly packed together that they literally are ripping spiral arms away from one another.

21. Photo album history of the universe.[37]

Since the big bang predicts that nearly all the galaxies will form at about the same time (see #18), and since galaxies change their appearance significantly as they age, images of portions of the universe at progressively greater and greater distances (and, because of light's finite velocity, farther and farther back in time) should show dramatic changes in the appearances of the galaxies. Hubble Space Telescope images verify the predicted changes in the appearances of galaxies.[38]

22. Ratio of ordinary matter to exotic matter.[39]

In a big bang universe, for the galaxies and stars to form and develop so that a site suitable for the support of physical life will be possible, the cosmos must exhibit a ratio of exotic matter (matter that does not interact well with radiation) to ordinary matter (matter that strongly interacts with radiation) that measures roughly five or six to one. Recent measurements reveal just such a ratio for the universe.[40]

23. Abundance of beryllium and boron in elderly stars.[41]

Long before the first stars can possibly form, the big bang fire-ball during the first few minutes after the creation event will generate tiny amounts of boron and beryllium if, and only if, the universe contains a significant amount of exotic matter. Astronomers have confirmed that primordial boron and beryllium exists in the amounts predicted by the big bang theory and their measurements of the amount of exotic matter.[42]

24. Numbers of Population I, II, and III stars.[43]

The big bang predicts that as the universe expands it will produce three distinct populations of stars. At its current age the big bang also predicts that astronomers should see certain specific numbers and masses of the three different populations. Astronomers do indeed see the predicted numbers and masses of stars for the three different populations.

25. Population, locations, and types of black holes and neutron stars.[44]

A big bang universe of the type that makes possible a site suitable for the support of physical life will after many billions of years of star burning produce a relatively small population of stellar mass black holes and a somewhat larger population of neutron stars in virtually every galaxy. Large galaxies are expected to produce supermassive (exceeding a million solar masses) black holes in their central cores. Astronomers, indeed, observe the predicted populations, locations, and types of black holes and neutron stars.[45]

26. Dispersion of star clusters and galaxy clusters.[46]

The big bang predicts that as the universe expands different types of star clusters and galaxy clusters will disperse at specific rates that will increase with time. It also predicts that the densest star clusters will not disperse. However, the orbital velocities of their stars about the cluster's center will "evolve" toward a predictable randomized condition known as virialization. The virial times depend on the cluster mass and size and on the individual masses of the stars. Astronomers observe the dispersal rates and virial times predicted by the big bang.

27. Number and type of space-time dimensions.[47]

A big bang universe of the type that makes possible a site suitable for the support of physical life must begin with ten rapidly expanding space-time dimensions. At about 10^{-43} seconds (about a ten millionth of a trillionth of a trillionth of a trillionth of a second) after the creation event six of the ten dimensions must cease expanding while the other four continue to expand at a rapid rate. Several experiments and calculations confirm that we live in such a universe.

28. **Masses and flavors of neutrinos.**[48]

All currently viable big bang models require that the dominant form of matter in the universe be a form of exotic matter called "cold dark matter." Astronomers and physicists already know that neutrinos are very plentiful in the universe and that they are "cold" and "dark." Recent experiments establish that neutrinos oscillate (that is, transform) from one flavor or type to another (the three neutrino flavors are electron, muon, and tau).[49] This oscillation implies that a neutrino particle must have a mass between a few billionths and a millionth of an electron mass. Such a range of masses for the neutrino satisfies the requirement for the viable big bang models.

29. **Populations and types of fundamental particles.**[50]

In the big bang the rapid cooling of the universe from a near infinitely high temperature and a near infinitely dense state will generate a zoo of different fundamental particles of predictable properties and predictable populations. Particle accelerator experiments which duplicate the temperature and density conditions of the early universe have verified all the types and populations of particles predicted within the energy limits of the particle accelerators.

30. **Cosmic density of protons and neutrons.**[51]

Four independent methods for determining the density of protons and neutrons in the universe establish that the density measured is the same as what the big bang predicts for a universe that contains the stars and planets necessary for life.

NOTES

ONE—The Awe-Inspiring Night Sky

1. George Roche, *A World Without Heroes: The Modern Tragedy* (Hillsdale, MI: Hillsdale College Press, 1987), page 120.
2. Hugh Ross, *Biblical Forecasts of Scientific Discoveries* (Pasadena, CA: Reasons To Believe, 1987).

TWO—My Skeptical Inquiry

1. The details of this calculation are presented in a short paper by the author called *Fulfilled Prophecy: Evidence for the Reliability of the Bible* (Pasadena, CA: Reasons To Believe, 1975).
2. A detailed account of my personal search for truth is given on an audiotape, *A Scientist Who Looked and Was Found* (Pasadena, CA: Reasons To Believe, 1988).
3. A detailed account of my personal search for truth is given on an audiotape, *An Astronomer's Quest* (Pasadena, CA: Reasons To Believe, 1993).

THREE—Big Bang—The Bible Taught It First!

1. Arno A. Penzias and Robert W. Wilson, "A Measurement of Excess Antenna Temperature at 4080 Mc/s," *Astrophysical Journal*, 142 (1965), pages 419-421.
2. George Gamow, "Expanding Universe and the Origin of the Elements," *Physical Review*, 70 (1946), pages 572-573.
3. Edwin Hubble, "A Relation Between Distance and Radial Velocity Among Extra-Galactic Nebulae," *Proceedings of the National Academy of Sciences*, 15 (1929), pages 168-173.
4. Georges Lemaître, "A Homogeneous Universe of Constant Mass and Increasing Radius Accounting for the Radial Velocity of Extra-Galactic Nebulae," *Monthly Notices of the Royal Astronomical Society*, 91 (1931), pages 483-490. The original paper appears in French in *Annales de la Société Scientifique de Bruxelles, Tome XLVII, Serie A, Premiere Partie* (April, 1927), page 49.
5. Albert Einstein, "Die Grundlage der allgemeinen Relativitätstheorie," *Annalen der Physik*, 49 (1916), pages 769-822. The English translation is in *The Principle of Relativity* by H. A. Lorentz, A. Einstein, H. Minkowski, and H. Weyl with notes by A. Sommerfeld and translated by W. Perrett and G. B. Jeffrey (London: Methuen and Co., 1923), pages 109-164.
6. Albert Einstein, "Kosmologische Betrachtungen zur allgemeinen Relativitätstheorie," *Sitzungsberichte der Königlich Preussichen Akademie der Wissenschaften* (1917), Feb. 8, pages 142-152. The English translation is in *The Principle of Relativity*, pages 175-188.
7. R. Laird Harris, Gleason L. Archer, and Bruce K. Waltke, *Theological Wordbook of the Old Testament*, 1 (Chicago: Moody, 1980), page 127.
8. Harris, Archer, and Waltke, vol. 2, page 916.
9. Harris, Archer, and Waltke, page 935.
10. Jack J. Lissauer, "It's Not Easy to Make the Moon," *Nature*, 389 (1997), pages 327-328; Sigeru Ida, Robin M. Canup, and Glen R. Stewart, "Lunar Accretion from an

Impact-Generated Disk," *Nature*, 389 (1997), pages 353-357; P. Jonathon Patchett, "Scum of the Earth After All," *Nature*, 382 (1996), page 758; Hugh Ross, *The Genesis Question* (Colorado Springs, CO: NavPress, 1998), pages 31-33.

11. Fred Hoyle, "A New Model for the Expanding Universe," *Monthly Notices of the Royal Astronomical Society*, 108 (1948), page 372.

FOUR—*The Discovery of the Twentieth Century*

1. Nigel Hawkes, "Hunt On for Dark Secret of Universe," *London Times*, 25 April 1992, page 1.
2. Hawkes, page 1.
3. The Associated Press, "U.S. Scientists Find a 'Holy Grail': Ripples at Edge of the Universe," *International Herald Tribune* (London), 24 April 1992, page 1.
4. The Associated Press, page 1.
5. Thomas H. Maugh II, "Relics of 'Big Bang' Seen for First Time," *Los Angeles Times*, 24 April 1992, pages A1, A30.
6. David Briggs, "Science, Religion, Are Discovering Commonality in Big Bang Theory," *Los Angeles Times*, 2 May 1992, pages B6-B7.
7. Stephen Strauss, "An Innocent's Guide to the Big Bang Theory: Fingerprint in Space Left by the Universe as a Baby Still Has Doubters Hurling Stones," *The Globe and Mail* (Toronto), 25 April 1992, page 1.
8. Richard C. Tolman, "Thermodynamic Treatment of the Possible Formation of Helium from Hydrogen," *Journal of the American Chemical Society* 44 (1922), pages 1902-1908.
9. George Gamow, "Expanding Universe and the Origin of the Elements," *Physical Review* 70 (1946), pages 572-573.
10. Ralph A. Alpher and Robert C. Herman, "Evolution of the Universe," *Nature* 162 (1948), pages 774-775.
11. Arno A. Penzias and Robert W. Wilson, "A Measurement of Excess Antenna Temperature at 4080 Mc/s," *Astrophysical Journal* 142 (1965), pages 419-421; Robert H. Dicke et al., "Cosmic Black-Body Radiation," *Astrophysical Journal* 142 (1965), pages 414-419.
12. George F. Smoot, "Comments and Summary on the Cosmic Background Radiation," *Proceedings of the International Astronomical Union Symposium, No. 104: Early Evolution of the Universe and Its Present Structure*, ed. G. O. Abell and G. Chincarini (Dordrecht, Holland; Boston, MA, USA: Reidel Publishing, 1983), pages 153-158.
13. Craig J. Hogan, "Experimental Triumph," *Nature* 344 (1990), pages 107-108; J. C. Mather et al., "A Preliminary Measurement of the Cosmic Microwave Background Spectrum by the Cosmic Background Explorer (COBE) Satellite," *Astrophysical Journal Letters* 354 (1990), pages L37-L40.
14. Hugh Ross, *The Fingerprint of God*, 2nd ed. rev. (Orange, CA: Promise Publishing, 1991), pages 87-88.
15. Ross, page 124.
16. George F. Smoot, et al., "Structure in the COBE Differential Microwave Radiometer First-Year Maps," *Astrophysical Journal Letters* 396 (1992), pages L1-L6; C. L. Bennett et al., "Preliminary Separation of Galactic and Cosmic Microwave Emission for the COBE Differential Microwave Radiometers," *Astrophysical Journal Letters* 396 (1992), pages L7-L12.
17. E. L. Wright, et al., "Interpretation of the Cosmic Microwave Background Radiation Anisotropy Detected by the COBE Differential Microwave Radiometer," *Astrophysical Journal Letters* 396 (1992), pages L13-L18.
18. Geoffrey Burbidge's comments were made on a radio talk show called Live From LA with host Phil Reid on KKLA in Los Angeles, CA. The program aired 11 May 1992 and included comments on the big bang ripples discovery from Drs. G. De Amici, Geoffrey Burbidge, Russell Humphreys, and Hugh Ross.
19. Ron Cowen, "Balloon Survey Backs COBE Cosmos Map," *Science News* 142 (1992), page 420.
20. S. Hancock, et al., "Direct Observation of Structure in the Cosmic Background Radiation," *Nature* 367 (1994), pages 333-338.

21. A. C. Clapp, et al., "Measurements of Anistropy in the Cosmic Microwave Background Radiation at Degree Angular Scales Near the Stars Sigma Herculis and Iota Draconis," *Astrophysical Journal Letters* 433 (1994), pages L57-L60.

22. C. L. Bennett, et al., "Four-Year COBE Cosmic Microwave Background Observations: Maps and Basic Results," *Astrophysical Journal Letters*, 464 (1996), pages L1-L4; C. M. Gutiérrez, et al., "New Cosmological Structures on Medium Angular Scales Detected with the Tenerife Experiments," *Astrophysical Journal Letters*, 480 (1997), pages L83-L86; E. S. Cheng, et al., "Detection of Cosmic Microwave Background Anisotropy by the Third Flight of the Medium-Scale Anisotropy Measurement," *Astrophysical Journal Letters*, 488 (1997), pages L59-L62; B. Femenia, et al., "The Instituto de Astrofísica de Canarias-Bartol Cosmic Microwave Background Anisotropy Experiment: Results of the 1994 Campaign," *Astrophysical Journal*, 498 (1998), pages 117-136; Angelica de Oliveira-Costa, et al., "Mapping the Cosmic Microwave Background Anisotropy: Combined Analysis of QMAP Flights," *Astrophysical Journal Letters*, 509 (1998), pages L77-L80; C. B. Netterfield, et al., "A Measurement of the Angular Power Spectrum of the Anisotropy in the Cosmic Microwave Background," *Astrophysical Journal*, 474 (1997), pages 47-66; S. R. Platt, "Anisotropy in the Microwave Sky at 90 GHz: Results from Python III," *Astrophysical Journal Letters*, 475 (1997), pages L1-L4; K. Coble, et al., "Anisotropy in the Cosmic Microwave Background at Degree Angular Scales: Python V Results," *Astrophysical Journal Letters*, 519 (1999), pages L5-L8; Bharat Ratra, et al., "Using White Dish CMB Anisotropy Data to Probe Open and Flat-Λ CDM Cosmogonies," *Astrophysical Journal*, 505 (1998), pages 8-11; Joanne C. Baker, et al., "Detection of Cosmic Microwave Background Structure in a Second Field with the Cosmic Anisotropy Telescope," *Monthly Notices of the Royal Astronomical Society*, 308 (1999), pages 1173-1178; Bharat Ratra, et al., "ARGO CMB Anisotropy Measurement Constraints on Open and Flat-Λ Cold Dark Matter Cosmogonies," *Astrophysical Journal*, 510 (1999), pages 11-19; Martin White, John E. Carlstrom, Mark Dragovan, and William L. Holzapfel, "Interferometric Observation of Cosmic Microwave Background Anisotropies," *Astrophysical Journal*, 514 (1999), pages 12-24; Bharat Ratra, et al., "Cosmic Microwave Background Anisotropy Constraints on Open and Flat-Λ Cold Dark Matter Cosmogonies from UCSB South Pole, ARGO, MAX. White Dish, and SuZIE Data," *Astrophysical Journal*, 517 (1999), pages 549-564; E. Torbet, et al, "A Measurement of the Angular Power Spectrum of the Microwave Background Made from the High Chilean Andes," *Astrophysical Journal Letters*, 521 (1999), pages L79-L82; A. D. Miller, et al., "A Measurement of the Angular Power Spectrum of the Cosmic Microwave Background from l = 100 to 400," *Astrophysical Journal Letters*, 524 (1999), pages L1-L4; E. M. Leitch, et al., "A Measurement of Anisotropy in the Cosmic Microwave Background on 7'-22' Scales," *Astrophysical Journal*, 532 (2000), pages 37-56.

23. Ron Cowen, "COBE: A Match Made in Heaven," *Science News* 143 (1993), page 43; J.C. Mather, et al., "Measurement of the Cosmic Microwave Background Spectrum by the COBE FIRAS Instrument," *Astrophysical Journal* 420 (1994), pages 439-444.

24. Katherine C. Roth, David M. Meyer, and Isabel Hawkins, "Interstellar Cyanogen and the Temperature of the Cosmic Microwave Background Radiation," *Astrophysical Journal* 413 (1993), pages L67-L71.

25. Antoinette Songaila, et al., "Measurement of the Microwave Background Temperature at Redshift 1.776," *Nature* 371 (1994), pages 43-45.

26. David M. Meyer, "A Distant Space Thermometer," *Nature* 371 (1994), page 13.

27. K. C. Roth, A. Songaila, L. L. Cowie, and J. Bechtold, "C I Fine-Structure Excitation by the CMBR at z = 1.973," *American Astronomical Society Meeting*, 189, #122.17, December, 1996.

28. R. Srianand, P. Petitjean, and C. Leadoux, "The Cosmic Microwave Background Radiation Temperature at a Redshift of 2.34," *Nature*, 408 (2000), pages 931-935

29. In 1998 Reasons To Believe produced a one-hour television documentary, *Journey Toward Creation*, that portrayed through astronomical images, video clips, and computer animations a simulated trip from planet Earth to the most distant entities in the universe, a journey toward the creation event itself. A video cassette is available: P. O. Box 5978, Pasadena, CA 91117.

30. Hugh Ross, *Beyond the Cosmos*, 2nd edition (Colorado Springs, CO: NavPress, 1999).
31. Hugh Ross and Guillermo Gonzalez, "You Must Be Here," *Facts for Faith*, vol. 1, no. 1 (2000), pages 36-41.
32. Stephen Hawking, *A Brief History of Time* (New York: Bantam Books, 1988), pages 163-165.

FIVE—Twenty-first Century Discoveries

1. James Glanz, "Breakthrough of the Year: Cosmic Motion Revealed," *Science*, 282 (1998), pages 2156-2157; Floyd E. Bloom, "Breakthroughs 1998," *Science*, 282 (1998), page 2193.
2. Lawrence M. Krauss, "The End of the Age Problem and the Case for a Cosmological Constant Revisited," *Astrophysical Journal*, 501 (1998), page 461.
3. Hugh Ross, *The Fingerprint of God*, 2nd edition (Orange, CA: NavPress, 1991), pages. 27-29; Immanuel Kant, "Universal Natural History and Theory of the Heavens," in *Theories of the Universe*, edited by Milton K. Munitz (Glencoe, IL: Free Press, 1957), pages 242-247.
4. Albert Einstein, "Kosmologische Betrachtungen zur allgemeinen Relativitätstheorie," in *Sitzungsherichte der Koniglich Preussischen Akademie der Wissenschaften* (1917), Feb. 8, pages 142-152. The English translation is in *The Principle of Relativity* by H. A. Lorentz, A. Einstein, H. Minkowski, and H. Weyl with notes by A. Sommerfeld and translated by W. Perrett and G. B. Jeffrey (London, UK: Methuen and Co., 1923), pages 175-188; Albert Einstein, "Die Grundlage der allgemeinen Relativitätstheorie," *Annalen der Physik*, 49 (1916), pages 769-822. The English translation is in *The Principle of Relativity*, pages 109-164.
5. A. Vibert Douglas, "Forty Minutes with Einstein," *Journal of the Royal Astronomical Society of Canada*, 50 (1956), p. 100.
6. Adam G. Riess, et al., "Observational Evidence from Supernovae for an Accelerating Universe and a Cosmological Constant," *Astronomical Journal*, 116 (1998), pages 1009-1038.
7. Richard C. Tolman and Morgan Ward, "On the Behavior of Non-Static Models of the Universe When the Cosmological Term Is Omitted," *Physical Review*, 39 (1932), pages 841-843; John D. Barrow and Joseph Silk, *The Left Hand of Creation: The Origin and Evolution of the Expanding Universe* (New York: Basic Books, 1983), page 32.
8. S. Perlmutter, et al., "Measurements of Ω and $\wedge$ from 42 High-Redshift Supernovae," *Astrophysical Journal*, 517 (1999), pages. 565-586.
9. James Glanz, "Has a Cosmic Standard Candle Flickered?" *Science*, 285 (1999), page 19.
10. Adam G. Riess, Alexei V. Filippenko, Weidong Li, and Brian P. Schmidt, "Is There an Indication of Evolution of Type Ia Supernovae from Their Rise Times?" *Astronomical Journal*, 118 (1999), pages 2668-2674; Hideyuki Umeda, Ken'ichi Nomoto, and Chiaki Kobayashi, "The Origin of the Diversity of Type Ia Supernovae and the Environmental Effects," *Astrophysical Journal Letters*, 522 (1999), pages L43-L47; Anthony Aguirre, "Intergalactic Dust and Observations of Type Ia Supernovae," *Astrophysical Journal*, 525 (1999), pages 583-593; Tomonori Totani and Chiaki Kobayashi, "Evolution of Dust Extinction and Supernova Cosmology," *Astrophysical Journal Letters*, 526 (1999), pages L65-L68; Persis S. Drell, Thomas J. Loredo, and Ira Wasserman, "Type Ia Supernovae, Evolution, and the Cosmological Constant," *Astrophysical Journal*, 530 (2000), pages 593-617.
11. Lev R. Yungelson and Mario Livio, "Supernova Rates: A Cosmic History," *Astrophysical Journal*, 528 (2000), pages 108-117; Greg Aldering, Robert Knop, and Peter Nugent, "The Rise Times of High- and Low-Redshift Type Ia Supernovae Are Consistent," *Astronomical Journal*, 119 (2000), pages 2110-2117.
12. S. Perlmutter, et al., page 581.
13. S. Perlmutter, et al., page 579.
14. Bharat Ratra, et al., "Cosmic Microwave Background Anisotropy Constraints on Open and Flat-L Cold Dark Matter Cosmogonies with UCSB South Pole, ARGO, MAX, White Dish, and SuZIE Data," *Astrophysical Journal*, 517 (1999), pages 549-564; Aaron D. Lewis, E. Ellingson, Simon L. Morris, and R. G. Carlberg, "X-Ray Mass

Estimates at z ~ 0.3 for the Canadian Network for Observational Cosmology Cluster Sample," *Astrophysical Journal,* 517 (1999), pages 587-608; Joseph J. Mohr, Benjamin Mathiesen, and August E. Evrard, "Properties of the Intracluster Medium in an Ensemble of Nearby Galaxy Clusters," *Astrophysical Journal,* 517 (1999), pages 627-649.

15. Raul Jimenez and Paolo Padoan, "The Ages and Distances of Globular Clusters with the Luminosity Function Method: The Case of M5 and M55," *Astrophysical Journal,* 498 (1998), pages 704-709; David S. Graff, Gregory Laughlin, and Katherine Freese, "MACHOs, White Dwarfs, and the Age of the Universe," *Astrophysical Journal,* 499 (1998), pages 7-19; Judith G. Cohen, John P. Blakeslee, and Anton Ryshov, "The Ages and Abundances of a Large Sample of M87 Globular Clusters," *Astrophysical Journal,* 496 (1998), pages 808-826; R. Buopnanno, et al., "The Ages of the Globular Clusters in the Fornax Dwarf Galaxy," *Astrophysical Journal Letters,* 501 (1998), pages L33-L36.

16. Hugh Ross, "News Report Hypes Cosmic Age Controversy," *Facts & Faith,* vol. 8, n. 4 (1994), pages 1-2.

17. *The Vancouver Sun,* October 1, 1999, page A1.

18. David S. Graff, Gregory Laughlin, and Katherine Freese, pages 7, 18.

19. P. De Barnardis, et al., "A Flat Universe from High-Resolution Maps of the Cosmic Microwave Background Radiation," *Nature,* 494 (2000), pages 955-959.

20. Max Tegmark's web site at the University of Pennsylvania: www.hep.upenn.edu/max/boompa_frames.html

21. E. Torbet, et al., "A Measurement of the Angular Power Spectrum of the Microwave Background Made from the High Chilean Andes," *Astrophysical Journal Letters,* 521 (1999), pages L79-L82; C. M. Gutiérrez, et al., "The Tenerife Cosmic Microwave Background Maps: Observations and First Analysis," *Astrophysical Journal,* 529 (2000), pages 47-55; Bharat Ratra, et al., "Cosmic Microwave Background Anisotropy Constraints on Open and Flat-L Cold Dark Matter Cosmogonies From USSB South Pole, ARGO, MAX, White Dish, and SuZIE Data," *Astrophysical Journal,* 517 (1999), pages 549-564; Graça Rocha, et al., "Python I, II, and III Cosmic Microwave Background Anisotropy Measurement Constraints on Open and Flat-L Cold Dark Matter Cosmogonies," *Astrophysical Journal,* 525 (1999), pages 1-9; James Glanz, "Microwave Hump Reveals Flat Universe," *Science,* 283 (1999), page 21.

22. S. Perlmutter, et al., "Measurements of Ω and Λ from 42 High-Redshift Supernovae," *Astrophysical Journal,* 517 (1999), pages 565-586; Megan Donahue and G. Mark Voit, "Ω_m from the Temperature-Redshift Distribution of EMSS Clusters of Galaxies," *Astrophysical Journal Letters,* 523 (1999), pages L37-L40; David H. Weinberg, et al., "Closing in on Ω_M: The Amplitude of Mass Fluctuations from Galaxy Clusters and the Lya Forest," *Astrophysical Journal,* 522 (1999), pages 563-568; G. Steigman and I. Tkachev, "Ω_B and Ω_o from MACHOs and Local Group Dynamics," *Astrophysical Journal,* 522 (1999), pages 793-801; J. Nevalainen, M. Markevitch, and W. Forman, "The Baryonic and Dark Matter Distribution in Abell 401," *Astrophysical Journal,* 526 (1999), pages 1-9; Joseph J. Mohr, Benjamin Mathiesen, and August E. Evrard, "Properties of the Intercluster Medium in an Ensemble of Nearby Galaxy Clusters," *Astrophysical Journal,* 517 (1999), pages 627-649; J. S. Alcaniz and J. A. S. Lima, "New Limits on Ω_Λ and Ω_M from Old Galaxies at High Redshift," *Astrophysical Journal Letters,* 521 (1999), pages L87-L90; N. A. Bahcall, et al., "The Mass-To-Light Function: Antibias and Ω_m." *Astrophysical Journal,* 541 (2000), pages 1-9; Kentaro Nagamine, Renyue Cen, and Jeremiah P. Ostriker, "Luminosity Density of Galaxies and Cosmic Star Formation Rate From Λ Cold Dark Matter Hydrodynamical Simulations," *Astrophysical Journal,* 541 (2000), pages 25-36; Stacy S. McGaugh, "Boomerang Data Suggest a Purely Baryonic Universe," *Astrophysical Journal Letters,* 541 (2000), pages L33-L36.

23. A. Melchiorri, et al., "A Measurement of Ω from the North American Test Flight of Boomerang," *Astrophysical Journal Letters,* 536 (2000), pages L63-L66.

24. Idit Zehavi and Avishai Dekel, "Evidence for a Positive Cosmological Constant from Flows of Galaxies and Distant Supernovae," *Nature,* 401 (1999), pages 252-254; Adam G. Riess, "Universal Peekaboo," *Nature,* 401 (1999), pages 219, 221.

25. Lawrence M. Krauss, page 461.

26. Lawrence M. Krauss, pages 461, 465.

27. James Glanz, "Microwave Hump Reveals Flat Universe," *Science*, 283 (1999), page 21; P. DeBarnardis, et al., pages 957-958; Wayne He, "Ringing in the New Cosmology," *Nature*, 404 (2000), pages 939-940.
28. Idit Zehavi and Avishai Dekel, page 252.
29. N. Straumann, "The Mystery of the Cosmic Vacuum Energy Density and the Accelerated Expansion of the Universe," *European Journal of Physics* (2000), in press.
30. S. Perlutter, et al., page 584.
31. Lawrence M. Krauss and Glenn D. Starkman, "Life, the Universe, and Nothing: Life and Death in an Ever-Expanding Universe," *Astrophysical Journal*, 531 (2000), pages 22-30.
32. Revelation 21–22, *The Holy Bible*; Hugh Ross, *Beyond the Cosmos*, 2nd edition (Colorado Springs, CO: NavPress, 1999), pages 217-228.
33. P. Jokeosen, et al., "Detection of Intergalactic Ionized Helium Absorption in a High-Redshift Quasar," *Nature*, 370 (1994), pages 35-39.
34. Yuri I. Izotov, Trinh X. Thuan, and Valentin A. Lipovetsky, "The Primordial Helium Abundance from a New Sample of Metal-Deficient Blue Compact Galaxies," *Astrophysical Journal*, 435 (1994), pages 647-667.
35. Yuri I. Izotov, et al., "Helium Abundance in the Most Metal-Deficient Blue Compact Galaxies: I Zw 18 and SBS 0335-052," *Astrophysical Journal*, 527 (1999), pages 757-777.
36. Yuri I. Izotov, et al., page 776.
37. D. R. Ballantyne, G. J. Ferland, and P. G. Martin, "The Primordial Helium Abundance: Toward Understanding and Removing the Cosmic Scatter in the dY/dZ Relation," *Astrophysical Journal*, 536 (2000), pages 773-777.
38. D. R. Ballantyne, G. J. Ferland, and P. G. Martin, page 777.
39. Yuri I. Izotov, et al., page 776.
40. Scott Burles, David Kirkman, and David Tytler, "Deuterium Toward Quasar Q0014+813," *Astrophysical Journal*, 519 (1999), pages 18-21; David Kirkman, et al., "QSO 0130-4021: A Third QSO Showing a Low Deuterium-To-Hydrogen Abundance Ratio," *Astrophysical Journal*, 529 (2000), pages 655-660; Sergei A. Levshakov, Wilhelm H, Kegel, and Fumio Takahara, "The D/H Ratio at z = 3.57 Toward Q1937-1009," *Astrophysical Journal Letters*, 499 (1998), pages L1-L4.
41. E. Casuso and J. E. Beckman, "Deuterium, Lithium, and the Hubble Deep Field," *Astronomical Journal*, 118 (1999), pages 1907-1911.
42. Sylvie Vauclair and Corinne Charbonnel, "Element Segregation in Low-Metallicity Stars and the Primordial Lithium Abundance," *Astrophysical Journal*, 502 (1998), pages 372-377; D. A. Lubowich, et al., "Deuterium in the Galactic Centre as a Result of Recent Infall of Low-Metallicity Gas," *Nature*, 405 (2000), pages 1025-1027; Takeru Ken Suzuki, Yuzuru Yoshii, and Timothy C. Beers, "Primordial Lithium Abundance as a Stringent Constraint on the Baryonic Content of the Universe," *Astrophysical Journal*, 540 (2000), pages 99-103; E. Vanioni-Flam, A. Coc, and M. Cassé, "Big Bang Nucleosynthesis Updates with the NACRE Compilation," Astronomy and Astrophysics, 360 (2000), pages 15-23.
43. E. Casuso and J. E. Beckman, page 1907.
44. A. Melchiorri, et al., "A Measurement of Ω from the North American Test Flight of Boomerang," *Astrophysical Journal Letters*, 536 (2000), pages L63-L66.
45. Aaron D. Lewis, E. Ellingson, Simon L. Morris, and R. G. Carlberg, "X-Ray Mass Estimates at z ~ 0.3 for the Canadian Network for Observational Cosmology Cluster Sample," *Astrophysical Journal*, 517 (1999), pages 587-608; Bo Qin and Xiang-Ping Wu, "Baryon Distribution in Galaxy Clusters as a Result of Sedimentation of Helium Nuclei," *Astrophysical Journal Letters*, 529 (2000), pages L1-L4; M. Fukugita, C. J. Hogan, and P. J. E. Peebles, "The Cosmic Baryon Budget," *Astrophysical Journal*, 503 (1998), pages 518-530.
46. Hugh Ross, *The Fingerprint of God*, 2nd edition, pages 89-90.
47. D. B. Haarsma, J. N. Hewitt, J. Lehár, and B. F. Burke, "The Radio Wavelength Time Delay of Gravitational Lens 0957+561," *Astrophysical Journal*, 510 (1999), pages 64-70; Kyu-Hyun Chae, "New Modeling of the Lensing Galaxy and Cluster of Q0957+561: Implications for the Global Value of the Hubble Constant," *Astrophysical Journal*, 524 (1999), pages 582-590; C. D. Fassnacht, et al., "A Determination of H_o with the Class

Gravitational Lens B1608+656. I Time Delay Measurements with the VLA," *Astrophysical Journal,* 527 (1999), pages 498-512; L. V. E. Koopmans and C. D. Fassnacht, "A Determination of H_o with the Class Gravitational Lens B1608+656. II. Mass Models and the Hubble Constant from Lensing," *Astrophysical Journal,* 527 (1999), pages 513-524; Liliya L. R. Williams and Prasenjit Saha, "Pixelated Lenses and H_o from Time-Delay Quasars," *Astronomical Journal,* 119 (2000), pages 439-450.

48. Masaru Watanabe, Takashi Ichikawa, and Sadanori Okamura, "An Unbiased Estimate of the Global Hubble Constant in the Region of Pisces-Perseus," *Astrophysical Journal,* 503 (1998), pages 503-553; Shoko Sakai, et al., "The Hubble Space Telescope Key Project on the Extragalactic Distance Scale. XXIV. The Calibration of Tully-Fisher Relations and the Value of the Hubble Constant," *Astrophysical Journal,* 529 (2000), pages 698-722; G. Theureau, "Kinematics of the Local Universe. VI. B-Band Tully-Fisher Relations and Mean Surface Brightness," *Astronomy and Astrophysics,* 331 (1998), pages 1-10; Gustav A. Tammann, *International Astronomical Union Symposium No. 183, Cosmological Parameters and the Evolution of the Universe,* editor K. Sato (Dordrecht, Netherlands: Kluwer, 1999), page 31.

49. Allan Sandage, "Bias Properties of Extragalactic Distance Indicators. VIII. Ho from Distance-Limited Luminosity Class and Morphological Type-Specific Luminosity Functions for Sb, Sbc, and Sc Galaxies Calibrated Using Cepheids," *Astrophysical Journal,* 527 (1999), pages 479-487; Jeremy R. Mould, et al., "The Hubble Space Telescope Key Project on the Extragalactic Distance Scale. XXVIII. Combining the Constraints on the Hubble Constant," *Astrophysical Journal,* 529 (2000), pages 786-794; Brad K. Gibson, Philip R. Maloney, and Shoko Sakai, "Has Blending Compromised Cepheid-Based Determinations of the Extragalactic Distance Scale?" *Astrophysical Journal Letters,* 530 (2000), pages L5-L8; Allan Sandage, R. A. Bell, and Michael J. Tripicco, "On the Sensitivity of the Cepheid Period-Luminosity Relation to Variations in Metallicity," *Astrophysical Journal,* 522 (1999), pages 250-275; G. Petural, et al., "Hubble Constant from SOSIE Galaxies and HIPPARCOS Geometrical Calibration," *Astronomy and Astrophysics,* 339 (1998), pages 671-677.

50. S. Perlmutter, et al., "Measurements of Ω and $\wedge$ from 42 High-Redshift Supernovae," *Astrophysical Journal,* 517 (1999), pages 565-586; Robert Tripp and David Branch, "Determination of the Hubble Constant Using a Two-Parameter Luminosity Correction for Type Ia Supernovae," *Astrophysical Journal,* 525 (1999), pages 209-214; A. Saha, et al., "Cepheid Calibration of the Peak Brightness of Type Ia Supernovae. IX. SN 1989B in NGC 3627," *Astrophysical Journal,* 522 (1999), pages 802-838; Saurabh Jha, et al, "The Type Ia Supernova 1998bu in M96 and the Hubble Constant," *Astrophysical Journal Supplement,* 125 (1999), pages 73-89; B. R. Parodi, A. Saha, A. Sandage, and G. A. Tammann, "Supernova Type Ia Luminosities. Their Dependence on Second Parameters, and the Value of H_o," *Astrophysical Journal,* 540 (2000), pages 634-651.

51. D. C. Homan and J. F. C. Wardle, "Direct Distance Measurements to Superluminal Radio Sources," *Astrophysical Journal,* 535 (2000), pages 575-585; James Glanz, "The First Step to Heaven," *Science,* 285 (1999), pages 1658-1661; J. R. Hernstein, et al., "A Geometric Distance to the Galaxy NGC 4258 from Orbital Motions in a Nuclear Gas Disk," *Nature,* 400 (1999), pages 539-541; E. F. Guinan, et al., "The Distance to the Large Magellanic Cloud from the Eclipsing Binary HV2274," *Astrophysical Journal Letters,* 509 (1998), pages L21-L24; G. Petural, et al., "Hubble Constant from SOSIE Galaxies and HIPPARCOS Geometrical Calibration," *Astronomy and Astrophysics,* 339 (1998), pages 671-677.

52. Volker Bromm, Paolo S. Coppi, and Richard B. Larson, "Forming the First Stars in the Universe: The Fragmentation of Primordial Gas," *Astrophysical Journal Letters,* 527 (1999), pages L5-L8.

53. Masayuki Y. Fujimoto, Yasufumi Ikeda, and Icko Iben, Jr., "The Origin of Extremely Metal-Poor Carbon Stars and the Search for Population III," *Astrophysical Journal Letters,* 529 (2000), page L25; A. Weiss, S. Cassisi, H. Schlattl, and M. Salaris, "Evolution of Low-Mass Metal-Free Stars Including Effects of Diffusion and External Pollution," *Astrophysical Journal,* 533 (2000), page 413.

54. Masayuki Y. Fujimoto, Yasufumi Ikeda, and Icko Iben, Jr., pages L25-L28; A. Weiss, S. Cassisi, H. Schlattl, and M. Salaris, pages 413-423.

55. Eugenio Carretta, Raffaele G. Gratton, Gisela Clementini, and Flavio Fusi Pecci, "Distances, Ages, and Epoch of Formation of Globular Clusters," *Astrophysical Journal*, 533 (2000), pages 215-235.

56. Brad K. Gibson, et al., "The Spectroscopic Age of 47 Tucanae," *Astronomical Journal*, 118 (1999), pages 1268-1272.

57. Jennifer A. Johnson, et al., "Hubble Space Telescope Observations of the Oldest Star Clusters in the Large Magellanic Cloud," *Astrophysical Journal*, 527 (1999), pages 199-218.

58. Paul W. Hodge, Andrew E. Dolphin, Toby R. Smith, and Mario Mateo, "Hubble Space Telescope Studies of the WLM Galaxy. I. The Age and Metallicity of the Globular Cluster," *Astrophysical Journal*, 521 (1999), pages 577-581.

59. R. Buonanno, et al., "The Ages of Globular Clusters in the Fornax Dwarf Galaxy," *Astrophysical Journal Letters*, 501 (1998), pages L33-L36.

60. Raul Jimenez and Paolo Padoan, "The Ages and Distances of Globular Clusters with the Luminosity Function Method: The Case of M5 and M55," *Astrophysical Journal*, 498 (1998), pages 704-709.

61. David S. Graff, Gregory Laughlin, and Katherine Freese, "MACHOs, White Dwarfs, and the Age of the Universe," *Astrophysical Journal*, 499 (1998), pages 7-19.

62. Judith G. Cohen, John Blakeslee, and Anton Ryzhov, "The Ages and Abundances of a Large Sample of M87 Globular Clusters," *Astrophysical Journal*, 496 (1998), pages 808-826.

63. Hugh Ross, *The Creator and the Cosmos*, 2nd edition, (Colorado Springs, CO: NavPress, 1995), pages 35-47.

64. S. Perlmutter, et al., pages 565-586; Aaron D. Lewis, E. Ellingson, Simon L. Morris, and R. G. Carlberg, pages 587-608; Joseph J. Mohr, Benjamin Mathiesen, and August E. Evrard, pages 627-649; N. A, Bahcall, et al., pages 1-9; Kentaro Nagamine, Renyue Cen, and Jeremiah P. Ostriker, pages 25-36; David H. Weinberg, et al., pages 563-568; J. Nevalainen, M. Markevitch, and W. Forman, pages 1-9; J. S. Alcaniz and J. A. S. Lima, pages L87-L90; Megan Donahue and G. Mark Voit, pages L37-L40; Asantha R. Cooray, "An Upper Limit on Ωm Using Lensed Arcs," *Astrophysical Journal*, 524 (1999), pages 504-509; Masashi Chiba and Yuzuru Yoshii, "New Limits on a Cosmological Constant from Statistics of Gravitational Lensing," *Astrophysical Journal*, 510 (1999), pages 42-53; Stephano Borgani, Piero Rosati, Paolo Tozzi, and Colin Norman, "Cosmological Constraints from the ROSAT Deep Cluster Survery," *Astrophysical Journal*, 517 (1999), pages 40-53; Neta A. Bahcall and Xiaohui Fan, "The Most Distant Clusters: Determining Ω_m. σ_8." *Astrophysical Journal*, 504 (1998), pages 1-6; James Robinson and Joseph Silk, "Star Formation As a Cosmological Probe," *Astrophysical Journal*, 539 (2000), pages 89-97; Esther M. Hu, Richard G. McMahon, and Lennox L. Cowie, "An Extremely Luminous Galaxy at z = 5.74," *Astrophysical Journal Letters*, 522 (1999), pages L9-L12; B. F. Roukema and G. A. Mamon, "Tangential Large Scale Structure as a Standard Ruler: Curvature Parameters from Quasars," *Astronomy and Astrophysics*, 358 (2000), pages 395-408; B. Novosyadlyj, et al, "Cosmological Parameters from Large Scale Structure Observations," *Astronomy and Astrophysics*, 356 (2000), pages 418-434; P. Valageas, "Weak Gravitational Lensing Effects on the Determination of Ω_m and Ω_Λ from SneIa," *Astronomy and Astrophysics*, 354 (2000), pages 767-786; J. F. Macias-Perez, et al., "Gravitational Lensing Statistics with Extragalactic Surveys," *Astronomy and Astrophysics*, 353 (2000), pages 419-426; David M. Wittman, et al., "Detection of Weak Gravitational Lensing Distortions of Distant Galaxies by Cosmic Dark Matter at Large Scales," *Nature*, 405 (2000), pages 143-148.

65. Karl Glazebrook, "The 2dFGRS – Galaxy Properties and Evolution," American Astronomical Society Meeting 196, #56.06, May 2000; R. Bennett, "Survey Confirms Composition of the Cosmos, *Science News*, 157 (2000), page 374.

66. R. Juszkiewicz, et al., "Evidence for a Low-Density Universe from the Relative Velocities of Galaxies," *Science*, 287 (2000), pages 109-112.

67. F. R. Pearce, et al., "A Simulation of Galaxy Formation and Clustering," *Astrophysical Journal Letters*, 521 (1999), pages L99-L102; Wesley N. Colley, et al., "Topology from the Simulated Sloan Digital Sky Survey," *Astrophysical Journal*, 529 (2000), pages 795-810.

68. Andrew Watson, "Case for Neutrino Mass Gathers Weight," *Science,* 277 (1997), pages 30-31.
69. Andrew Watson, page 31.
70. Dennis Normile, "Heavy News on Solar Neutrinos," *Science,* 280 (1998), page 1839.
71. Dennis Normile, "Weighing In on Neutrino Mass," *Science,* 280 (1998), pages 1689-1690.
72. Dennis Normile, "New Experiments Step Up Hunt for Neutrino Mass," *Science,* 276 (1997), page 1795.
73. F. Gatti, et al., "Detection of Environmental Fine Structure in the Low-Energy b-Decay Spectrum of 187Re," *Nature,* 397 (1997), pages 137-139.
74. Ron Cowen, "Votes Cast For and Against the WIMP Factor," *Science News,* 157 (2000), page 135.
75. Hugh Ross, *The Fingerprint of God,* 2nd edition, pages 39-138.

SIX—*Einstein's Challenge*

1. Immanuel Kant, "Universal Natural History and Theory of the Heavens," *Theories of the Universe,* ed. Milton K. Munitz (Glencoe, IL: Free Press, 1957), page 240.
2. Rudolf Thiel, *And There Was Light: The Discovery of the Universe* (New York: Alfred A. Knopf, 1957), page 218; John Herman Randall, Jr., *The Career of Philosophy,* vol. 2 (New York: Columbia University Press, 1965), page 113; Kant, "Universal Natural History and Theory of the Heavens," pages 242-247.
3. Hugh Ross, *The Fingerprint of God,* 2nd ed. rev. (Orange, CA: Promise Publishing, 1991), pages 27-38.
4. Albert Einstein, "Zur Elektrodynamik bewegter Körper," *Annalen der Physik* 17 (1905), pages 891-921 [Hendrik A. Lorentz, et al., *The Principle of Relativity,* with notes by Arnold Sommerfeld, trans. W. Perrett and G. B. Jeffrey (London: Methuen and Co., 1923), pages 35-65]; Albert Einstein, "Ist die Trägheit eines Körpers von seinem Energieinhalt abhängig?" *Annalen der Physik* 18 (1905), pages 639-644 [Lorentz, et al., *The Principle of Relativity,* pages 67-71].
5. Robert Martin Eisberg, *Fundamentals of Modern Physics* (New York: John Wiley & Sons, 1961), pages 37-38, 75-76, 580-592; John D. Jackson, *Classical Electrodynamics* (New York: John Wiley and Sons, 1962), pages 352-369; S. K. Lamoreaux, et al., "New Limits on Spatial Anisotropy from Optically Pumped ^{201}Hg and ^{199}Hg," *Physical Review Letters* 57 (1986), pages 3125-3128. This recent experiment confirms the predictions of special relativity to better than one part in 10^{21}.
6. Albert Einstein, "Die Feldgleichungen der Gravitation," *Sitzungsberichte der Königlich Preussischen Akademie der Wissenschaften,* 25 November 1915, pages 844-847 (the following reference includes this reference); Albert Einstein, "Die Grundlage der allgemeinen Relativitätstheorie," *Annalen der Physik* 49 (1916), pages 769-822 [Lorentz, et al., *The Principle of Relativity,* pages 109-164].
7. Albert Einstein,"Kosmologische Betrachtungen zur allgemeinen Relativitätstheorie," *Sitzungsberischte der Königlich Preussischen Akademie der Wissenschaften,* Feb. 8, 1917, pages 142-152. The English translation is in *The Principle of Relativity* by H. A. Lorentz, A. Einstein, H. Minkowski, and H. Weyl with notes by A. Sommerfield and translated by W. Perrett and G. B. Jeffrey (London, UK: Methuen and Co., 1923), pages 175-188.
8. Einstein, "Die Grundlage der allgemeinen Relativitätstheorie," pages 769-822 [Lorentz, et al., pages 109-164].
9. A. Vibert Douglas, "Forty Minutes with Einstein," *Journal of the Royal Astronomical Society of Canada* 50 (1956), page 100.
10. Lincoln Barnett, *The Universe and Dr. Einstein* (New York: William Sloane Associates, 1948), page 106.
11. Edwin Hubble, "A Relation Between Distance and Radial Velocity Among Extra-Galactic Nebulae," *Proceedings of the National Academy of Sciences* 15 (1929), pages 168-173.
12. Albert Einstein, *Out of My Later Years* (New York: Philosophical Library, 1950), page 27.

13. Hugh Ross, *Beyond the Cosmos,* 2nd edition (Colorado Springs, CO: NavPress, 1999), pages 151-193.

SEVEN—*Closing Loopholes: Round One*

1. Arthur S. Eddington, "The End of the World: From the Standpoint of Mathematical Physics," *Nature,* 127 (1931), page 450.
2. Arthur S. Eddington, "On the Instability of Einstein's Spherical World," *Monthly Notices of the Royal Astronomical Society,* 90 (1930), page 672.
3. Hubert P. Yockey, "On the Information Content of Cytochrome c," *Journal of Theoretical Biology,* 67 (1977), pages 345-376; Hubert P. Yockey, "Self Organization Origin of Life Scenarios and Information Theory," *Journal of Theoretical Biology,* 91 (1981), pages 13-31; James A. Lake, "Evolving Ribosome Structure: Domains in Archaebacteria, Eubacteria, Eocytes, and Eukaryotes," *Annual Review of Biochemistry,* 54 (1985), pages 507-530; M. J. Dufton, "Genetic Code Redundancy and the Evolutionary Stability of Protein Secondary Structure," *Journal of Theoretical Biology* 116 (1985), pages 343-348; Hubert P. Yockey, "Do Overlapping Genes Violate Molecular Biology and the Theory of Evolution?" *Journal of Theoretical Biology* 80 (1979), pages 21-26; John Abelson, "RNA Processing and the Intervening Sequence Problem," *Annual Review of Biochemistry,* 48 (1979), pages 1035-1069; Ralph T. Hinegardner and Joseph Engleberg, "Rationale for a Universal Genetic Code," *Science* 142 (1963), pages 1083-1085; Hans Neurath, "Protein Structure and Enzyme Action," *Reviews of Modern Physics* 31 (1959), pages 185-190; Fred Hoyle and Chandra Wickramasinghe, *Evolution from Space* (New York: Simon and Schuster, 1981), pages 14-97; Charles B. Thaxton, Walter L. Bradley, and Roger Olsen, *The Mystery of Life's Origin* (New York: Philosophical Library, 1984); Robert Shapiro, *Origins* (New York: Summit Books, 1986), pages 117-131; Hugh Ross, *Genesis One: A Scientific Perspective,* 2nd ed. rev. (Pasadena, CA: Reasons To Believe, 1983), pages 9-10; Hubert P. Yockey, "A Calculation of the Probability of Spontaneous Biogenesis by Information Theory," *Journal of Theoretical Biology* 67 (1977), pages 377-398; W. W. Duley, "Evidence Against Biological Grains in the Interstellar Medium," *Quarterly Journal of the Royal Astronomical Society,* 25 (1984), pages 109-113; Randall A. Kok, John A. Taylor, and Walter L. Bradley, "A Statistical Examination of Self-Ordering of Amino Acids in Proteins," *Origins of Life and Evolution of the Biosphere,* 18 (1988), pages 135-142; John D. Barrow and Frank J. Tipler, *The Anthropic Cosmological Principle* (New York: Oxford University Press, 1986), pages 560-570; Hubert P. Yockey, *Information Theory and Molecular Biology* (Cambridge, U.K.: Cambridge University Press, 1992), pages 131-309.
4. Herman Bondi and T. Gold, "The Steady-State Theory of the Expanding Universe," *Monthly Notices of the Royal Astronomical Society,* 108 (1948), pages 252-270; Fred Hoyle, "A New Model for the Expanding Universe," *Monthly Notices of the Royal Astronomical Society,* 108 (1948), pages 372-382.
5. Herman Bondi, *Cosmology,* 2nd ed. rev. (Cambridge, U.K.: Cambridge University Press, 1960), page 140; Hoyle, "A New Model for the Expanding Universe," page 372.
6. Fred Hoyle, *The Nature of the Universe,* 2nd ed. rev. (Oxford, U.K.: Basil Blackwell, 1952), page 111; Fred Hoyle, "The Universe: Past and Present Reflections," *Annual Reviews of Astronomy and Astrophysics,* 20 (1982), page 3.
7. Ross, *The Fingerprint of God,* pages 81-96; J.C. Mather, et al., "Measurement of the Cosmic Microwave Background Spectrum by the COBE FIRAS Instrument," *Astrophysical Journal,* 420 (1994), pages 439-444; Alan Dressler, et al., "New Images of the Distant, Rich Cluster CL 0939+4713 with WFPC2," *Astrophysical Journal Letters* 435 (1994), pages L23-L26. J. C. Mather, et al., "Meaurement of the Cosmic Microwave Background Spectrum by the COBE FIRAS Instrument," *Astrophysical Journal,* 420 (1994), pages 439-444; Alan Dressler, et al., "New Images of the Distant, Rich Cluster CL 0939+4713 with WFPC2," *Astrophysical Journal Letters,* 435 (1994), pages L23-L26.
8. Sir James H. Jeans, *Astronomy and Cosmogony,* 2nd ed. rev. (Cambridge, U.K.: Cambridge University Press, 1929), pages 421-422.
9. Thomas L. Swihart, *Astrophysics and Stellar Astronomy* (New York: John Wiley & Sons, 1968), pages 157-158.

10. Donald Hamilton, "The Spectral Evolution of Galaxies. I. An Observational Approach," *Astrophysical Journal* 297 (1985), pages 371-389.

11. Ross, *The Fingerprint of God*, pages 81-96; J. C. Mather, et al., pages 439-444; Dressler, et al., pages L23-L26.

12. Paul S. Wesson, "Olber's Paradox and the Spectral Intensity of the Extragalactic Background Light," *Astrophysical Journal* 367, 1 February 1991, pages 399-406.

13. Hugh Ross, *The Fingerprint of God*, 2nd edition, pages 69-96.

14. Robert Jastrow, *God and the Astronomers*, 2nd edition (New York: W. W. Norton, 1992), pages 67-85.

15. Fred Hoyle, Geoffrey Burbidge, and Jayant V. Narlikar, *A Different Approach to Cosmology* (Cambridge, UK: Cambridge University Press, 2000), pages 65-115.

16. One of the more spectacular evidences for the universe maturing with time was a recently announced Hubble Space Telescope discovery (Mark A. Stein, "Hubble's Galaxy Photos Show Universe in Flux," *Los Angeles Times*, 2 December 1992, pages B1, B4). A team led by astronomer Alan Dressler found that for a galaxy cluster four billion light years distant (and hence four billion years younger than ours) the ratio of younger (spiral shaped) galaxies to older galaxies (elliptical shaped) was about six times higher than for our own galaxy cluster. For more details see my article, "Galaxy Formation Supports Creation," *Facts & Faith*, the Quarterly Newsletter of Reasons To Believe, Spring 1993, pages 2-3. For a list of references to additional evidences for the evolution of the universe see *The Fingerprint of God*, pages 81-82, 93-94.

17. Hoyle, Burbidge, and Narlikar, pages 107-337.

18. Gretchen Vogel, "Hubble Gives a Quasar House Tour," *Science*, 274 (1996), page 1468.

19. Faye Flam, "The Space Telescope Spies on Ancient Galaxy Menageries," *Science*, 266 (1994), page 1806; Hugh Ross, "Hubble Space Telescope Captures Infancy of Cosmos," *Facts & Faith*, vol. 9, no. 2, pages 1-2.

20. S. J. Warren, P. C. Hewett, and P. S. Osmer, "A Wide-Field Multicolor Survey for High-Redshift Quasars, $z \geq 2.2$. III. The Luminosity," *Astrophysical Journal*, 421 (1994), pages 412-433; M. Schmidt, D. P. Schneider, and J. E. Gunn, "Spectroscopic CCD Surveys for Quasars at Large Redshift. IV. Evolution of the Luminosity Function From Quasars Detected by Their Lyman-Alpha Emission," *Astronomical Journal*, 110 (1995), pages 68-77; J. D. Kennefict, S. G. Djorgovski, and R. R. de Carvalho, "The Luminosity Function of $z > 4$ Quasars from the Second Palomar Sky Survey," *Astronomical Journal*, 110 (1995), pages 2553-2565; J. P. Ostriker and J. Heisler, "Are Cosmologically Distant Objects Obscured by Dust: A Test Using Quasars," *Astrophysical Journal*, 278 (1984), pages 1-10; P. A. Shaver et al., "Decrease in the Space Density of Quasars at High Redshift," *Nature*, 384 (1996), pages 439-441; B. J. Boyle and T. di Matteo, "Limits of Dust Obscuration in QSOs," *Monthly Notices of the Royal Astronomical Society*, 277 (1995), pages L63-L66; Patrick S. Osmer, "The Sharp End of Quasars," *Nature*, 384 (1996), page 416.

21. G. S. Wasserburg and Y.-Z. Qian, "A Model of Metallicity Evolution in the Early Universe," *Astrophysical Journal Letters*, 538 (2000), pages L99-L102.

22. G. S. Bisnovatyi-Kogan, "At the Border of Eternity," *Science*, 279 (1998), page 1321.

23. D. C. Homan and J. F. C. Wardle, "Direct Distance Measurements to Superluminal Radio Sources," *Astrophysical Journal*, 535 (2000), pages 575-585.

24. Abraham Loeb and Eli Waxman, "Cosmic γ-Ray Background from Structure Formation in the Intergalactic Medium," *Nature*, 405 (2000), pages 156-158; A. Melchiorri, et al., "A Measurement of Ω from the North American Test Flight of Boomerang," *Astrophysical Journal Letters*, 536 (2000), pages L63-L66; M. Fukugita, C. J. Hogan, and P. J. E. Peebles, "The Cosmic Baryon Budget," *Astrophysical Journal*, 503 (1998), pages 518-530; Bo Qin and Xiang-Ping Wu, "Baryon Distribution in Galaxy Clusters as a Result of Sedimentation of Helium Nuclei," *Astrophysical Journal Letters*, 529 (2000), pages L1-L4; Sean G. Ryan, et al., "Primordial Lithium and Big Bang Nucleosynthesis," *Astrophysical Journal Letters*, 530 (2000), pages L57-L60.

25. S. Perlmutter, et al., "Measurements of Ω and $\wedge$ from 42 High-Redshift Supernovae," *Astrophysical Journal*, 517 (1999), pages 565-586; A Mechiorri, et al, pages L63-L66; P. deBernardis, et al., "A Flat Universe from High-Resolution Maps of the Cosmic Microwave Background Radiation," *Nature*, 404 (2000), pages 955-959; R. G. Carlberg,

et al., "The Ω_M-Ω_Λ Dependence of the Apparent Cluster Ω," *Astrophysical Journal,* 516 (1999), pages 552-558; Aaron D. Lewis, E. Ellington, Simon L. Morris, and R. G. Carlberg, "X-Ray Mass Estimates at z ~ 0.3 for the Canadian Network for Observational Cosmology Cluster Sample," *Astrophysical Journal,* 517 (1999), pages 587-608.

26. J. C. Mather, et al., "Measurement of the Cosmic Microwave Background Spectrum by the COBE FIRAS Instrument," *Astrophysical Journal,* 420 (1994), pages 439-444; P. deBernardis, et al., pages 955-959.

27. Fred Hoyle, Geoffrey Burbidge, and Jayant V. Narlikar.

28. John Gribbin, "Oscillating Universe Bounces Back," *Nature* 259 (1976), pages 15-16.

EIGHT—Closing Loopholes: Round Two

1. Robert H. Dicke, et al., "Cosmic Black-Body Radiation," *Astrophysical Journal Letters* 142 (1965), page 415.

2. Dicke, et al., pages 414-415.

3. S. Perlmutter, et al., pages 565-586; Aaron D. Lewis, E. Ellingson, Simon L. Morris, and R. G. Carlberg, pages 587-608; Joseph J. Mohr, Benjamin Mathiesen, and August E. Evrard, pages 627-649; N. A, Bahcall, et al., pages 1-9; Kentaro Nagamine, Renyue Cen, and Jeremiah P. Ostriker, pages 25-36; David H. Weinberg, et al., pages 563-568; J. Nevalainen, M. Markevitch, and W. Forman, pages 1-9; J. S. Alcaniz and J. A. S. Lima, pages L87-L90; Megan Donahue and G. Mark Voit, pages L37-L40; Asantha R. Cooray, "An Upper Limit on Ω_m Using Lensed Arcs," *Astrophysical Journal,* 524 (1999), pages 504-509; Masashi Chiba and Yuzuru Yoshii, "New Limits on a Cosmological Constant from Statistics of Gravitational Lensing," *Astrophysical Journal,* 510 (1999), pages 42-53; Stephano Borgani, Piero Rosati, Paolo Tozzi, and Colin Norman, "Cosmological Constraints from the ROSAT Deep Cluster Survery," *Astrophysical Journal,* 517 (1999), pages 40-53; Neta A. Bahcall and Xiaohui Fan, "The Most Distant Clusters: Determining Ω am σ_8." *Astrophysical Journal,* 504 (1998), pages 1-6; James Robinson and Joseph Silk, "Star Formation As a Cosmological Probe," *Astrophysical Journal,* 539 (2000), pages 89-97; Esther M. Hu, Richard G. McMahon, and Lennox L. Cowie, "An Extremely Luminous Galaxy at z = 5.74," *Astrophysical Journal Letters,* 522 (1999), pages L9-L12; B. F. Roukema and G. A. Mamon, "Tangential Large Scale Structure as a Standard Ruler: Curvature Parameters from Quasars," *Astronomy and Astrophysics,* 358 (2000), pages 395-408; B. Novosyadlyj, et al., "Cosmological Parameters from Large Scale Structure Observations," *Astronomy and Astrophysics,* 356 (2000), pages 418-434; P. Valageas, "Weak Gravitational Lensing Effects on the Determination of Ω_m and Ω_Λ from SneIa," *Astronomy and Astrophysics,* 354 (2000), pages 767-786; J. F. Macias-Perez, et al., "Gravitational Lensing Statistics with Extragalactic Surveys," *Astronomy and Astrophysics,* 353 (2000), pages 419-426; Karl Glazebrook, "The 2dFGRS – Galaxy Properties and Evolution," American Astronomical Society Meeting 196, #56.06, May, 2000; R. Bennett, "Survey Confirms Composition of the Cosmos," *Science News,* 157 (2000), page 374; R. Juszkiewicz, et al, "Evidence for a Low-Density Universe from the Relative Velocities of Galaxies," *Science,* 287 (2000), pages 109-112; F. R. Pearce, et al., "A Simulation of Galaxy Formation and Clustering," *Astrophysical Journal Letters,* 521 (1999), pages L99-L102; Wesley N. Colley, et al., "Topology from the Simulated Sloan Digital Sky Survey," *Astrophysical Journal,* 529 (2000), pages 795-810.

4. Alan H. Guth and Marc Sher, "The Impossibility of a Bouncing Universe," *Nature* 302 (1983), pages 505-507; Sidney A. Bludman, "Thermodynamics and the End of a Closed Universe," *Nature* 308 (1984), pages 319-322.

5. Igor D. Novikov and Yakob B. Zel'dovich, "Physical Processes Near Cosmological Singularities," *Annual Review of Astronomy and Astrophysics* 11 (1973), pages 387-412.

6. Arnold E. Sikkema and Werner Israel, "Black-hole Mergers and Mass Inflation in a Bouncing Universe," *Nature* 349 (1991), pages 45-47.

7. André Linde, "Self-Reproducing Universe," lecture given at the Centennial Symposium on Large Scale Structure, California Institute of Technology, Pasadena, CA, 27 September 1991.

8. Linde, "Self-Reproducing Universe."

9. Hugh Ross, *Beyond the Cosmos,* 2nd edition (Colorado Springs, CO: NavPress, 1999), pages 27-46.

10. Jaume Garriga and Alexander Vilenkin, "Recycling Universe," *Physical Review D,* 57 (1998), pages 2230-2244; E. Rebhan, "'Soft Bang' Instead of 'Big Bang': Model of an Inflationary Universe Without Singularities and with Eternal Physical Past Time," *Astronomy and Astrophysics,* 353 (2000), pages 1-9; J. M. Overduin, "Nonsingular Models with a Variable Cosmological Term," *Astrophysical Journal Letters,* 517 (1999), pages L1-L4; Mark Sincell, "Heretical Idea Faces Its Sternest Test," *Science,* 287 (2000), pages 572-573.

11. Redouane Fakir, "General Relativistic Cosmology with No Beginning of Time," *Astrophysical Journal,* 537 (2000), pages 533-536.

12. Stephen Hawking and Roger Penrose, "The Singularities of Gravitational Collapse and Cosmology," *Proceedings of the Royal Society of London,* Series A, 314 (1970), pages 529-548; Stephen W. Hawking and George F. R. Ellis, *The Large Scale Structure of Space-Time* (Cambridge, UK: Cambridge University Press, 1970); Jacob D. Bekenstein, "Nonsingular General-Relativistic Cosmologies," *Physical Review,* D, 11 (1975), pages 2072-2075; Leonard Parker and Yi Wang, "Avoidance of Singularities in Relativity Through Two-Body Interactions," *Physical Review,* D, 42 (1990), pages 1877-1883; Arvind Borde, "Open and Closed Universes, Initial Singularities, and Inflation," *Physical Review,* D, 50 (1994), pages 3692-3702; Arvind Borde and Alexander Vilenkin, "Eternal Inflation and the Initial Singularity," *Physical Review Letters,* 72 (1994), pages 3305-3308; Arvind Borde and Alexander Vilenkin, "Violation of the Weak Energy Condition in Inflating Spacetimes," *Physical Review D,* 56 (1997), pages 717-723.

13. Redouane Fakir, page 533.

14. Redouane Fakir, page 536.

15. A. Melchiorri, et al., "A Measurement of Ω from the North American Test Flight of Boomerang," *Astrophysical Journal Letters,* 536 (2000), pages L63-L66.

16. Hugh Ross, *The Fingerprint of God,* 2nd edition (Orange, CA: Promise Publishing, 1991), pages 98-105.

17. Albert Einstein,"Kosmologische Betrachtungen zur allgemeinen Relativitätstheorie," *Sitzungsberichte der Königlich Preussischen Akademie der Wissenschaften,* Feb. 8, 1917, pages 142-152. The English translation is in *The Principle of Relativity* by H. A. Lorentz, A. Einstein, H. Minkowski, and H. Weyl with notes by A. Sommerfield and translated by W. Perrett and G. B. Jeffrey (London, UK: Methuen and Co., 1923), pages 175-188.

18. Arthur S. Eddington, "On the Instability of Einstein's Spherical World," *Monthly Notices of the Royal Astronomical Society,* 90 (1930), pages 668-678; Hugh Ross, pages 64-67.

19. C. Brans and R. H. Dicke, "Mach's Principle and a Relativistic Theory of Gravitation," *Physical Review,* 124 (1961), pages 925-935.

20. D. B. Guenther, "Testing the Constancy of the Gravitational Constant Using Helioseismology," *Astrophysical Journal,* 498 (1998), pages 871-876.

21. Mark Sincell, "Heretical Idea Faces Its Sternest Test," *Science,* 287 (2000), pages 572-573.

22. Alexander Y. Potekhin, et al., "Testing Cosmological Variability of the Proton-To-Electron Mass Ratio Using the Spectrum of PKS 0528-250," *Astrophysical Journal,* 505 (1998), pages 523-528.

23. Mario Livio and Massimo Stiavelli, "Does the Fine-Structure Constant Really Vary in Time?" *Astrophysical Journal Letters,* 507 (1998), pages L13-L15.

24. Mario Livio and Massimo Stiavelli, page L14.

25. L. H. Ford and Thomas A. Roman, "Classical Scalar Fields and Violations of the Second Law," gr-qc/0009076, Sept. 21, 2000, preprint.

26. Charles W. Misner, Kip S. Thorne, and John Archibald Wheeler, *Gravitation* (San Francisco, CA: W. H. Freeman, 1973), page 752.

NINE—Science Discovers Time Before Time

1. Eric J. Lerner, *The Big Bang Never Happened* (New York: Random House, 1991), pages 120, 295-318.
2. Lerner, pages 7-8.
3. Lerner, pages 283-291, 300-301.
4. Hugh Ross, *The Fingerprint of God*, 2nd ed. rev. (Orange, CA: Promise Publishing, 1991), pages 53-68, 111-118.
5. Roger Penrose, "An Analysis of the Structure of Space-time," *Adams Prize Essay*, Cambridge University (1966); Stephen W. Hawking, "Singularities and the Geometry of Space-time," *Adams Prize Essay*, Cambridge University (1966); Stephen W. Hawking and George F. R. Ellis, "The Cosmic Black-Body Radiation and the Existence of Singularities in Our Universe," *Astrophysical Journal* 152 (1968), pages 25-36; Stephen Hawking and Roger Penrose, "The Singularities of Gravitational Collapse and Cosmology," *Proceedings of the Royal Society of London*, series A, 314 (1970), pages 529-548.
6. Hawking and Penrose, pages 529-548.
7. Jacob D. Bekenstein, "Nonsingular General-Relativistic Cosmologies," *Physical Review* D, 11 (1975), pages 2072-2075; Leonard Parker and Yi Wang, "Avoidance of Singularities in Relativity Through Two-Body Interactions," *Physical Review* D, 42 (1990), pages 1877-1883; Arvind Borde, "Open and Closed Universes, Initial Singularities, and Inflation," *Physical Review* D, 50 (1994), pages 3692-3702; Arvind Borde and Alexander Vilenkin, "Eternal Inflation and the Initial Singularity," *Physical Review Letters*, 72 (1994), pages 3305-3308; Arvind Borde and Alexander Vilenkin, "Violation of the Weak Energy Condition in Inflating Spacetimes," *Physical Review* D, 56 (1997), pages 717-723.
8. John Boslough, "Inside the Mind of a Genius," *Reader's Digest* (February 1984), page 120.
9. Albert Einstein, "Die Feldgleichungen der Gravitation," *Sitzungsberichte der Königlich Preussischen Akademie der Wissenschaften*, 25 November 1915, pages 844-847; Albert Einstein, "Die Grundlage der allgemeinen Relativitätstheorie," *Annalen der Physik* 49 (1916), pages 769-822 [Hendrik A. Lorentz, et al., *The Principle of Relativity*, with notes by Arnold Sommerfeld, trans. W. Perrett and G. B. Jeffrey (London: Methuen, 1923), pages 109-164]; Albert Einstein, "Erklärung der Perihelbewegung des Merkur aus der allgemeinen Relativitätstheorie," *Sitzungsberichte der Königlich Preussischen-Akademie der Wissenschaften*, 18 November 1915, pages 831-839.
10. F. W. Dyson, Arthur S. Eddington, and C. Davidson, "A Determination of the Deflection of Light by the Sun's Gravitational Field, from Observations Made at the Total Eclipse of May 29, 1919," *Philosophical Transactions of the Royal Society of London*, series A, 220 (1920), pages 291-333.
11. Steven Weinberg, *Gravitation and Cosmology: Principles and Applications of the General Theory of Relativity* (New York: J. Wiley and Sons, 1972), page 198; Irwin I. Shapiro et al., "Mercury's Perihelion Advance: Determination by Radar," *Physical Review Letters* 28 (1972), pages 1594-1597; R. V. Pound and J. L. Snider, "Effect of Gravity on Nuclear Resonance," *Physical Review Letters* 13 (1964), pages 539-540.
12. C. Brans and Robert H. Dicke, "Mach's Principle and a Relativistic Theory of Gravitation," *Physical Review* 124 (1961), pages 925-935; J. W. Moffat, "Consequences of a New Experimental Determination of the Quadrupole Moment of the Sun for Gravitation Theory," *Physical Review Letters* 50 (1983), pages 709-712; George F. R. Ellis, "Alternatives to the Big Bang," *Annual Reviews of Astronomy and Astrophysics* 22 (1984), pages 157-184.
13. Irwin I. Shapiro, Charles C. Counselman III, and Robert W. King, "Verification of the Principle of Equivalence for Massive Bodies," *Physical Review Letters* 36 (1976), pages 555-558.
14. R. D. Reasenberg, et al., "Viking Relativity Experiment: Verification of Signal Retardation by Solar Gravity," *Astrophysical Journal Letters* 234 (1979), pages 219-221.
15. R. F. C. Vessot et al., "Test of Relativistic Gravitation with a Space- Borne Hydrogen Maser," *Physical Review Letters* 45 (1980), pages 2081-2084.

16. J. H. Taylor, "Gravitational Radiation and the Binary Pulsar," *Proceedings of the Second Marcel Grossman Meeting on General Relativity*, part A, ed. Remo Ruffini (Amsterdam: North-Holland Publishing, 1982), pages 15-19.
17. J. H. Taylor, et al., "Experimental Constraints on Strong-field Relativistic Gravity," *Nature* 355 (1992), pages 132-136.
18. Roger Penrose, *Shadows of the Mind: A Search for the Missing Science of Consciousness* (New York: Oxford University Press, 1994), page 230.
19. Ron Cowen, "Einstein's General Relativity: It's a Drag," *Science News*, 152 (1997), page 308.
20. Peter G. Jonker, Mariano Méndez, and Michiel van der Klis, "Discovery of a New Third Kilohertz Quasi-Periodic Oscillation in 4U 1608-52, 4U 1728-34, and 4U 1636-53: Sidebands to the Lower Kilohertz Quasi-Periodic Oscillation?" *Astrophysical Journal Letters*, 540 (2000), pages L29-L32.
21. G. S. Bisnovatyi-Kogan, "At the Border of Eternity," *Science*, 279 (1998), page 1321.
22. Stephen Battersky, "A Ring in Truth," *Nature*, 392 (1998), page 548.
23. Andrew Watson, "Einstein's Theory Rings True," *Science*, 280 (1998), page 205.
24. Ignazio Ciufolini, et al., "Test of General Relativity and Measurement of the Lense-Thirring Effect with Two Earth Satellites," *Science*, 279 (1998), pages 2100-2103.
25. Ignazio Ciufolini, et al., page 2102.
26. K. C. Cole, "Massive Blast Deep in Space Puzzles Experts," *Los Angeles Times*, May 7, 1998, pages A1, A32.
27. Ralph Wijers, "The Burst, the Burster, and Its Lair," *Nature*, 393 (1998), pages 13-14.

TEN—*A God Outside of Time, But Knowable*

1. Hugh Ross, *Beyond the Cosmos*, 2nd edition (Colorado Springs, CO: NavPress, 1999).
2. Paul Kurtz, *Free Inquiry* (Winter 1992/93), pages 10-15.
3. John Maddox, "Down with the Big Bang," *Nature* 340 (1989), page 425.
4. Eric J. Lerner, *The Big Bang Never Happened* (New York: Random House, 1991); Eric J. Lerner, "The Big Bang Never Happened," *Discover* (June 1988), pages 70-79.
5. Jean-Claude Pecker, "Big Bangs, Plural: A Heretical View," *Free Inquiry* (Winter 1992/93), pages 10-11.
6. Milton Rothman, "What Went Before?" *Free Inquiry* (Winter 1992/93), page 12.
7. Victor J. Stenger, "The Face of Chaos," *Free Inquiry* (Winter 1992/93), page 14.
8. Adolf Grünbaum, "Pseudo-Creation of the 'Big Bang,'" *Free Inquiry* (Winter 1992/93), page 15.
9. Maddox, page 425.
10. Donald Lynden-Bell, J. Katz, and J. H. Redmount, "Sheet Universes and the Shapes of Friedmann Universes," *Monthly Notices of the Royal Astronomical Society* 239 (1989), page 201.
11. J. R. Hernstein, et al., "A Geometric Distance to the Galaxy NGC 4258 from Orbital Motions in a Nuclear Gas Disk," *Nature*, 400 (1999), pages 539-541; D. C. Homan, and J. F. C. Wardle, "Direct Distance Measurements to Superluminal Radio Sources," *Astrophysical Journal*, 535 (2000), pages 575-585.
12. Rothman, page 12.
13. Augustine of Hippo, "Confessions, Book Eleven, Chapters 10-14," *The Fathers of the Church*, vol. 21, *Confessions*, trans. Vernon J. Bourke (New York: Fathers of the Church, Inc., 1953), pages 339-344.
14. Fred Hoyle, *Quarterly Journal of the Royal Astronomical Society* 1 (1960), pages 28-39; Robert Jastrow and A. G. W. Cameron, ed., *Origin of the Solar System* (New York: Academic Press, 1963).
15. Lerner, *The Big Bang Never Happened*, pages 23-25.

ELEVEN—*A Brief Look at* **A Brief History of Time**

1. Stephen W. Hawking, *A Brief History of Time: From the Big Bang to Black Holes* (New York: Bantam Books, April, 1988), page 171.
2. Bryan Appleyard, "A Master of the Universe," *Sunday Times Magazine* (London), 19 July 1988, page 29.

3. Carl Sagan, "Introduction," *A Brief History of Time: From the Big Bang to Black Holes* (New York: Bantam Books, 1988), page x.
4. John Boslough, "Inside the Mind of a Genius," *Reader's Digest* (February 1984), page 120.
5. James B. Hartle and Steven W. Hawking, "Wave Function of the Universe," *Physical Review D* 28 (1983), pages 2960-2975.
6. Leon Jaroff, "Roaming the Cosmos," *Time*, 8 February 1988, page 60; Hawking, pages 136, 141.
7. Hawking, page 136.
8. Heinz R. Pagels, *Perfect Symmetry: The Search for the Beginning of Time* (New York: Simon & Schuster, 1985), page 243.
9. Frank Tipler, "The Mind of God," *The Times Higher Education Supplement* (London), 14 October 1988, page 23.
10. Hawking, page 139.
11. 2 Timothy 1:9 and Titus 1:2. See also table 10.1, page 110.
12. Hawking, page 122.
13. Hawking, page 140.
14. Hawking, page 13.
15. Hawking, page 12.
16. Hawking, page 166.
17. Hawking, page 169.
18. Hawking, page 175.
19. Stanley L. Jaki, *Cosmos and Creator* (Edinburgh, U.K.: Scottish Academic Press, 1980), pages 49-54; Stanley L. Jaki, *God and the Cosmologists* (Washington, DC: Regnery Gateway, 1989), pages 104-109.
20. Hawking, page 168.
21. Hawking, page 126.
22. Hugh Ross, *The Fingerprint of God*, 2nd ed. rev. (Orange, CA: Promise, 1991), pages 124-128.
23. Hawking, page 174.

TWELVE—A Modern-Day Goliath

1. Allen Emerson, "A Disorienting View of God's Creation," *Christianity Today*, 1 February 1985, page 19.
2. Paul Davies, *God and the New Physics* (New York: Simon and Schuster, 1983), pages 25-43, specifically pages 38-39.
3. Hugh Ross, *Beyond the Cosmos*, 2nd edition (Colorado Springs, CO: NavPress, 1999), pages 34-46.
4. Davies, *God and the New Physics*, pages 167-174.
5. Hebrews 11:3, *The Holy Bible*.
6. Paul Davies, *Superforce: The Search for a Grand Unified Theory of Nature* (New York: Simon and Schuster, 1984), page 243.
7. Paul Davies, *The Cosmic Blueprint: New Discoveries in Nature's Creative Ability to Order the Universe* (New York: Simon and Schuster, 1988), page 141.
8. Davies, *The Cosmic Blueprint*, page 203.
9. Paul Davies, *The Fifth Miracle: The Search for the Origin and Meaning of Life* (New York: Simon & Schuster, 1999), pages 93, 120.
10. Richard J. Gott III, "Creation of Open Universes from de Sitter Space," *Nature*, 295 (1982), page 306.
11. Heinz R. Pagels, "Uncertainty and Complementarity," *The World Treasury of Physics, Astronomy, and Mathematics*, ed. Timothy Ferris (Boston, MA: Little, Brown and Co., 1991), pages 106-108.
12. Nick Herbert, *Quantum Reality: Beyond the New Physics: An Excursion into Metaphysics and the Meaning of Reality* (New York: Anchor Books, Doubleday, 1987), pages 16-29; Stanley L. Jaki, *Cosmos and Creator* (Edinburgh, U.K.: Scottish Academic Press, 1980), pages 96-98; James Jeans, "A Universe of Pure Thought," *Quantum Questions*, ed. Ken Wilber (Boston, MA: New Science Library, Shambhala, 1985), pages 140-144; Ken Wilber, *Quantum Questions* (Boston, MA: New Science Library, Shambhala,

1985), pages 145-146; Paul Teller, "Relativity, Relational Holism, and the Bell Inequalities," *Philosophical Consequences of Quantum Theory: Reflections on Bell's Theorem*, ed. James T. Cushing and Eman McMullin (Notre Dame, IN: University of Notre Dame Press, 1989), pages 216-223.
13. James S. Trefil, *The Moment of Creation* (New York: Charles Scribner's Sons, 1983), pages 91-101.
14. David Dvorkin, "Why I Am Not a Jew," *Free Inquiry* 10, no. 2 (1990), page 34. David Dvorkin points out that orthodox Jews and fundamentalist Christians share many beliefs in common and also share the tendency to add dogmas to their doctrines.

THIRTEEN—The Divine Watchmaker

1. William Paley, *Natural Theology on Evidence and Attributes of Deity*, 18th ed. rev. (Edinburgh, U.K.: Lackington, Allen and Co., and James Sawers, 1818), pages 12-14.
2. David Hume, *Dialogues Concerning Natural Religion*, Fontana Library Edition (London: Collins, 1963), pages 154-156.
3. Jacques Monod, *Chance and Necessity* (London: Collins, 1972), page 110 (emphasis in original).
4. Richard Dawkins, *The Blind Watchmaker: Why the Evidence of Evolution Reveals a Universe Without Design* (New York: W. W. Norton, 1987), page 5 (emphasis in original).
5. Stephen Jay Gould, *The Panda's Thumb: More Reflections in Natural History* (New York: W. W. Norton, 1980).
6. Steven M. Block, "Real Engines of Creation," *Nature,* 386 (1997), pages 217-219; Hiroyuki Noji, Ryohei Yasuda, Masasuke Yoshida, and Kazuhiko Kinosita Jr., "Direct Observation of the Roatation of F1-ATPase," *Nature,* 386 (1997), pages 299-302.
7. Michael Groll et al., "Structure of 26S Proteasome from Yeast at 2.4 A° Resolution," *Nature,* 386 (1997), pages 463-471.
8. Hugh Ross, *The Genesis Question* (Colorado Springs, CO: NavPress, 1998), pages 50-57.
9. J. Raloff, "Earth Day 1980: The 29th Day?" *Science News* 117 (1980), page 270; Roger Lewin, "No Dinosaurs This Time," *Science,* 221 (1983), page 1169.
10. Paul R. Ehrlich, Anne H. Ehrlich, and J. P. Holdren, *Ecoscience: Population, Resources, Environment* (San Francisco, CA: W. H. Freeman, 1977), page 142; Paul R. Ehrlich and Anne H. Ehrlich, *Extinction: The Causes and Consequences of the Disappearance of Species* (New York: Ballantine, 1981), page 33.
11. Ehrlich and Ehrlich, page 23.
12. Peter Gordon, "The Panda's Thumb Revisited: An Analysis of Two Arguments Against Design," *Origins Research,* 7, no. 1 (1984), pages 12-14.
13. Hideki Endo, et al., "Role of the Giant Panda's 'Pseudo-Thumb,'" *Nature,* 397 (1999), pages 309-310.

FOURTEEN—A "Just Right" Universe

1. Richard Swinburne, "Argument from the Fine-Tuning of the Universe," *Physical Cosmology and Philosophy*, ed. John Leslie (New York: Macmillan, 1991), page 160; Hugh Ross, *The Fingerprint of God*, 2nd ed. rev. (Orange, CA: Promise, 1991), page 122.
2. Ross, pages 122-123.
3. Fred Hoyle, *Galaxies, Nuclei, and Quasars* (New York: Harper and Row, 1965), pages 147-150; Fred Hoyle, "The Universe: Past and Present Reflection," *Annual Reviews of Astronomy and Astrophysics* 20 (1982), page 16; Ross, pages 126-127.
4. Fred Hoyle, *The Nature of the Universe*, 2nd ed. rev. (Oxford, U.K.: Basil Blackwell, 1952), page 109; Fred Hoyle, *Astronomy and Cosmology: A Modern Course* (San Francisco, CA: W. H. Freeman, 1975), pages 684-685; Hoyle, "The Universe: Past and Present Reflection," page 3; Hoyle, *Astronomy and Cosmology*, page 522.
5. Hoyle, *The Nature of the Universe*, page 111.
6. Hoyle, "The Universe: Past and Present Reflection," page 16.
7. H. Oberhummer, A. Csótó, and H. Schlattl, "Stellar Production Rates of Carbon and Its Abundance in the Universe," *Science,* 289 (2000), pages 88-90.
8. Oberhummer, Csótó, and Schlattl, page 90.

9. John D. Barrow and Frank J. Tipler, *The Anthropic Cosmological Principle* (New York: Oxford University Press, 1986), page 400.

10. James S. Trefil, *The Moment of Creation* (New York: Collier Books, Macmillan, 1983), pages 127-134.

11. Lawrence M. Krauss, "The End of the Age Problem and the Case for a Cosmological Constant Revisited," *Astrophysical Journal*, 501 (1998), page 461.

12. George F. R. Ellis, "The Anthropic Principle: Laws and Environments," in *The Anthropic Principle*, F. Bertola and U. Curi, ed. (New York: Cambridge University Press, 1993), page 30; D. Allan Bromley, "Physics: Atomic and Molecular Physics," *Science* 209 (1980), page 116.

13. George F. R. Ellis, page 30; H. R. Marston, S. H. Allen, and S. L. Swaby, "Iron Metabolism in Copper-Deficient Rats," *British Journal of Nutrition* 25 (1971), pages 15-30; K. W. J. Wahle and N. T. Davies, "Effect of Dietary Copper Deficiency in the Rat on Fatty Acid Compostion of Adipose Tissue and Desaturase Activity of Liver Microsomes," *British Journal of Nutrition* 34 (1975), pages 105-112; Walter Mertz, "The Newer Essential Trace Elements, Chromium, Tin, Vanadium, Nickel, and Silicon," *Proceedings of the Nutrition Society*, 33 (1974), pages 307-313.

14. Christopher C. Page, et al., "Natural Engineering Principles of Electron Tunneling in Biological Oxidation-Reduction," *Nature*, 402 (1999), pages 47-52.

15. John P. Cox and R. Thomas Giuli, *Principles of Stellar Structure, Volume II: Applications to Stars* (New York: Gordon and Breach, 1968), pages 944-1028.

16. In my books on this subject the list of known characteristics of the universe that must be fine-tuned for physical life to be possible grew from 15 in 1989, to 16 in 1991, to 25 in 1993, to 26 in 1995, and now to 35.

17. Ross, pages 120-128; Barrow and Tipler, pages 123-457; Bernard J. Carr and Martin J. Rees, "The Anthropic Principle and the Structure of the Physical World," *Nature*, 278 (1979), pages 605-612; John M. Templeton, "God Reveals Himself in the Astronomical and in the Infinitesimal," *Journal of the American Scientific Affiliation* (December 1984), pages 194-200; Jim W. Neidhardt, "The Anthropic Principle: A Religious Response," *Journal of the American Scientific Affiliation* (December 1984), pages 201-207; Brandon Carter, "Large Number Coincidences and the Anthropic Principle in Cosmology," *Proceedings of the International Astronomical Union Symposium No. 63: Confrontation of Cosmological Theories with Observational Data*, ed. M. S. Longair (Boston, MA: Reidel Publishing, 1974), pages 291-298; John D. Barrow, "The Lore of Large Numbers: Some Historical Background to the Anthropic Principle," *Quarterly Journal of the Royal Astronomical Society*, 22 (1981), pages 404-420; Alan Lightman, "To the Dizzy Edge," *Science*, 82 (October 1982), pages 24-25; Thomas O'Toole, "Will the Universe Die by Fire or Ice?" *Science*, 81 (April 1981), pages 71-72; Hoyle, *Galaxies, Nuclei, and Quasars*, pages 147-150; Bernard J. Carr, "On the Origin, Evolution, and Purpose of the Physical Universe," *Physical Cosmology and Philosophy*, ed. John Leslie (New York: Macmillan, 1990), pages 134-153; Swinburne, pages 154-173; R. E. Davies and R. H. Koch, "All the Observed Universe Has Contributed to Life," *Philosophical Transactions of the Royal Society of London*, series B, 334 (1991), pages 391-403; George F. R. Ellis, pages 27-30; Hubert Reeves, "Growth of Complexity in an Expanding Universe," in *The Anthropic Principle*, ed. F. Bertola and U. Curi (New York: Cambridge University Press, 1993), pages 67-84; Oberhummer, Csótó, and Schlattl, pages 88-90; Lawrence M. Krauss, pages 461-466; Christopher C. Page, et al., pages 47-52; S. Perlmutter, et al., "Measurements of Ω and $\wedge$ from 42 High-Redshift Supernovae," *Astrophysical Journal*, 517 (1999), pages 565-586; P. deBarnardis, et al., "A Flat Universe from High-Resolution Maps of the Cosmic Microwave Background Radiation, *Nature*, 494 (2000), pages 955-959; A. Melchiorri, et al., "A Measurement of Ω from the North American Test Flight of Boomerang," *Astrophysical Journal Letters*, 536 (2000), pages L63-L66; Lawrence M. Krauss and Glenn D. Starkman, "Life, the Universe, and Nothing: Life and Death in an Ever-Expanding Universe," *Astrophysical Journal*, 531 (2000), pages 22-30; Volker Bromm, Paolo S. Coppi, and Richard B. Larson, "Forming the First Stars in the Universe: The Fragmentation of Primordial Gas, "*Astrophysical Journal Letters*, 527 (1999), pages L5-L8; Jaume Garriga, Takahiro Tanaka, and Alexander Vilenkin, "Density Parameter and the Anthropic Principle,"

Physical Review D, 60 (1999), pages 5-21; Jaume Garriga and Alexander Vilenkin, "On Likely Values of the Cosmological Constant," *Physical Review* D, 61 (2000), pages 1462-1471; Max Tegmark and Martin Rees, "Why is the Cosmic Microwave Background Fluctuation Level 10^{-5}?" *Astrophysical Journal*, 499 (1998), pages 526-532; Jaume Garriga, Mario Livio, and Alexander Vilenkin, "Cosmological Constant and the Time of Its Dominance," *Physical Review* D, 61 (2000), in press; Peter G. van Dokkum, et al., "A High Merger Fraction in the Rich Cluster MS 1054-03 at z = 0.83: Direct Evidence for Hierarchical Formation of Massive Galaxies," *Astrophysical Journal Letters*, 520 (1999), pages L95-L98; Theodore P. Snow and Adolf N. Witt, "The Interstellar Carbon Budget and the Role of Carbon in Dust and Large Molecules," *Science*, 270 (1995), pages 1455-1457; Elliott H. Lieb, Michael Loss, and Jan Philip Solovej, "Stability of Matter in Magnetic Fields," *Physical Review Letters*, 75 (1995), pages 985-989; B. Edvardsson et al., "The Chemical Evolution of the Galactic Disk. I. Analysis and Results," *Astronomy & Astrophysics*, 275 (1993), pages 101-152; Hugh Ross, "Sparks in the Deep Freeze," *Facts & Faith*, vol. 11, n. 1 (1997), pages 5-6; T. R. Gabella and T. Oka, "Detection of H_3^+ in Interstellar Space," *Nature*, 384 (1996), pages 334-335; David Branch, "Density and Destiny," *Nature*, 391 (1998), page 23; Andrew Watson, "Case for Neutrino Mass Gathers Weight," *Science*, 277 (1997), pages 30-31; Dennis Normile, "New Experiments Step Up Hunt for Neutrino Mass," *Science*, 276 (1997), page 1795; Joseph Silk, "Holistic Cosmology," *Science*, 277 (1997), page 644; Frank Wilczek, "The Standard Model Transcended," *Nature*, 394 (2 July 1998), pages 13-15; Limin Wang, et al, "Cosmic Concordance and Quintessence," *Astrophysical Journal*, 530 (2000), pages 17-35; Robert Irion, "A Crushing End for our Galaxy," *Science*, 287 (2000), pages 62-64; Roland Buser, "The Formation and Early Evolution of the Milky Way Galaxy," *Science*, 287 (2000), pages 69-74; Joss Bland-Hawthorn and Ken Freeman, "The Baryon Halo of the Milky Way: A Fossil Record of Its Formation," *Science*, 287 (2000), pages 79-83; Robert Irion, "Supernova Pumps Iron in Inside-Out Blast, *Science*, 287 (2000), pages 203-205; Gary Gibbons, "Brane-Worlds," *Science*, 287 (2000), pagegs 49-50; Anatoly Klypin, Andrey V. Kravtsov, and Octavio Valenzuela, "Where Are the Missing Galactic Satellites?" *Astrophysical Journal*, 522 (1999), pages 82-92; Inma Dominguez, et al, "Intermediate-Mass Stars: Updated Models," *Astrophysical Journal*, 524 (1999), pages 226-241;
J. Iglesias-Páramo and J. M. Vilchez, "On the Influence of the Environment in the Star Formation Rates of a Sample of Galaxies in Nearby Compact Groups," *Astrophysical Journal*, 518 (1999), pages 94-102; Dennis Normile, "Weighing In on Neutrino Mass," *Science*, 280 (1998), pages 1689-1690; Eric Gawiser and Joseph Silk, "Extracting Primordial Density Fluctuations," *Science*, 280 (1998), pages 1405-1411; Joel Primack, "A Little Hot Dark Matter Matters," *Science*, 280 (1998), pages 1398-1400; Stacy S. McGaugh and W. J. G. de Blok, "Testing the Dark Matter Hypothesis with Low Surface Brightness Galaxies and Other Evidence," *Astrophysical Journal*, 499 (1998), pages 41-65; Nikos Prantzos and Joseph Silk, "Star Formation and Chemical Evolution in the Milky Way: Cosmological Implications," *Astrophysical Journal*, 507 (1998), pages 229-240; P. Weiss, "Time Proves Not Reversible at Deepest Level," *Science News*, 154 (1998), page 277; E. Dwek, et al., "The COBE Diffuse Infrared Background Experiment Search for the Cosmic Infrared Background. IV. Cosmological Implications," *Astrophysical Journal*, 508 (1998), page 106-122; G. J. Wasserburg and Y.-Z. Qian, "A Model of Metallicity Evolution in the Early Universe," *Astrophysical Journal Letters*, 538 (2000), pages L99-L102; Ron Cowen, "Cosmic Axis Begets Cosmic Controversy," *Science News*, 151 (1997), page 287.

18. Hoyle, "The Universe," page 16.
19. Paul Davies, *God and the New Physics* (New York: Simon & Schuster, 1983), pages viii, 3-42, 142-143.
20. Paul Davies, *Superforce* (New York: Simon & Schuster, 1984), page 243.
21. Paul Davies, *The Cosmic Blueprint* (New York: Simon & Schuster, 1988), page 203; Paul Davies, "The Anthropic Principle," *Science Digest* 191, no. 10 (October 1983), page 24.
22. George Greenstein, *The Symbiotic Universe* (New York: William Morrow, 1988), page 27.

23. Tony Rothman, "A 'What You See Is What You Beget' Theory," *Discover* (May 1987), page 99.

24. Carr and Rees, page 612.

25. Carr, page 153 (emphasis in the original).

26. Freeman Dyson, *Infinite in All Directions* (New York: Harper and Row, 1988), page 298.

27. Henry Margenau and Roy Abraham Varghese, ed., *Cosmos, Bios, and Theos* (La Salle, IL: Open Court, 1992), page 52.

28. Margenau and Varghese, ed., page 83.

29. Stuart Gannes, *Fortune*, 13 October 1986, page 57.

30. Fang Li Zhi and Li Shu Xian, *Creation of the Universe*, trans. T. Kiang (Singapore: World Scientific, 1989), page 173.

31. Roger Penrose, in the movie *A Brief History of Time* (Burbank, CA: Paramount Pictures Incorporated, 1992).

32. George F. R. Ellis, page 30.

33. Stephen Hawking, *A Brief History of Time* (New York: Bantam Books, April 1988), page 127.

34. Edward Harrison, *Masks of the Universe* (New York: Collier Books, Macmillan, 1985), pages 252, 263.

35. John Noble Wilford, "Sizing Up the Cosmos: An Astronomer's Quest," *New York Times*, 12 March 1991, page B9.

36. Tim Stafford, "Cease-fire in the Laboratory," *Christianity Today*, 3 April 1987, page 18.

37. Robert Jastrow, "The Secret of the Stars," *New York Times Magazine*, 25 June 1978, page 7.

38. Robert Jastrow, *God and the Astronomers* (New York: W. W. Norton, 1978), page 116.

39. Swinburne, page 165.

40. William Lane Craig, "Barrow and Tipler on the Anthropic Principle Versus Divine Design," *British Journal of Philosophy and Science*, 38 (1988), page 392.

41. Joseph Silk, *Cosmic Enigma* (1993), pages 8-9.

42. NCSE staff, *Education and Creationism Don't Mix* (Berkeley, CA: National Center for Science Education, 1985), page 3; Eugenie C. Scott, "Of Pandas and People," *National Center for Science Education Reports* (January-February 1990), page 18; Paul Bartelt, "Patterson and Gish at Morningside College," *The Committees of Correspondence*, Iowa Committee of Correspondence Newsletter, vol. 4, no. 4 (October 1989), page 1.

43. *Education and Creationism Don't Mix*, page 3; Eugenie C. Scott and Henry P. Cole, "The Elusive Scientific Basis of Creation Science," *The Quarterly Review of Biology* (March 1985), page 297.

44. Ilya Prigogine and Isabelle Stengers, *Order Out Of Chaos: Man's New Dialogue with Nature* (New York: Bantam Books, 1984).

45. Barrow and Tipler.

46. Barrow and Tipler, pages 676-677.

47. Barrow and Tipler, pages 676-677, 682; Martin Gardner, "Notes of a Fringe-Watcher: Tipler's Omega Point Theory," *Skeptical Inquirer*, 15, no. 2 (1991), pages 128-132.

48. Frank J. Tipler, *The Physics of Immortality: Modern Cosmology, God, and the Resurrection of the Dead* (New York: Doubleday, 1994).

49. Martin Gardner, "WAP, SAP, PAP, and FAP," *The New York Review of Books*, vol. 23, no. 8, 8 May 1986, pages 22-25.

50. Roger Penrose, *The Emperor's New Mind* (New York: Oxford University Press, 1989), pages 3-145, 374-451; Roger Penrose, *Shadows of the Mind* (New York: Oxford University Press, 1994), pages 7-208.

51. Frank J. Tipler, pages 253-255.

52. Frank J. Tipler, pages 256-257.

53. Gardner, "Notes of a Fringe-Watcher," page 132.

FIFTEEN—A Layperson's Guide to Alternate Cosmologies

1. Hugh Ross, *The Fingerprint of God*, 2nd edition (Orange, CA: Promise, 1991), pages 27-118.

2. Hugh Ross, *Beyond the Cosmos*, 2nd edition (Colorado Springs, CO: NavPress, 1999), pages 34-46.

SIXTEEN—Earth: The Place for Life

1. Iosef S. Shklovskii and Carl Sagan, *Intelligent Life in the Universe* (San Francisco, CA: Holden-Day, 1966), pages 343-350.
2. Shklovskii and Sagan, page 413.
3. Dava Sobel, "Is Anybody Out There?" *Life* (September 1992), page 62.
4. Pieter G. van Dokkum, et al., "A High Merger Fraction in the Rich Cluster MS 1054-03 at z = 0.83: Direct Evidence for Hierarchical Formation of Massive Galaxies," *Astrophysical Journal Letters*, 520 (1999), pages L95-L98.
5. Anatoly Klypin, Andrey V. Kravtsov, and Octavio Valenzuela, "Where Are the Missing Galactic Satellites?" *Astrophysical Journal*, 522 (1999), pages 82-92; Roland Buser, "The Formation and Early Evolution of the Milky Way Galaxy," *Science*, 287 (2000), pages 69-74.
6. Robert Irion, "A Crushing End for our Galaxy," *Science*, 287 (2000), pages 62-64.
7. Ron Cowen, "Were Spiral Galaxies Once More Common," *Science News* 142 (1992), page 390; Alan Dressler, et al., "New Images of the Distant, Rich Cluster CL 0939+4713 with WFPC2," *Astrophysical Journal Letters* 435 (1994), pages L23-L26.
8. R. E. Davies and R. H. Koch, "All the Observed Universe Has Contributed to Life," *Philosophical Transactions of the Royal Society of London*, series B, 334 (1991), pages 391-403.
9. John Maddox, "The Anthropic View of Nucleosynthesis," *Nature* 355 (1992), page 107.
10. Robert H. Dicke, "Dirac's Cosmology and Mach's Principle," *Nature* 192 (1961), page 440.
11. Yu N. Mishurov and L. A. Zenina, "Yes, the Sun Is Located Near the Corotation Circle," *Astronomy & Astrophysics*, 341 (1999), pages 81-85.
12. Guillermo Gonzalez, "Solar System Bounces in the Right Range for Life," *Facts & Faith*, vol. 11, n. 1 (1997), pages 4-5; Guillermo Gonzalez, "Is the Sun Anomalous?" *Astronomy & Geophysics*, in press (2000).
13. Ray White III and William C. Keel, "Direct Measurement of the Optical Depth in a Spiral Galaxy," *Nature*, 359 (1992), pages 129-130; W. C. Keel and R. E. White III, "HST and ISO Mapping of Dust in Silhouetted Spiral Galaxies," *American Astronomical Society Meeting*, 191, #75.01, December, 1997; Raymond E. White III, William C. Keel, and Christopher J. Conselice, "Seeing Galaxies Through Thick and Thin. I Optical Opacity Measures in Overlapping Galaxies," *Astrophysical Journal*, 542 (2000), pages 761-778.
14. Psalm 8:1-3, 19:1-4, 50:6, 89:5, 97:6; Romans 1:20, *The Holy Bible*.
15. Michael H. Hart, "Habitable Zones About Main Sequence Stars," *Icarus* 37 (1979), pages 351-357.
16. George Abell, *Exploration of the Universe* (New York: Holt, Rinehart, and Winston, 1964), pages 244-247; John C. Brandt and Paul W. Hodge, *Solar System Astrophysics* (New York: McGraw-Hill, 1964), pages 395-416.
17. Charles B. Thaxton, Walter L. Bradley, and Roger L. Olsen, *The Mystery of Life's Origin: Reassessing Current Theories* (New York: Philosophical Library, 1984), pages 43-46, 73-94.
18. John Vanermeer, et al., "Hurricane Disturbance and Tropical Tree Species Diversity," *Science*, 290 (2000), pages 788-791.
19. Nicholas R. Bates, Anthony H. Knap, and Anthony F. Michaels, "Contribution of Hurricanes to Local and Global Estimates of Air-Sea Exchange of CO_2," *Nature*, 395 (1998), pages 58-61.
20. D. M. Murphy, et al, "Influence of Sea Salt on Aerosol Radiative Properties in the Southern Ocean Marine Boundary Layer, *Nature*, 392 (1998), pages 62-65.
21. Gregory S. Jenkins, Hall G. Marshall, and W. R. Kuhn, "Pre-Cambrian Climate: The Effects of Land Area and Earth's Rotation Rate," *Journal of Geophysical Research*, Series D, 98 (1993), pages 8785-8791; K. J. Zahnle and J.C.G. Walker, "A Constant Daylength During the Precambrian Era?" *Precambrian Research* 37 (1987), pages 95-105;

R. Monastersky, "Speedy Spin Kept Early Earth From Freezing," *Science News,* 143 (1993), page 373.

22. W. R. Kuhn, J .C. G. Walker, and H. G. Marshall, "The Effect on Earth's Surface Temperature from Variations in Rotation Rate, Continent Formation, Solar Luminosity, and Carbon Dioxide," *Journal of Geophysical Research,* 94 (1989), pages 11, 129-11, 136; R. Monastersky, page 373.

23. The editors, "Our Friend Jove," *Discover* (July 1993), page 15.

24. Hugh Ross, "Dinosaurs' Disappearance No Longer a Mystery," *Facts & Faith,* vol. 5, no. 3 (1991), pages 1-3.

25. Mordecai-Mark Lac Low and Kevin Zahnle, "Explosion of Comet Shoemaker-Levy 9 on Entry into the Jovian Atmosphere," *Astrophysical Journal Letters,* 434 (1994), pages L33-L36; Ron Cowen, "By Jupiter! Comet Crashes Dazzle and Delight," *Science News* 146 (1994), page 55.

26. The editors, page 15.

27. Jacques Laskar, "Large-Scale Chaos in the Solar System," *Astronomy and Astrophysics,* 287 (1994), page 112.

28. Neil F. Comins, *What If The Moon Didn't Exist?* (New York: HarperCollins, 1993), pages 53-65.

29. Neil F. Comins, pages 4-5, 58; W. R. Kuhn, J. C. G. Walker, and H. G. Marshall, "The Effect on Earth's Surface Temperature from Variations in Rotation Rate, Continent Formation, Solar Luminosity, and Carbon Dioxide," *Journal of Geophysical Research* ,94 (1989), pages 11, 129-131, 136.

30. Neil F. Comins, pages 2-8; H. E. Newsom and S. R. Taylor, "Geochemical Implications of the Formation of the Moon by a Single Giant Impact," *Nature,* 338 (1989), pages 29-34; Hugh Ross, "Lunar Origin Update," *Facts & Faith,* vol. 9, n. 1 (1995), pages 1-3; Jack J. Lissauer, "It's Not Easy to Make the Moon," *Nature,* 389 (1997), pages 327-328; Sigeru Ida, Robin M. Canup, and Glen R. Stewart, "Lunar Accretion from an Impact-Generated Disk," *Nature,* 389 (1997), pages 353-357.

31. Louis A. Codispoti, "The Limits to Growth," *Nature,* 387 (1997), pages 237; Kenneth H. Coale, "A Massive PhytoPlankton Bloom Induced by an Ecosystem-Scale Iron Fertilization Experiment in the Equatorial Pacific Ocean," *Nature,* 383 (1996), pages 495-499.

32. P. Jonathan Patchett, "Scum of the Earth After All," *Nature,* 382 (1996), page 758.

33. William R. Ward, "Comments on the Long-Term Stability of the Earth's Oliquity," *Icarus,* 50 (1982), pages 444-448; Carl D. Murray, "Seasoned Travellers," *Nature,* 361 (1993), pages 586-587; Jacques Laskar and P. Robutel, "The Chaotic Obliquity of the Planets," *Nature,* 361 (1993), pages 608-612; Jacques Laskar, F. Joutel, and P. Robutel, "Stabilization of the Earth's Obliquity by the Moon," *Nature,* 361 (1993), pages 615-617.

34. Hugh Ross, *Big Bang Model Refined by Fire* (Pasadena, CA: Reasons To Believe, 1998), pages 6-14.

35. John Emsley, *The Elements,* 3rd edition (Oxford, UK: Clarendon Press, 1998), pages 24, 40, 56, 58, 60, 62, 78, 102, 106, 122, 130, 138, 152, 160, 188, 198, 214, 222, 230.

36. A French observatory maintains an up-to-date database on every extrasolar planet that has been discovered. The web site address for this database is http://www.obspm.fr/encycl/encycl.html.

37. S. H. Rhie, et al., "On Planetary Companions to the MACHO 98-BLG-35 Microlens Star," *Astrophysical Journal,* 533 (2000), pages 378-391.

38. Ron Cowen, "Less Massive Than Saturn?" *Science News,* 157 (2000), pages 220-222; Hugh Ross, "Planet Quest—A Recent Success," *Connections,* vol. 2, no. 2 (2000), pages 1-2.

39. G. Gonzalez, "Spectroscopic Analyses of the Parent Stars of Extrasolar Planetary Systems," *Astronomy & Astrophysics,* 334 (1998), pages 221-238; Guillermo Gonzalez, "New Planets Hurt Chances for ETI," *Facts & Faith,* vol. 12, no. 4 (1998), pages 2-4.

40. Davies and Koch, pages 391-403; Hart, pages 351-357; Ward, pages 444-448; Murray, pages 586-587; Laskar and Robutel, pages 608-612; Laskar, Joutel, and Robutel, pages 615-617; Newsom and Taylor, pages 29-34; Kaula, pages 1191-1196; Robert T. Rood and James S. Trefil, *Are We Alone? The Possibility of Extraterrestrial Civilizations* (New York: Scribner's Sons, 1983); John D. Barrow and Frank J. Tipler, *The Anthropic*

Cosmological Principle (New York: Oxford University Press, 1986), pages 510-575; Don L. Anderson, "The Earth as a Planet: Paradigms and Paradoxes," *Science* 22, no. 3 (1984), pages 347-355; I. H. Campbell and S. R. Taylor, "No Water, No Granite—No Oceans, No Continents," *Geophysical Research Letters,* 10 (1983), pages 1061-1064; Brandon Carter, "The Anthropic Principle and Its Implications for Biological Evolution," *Philosophical Transactions of the Royal Society of London*, series A, 310 (1983), pages 352-363; Allen H. Hammond, "The Uniqueness of the Earth's Climate," *Science* 187 (1975), page 245; Owen B. Toon and Steve Olson, "The Warm Earth," *Science*, 85 (October 1985), pages 50-57; George Gale, "The Anthropic Principle," *Scientific American* 245, no. 6 (1981), pages 154-171; Hugh Ross, *Genesis One: A Scientific Perspective* (Pasadena, CA: Reasons To Believe, 1983), pages 6-7; Ron Cottrell, *The Remarkable Spaceship Earth* (Denver, CO: Accent Books, 1982); Ter D. Haar, "On the Origin of the Solar System," *Annual Review of Astronomy and Astrophysics* 5 (1967), pages 267-278; George Greenstein, *The Symbiotic Universe* (New York: William Morrow, 1988), pages 68-97; John M. Templeton, "God Reveals Himself in the Astronomical and in the Infinitesimal," *Journal of the American Scientific Affiliation* (December 1984), pages 196-198; Michael H. Hart, "The Evolution of the Atmosphere of the Earth," *Icarus*, 33 (1978), pages 23-39; Tobias Owen, Robert D. Cess, and V. Ramanathan, "Enhanced CO^2 Greenhouse to Compensate for Reduced Solar Luminosity on Early Earth," *Nature* 277 (1979), pages 640-641; John Gribbin, "The Origin of Life: Earth's Lucky Break," *Science Digest* (May 1983), pages 36-102; P .J. E. Peebles and Joseph Silk, "A Cosmic Book of Phenomena," *Nature* 346 (1990), pages 233-239; Michael H. Hart, "Atmospheric Evolution, the Drake Equation, and DNA: Sparse Life in an Infinite Universe," *Philosophical Cosmology and Philosophy*, ed. John Leslie (New York: Macmillan, 1990), pages 256-266; Stanley L. Jaki, *God and the Cosmologists* (Washington, DC: Regnery Gateway, 1989), pages 177-184; R. Monastersky, page 373; the editors, page 15; Jacques Laskar, pages 109-113; Richard A. Kerr, "The Solar System's New Diversity," *Science,* 265 (1994), pages 1360-1362; Richard A. Kerr, "When Comparative Planetology Hit Its Target," *Science,* 265 (1994), page 1361; W. R. Kuhn, J. C. G. Walker, and H. G. Marshall, pages 11,129-131,136; Gregory S. Jenkins, Hal G. Marshall and W. R. Kuhn, pages 8785-8791; K. J. Zahnle and J. C. G. Walker, pages 95-105; M. J. Newman and R. T. Roos, "Implications of the Solar Evolution for the Earth's Early Atmosphere," *Science,* 198 (1977), pages 1035-1037; J. C. G. Walker and K. J. Zahnle, "Lunar Nodal Tides and Distance to the Moon During the Precambrian," *Nature,* 320 (1986), pages 600-602; J. F. Kasting and J. B. Pollack, "Effects of High CO^2 Levels on Surface Temperatures and Atmospheric Oxidation State of the Early Earth," *Journal of Atmospheric Chemistry,* 1 (1984), pages 403-428; H. G. Marshall, J. C. G. Walker, and W. R. Kuhn, "Long Term Climate Change and the Geochemical Cycle of Carbon," *Journal of Geophysical Research* 93 (1988), pages 791-801; Pieter G. van Dokkum, et al., pages L95-L98; Anatoly Klypin, Andrey V. Kravtsov, and Octavio Valenzuela, pages 82-92; Roland Buser, pages 69-74; Robert Irion, pages 62-64; D. M. Murphy, et al., pages 62-65; Neil F. Comins., pages 2-8; 53-65; W. R. Kuhn, J. C. G. Walker, and H. G. Marshall, pages 11, 129-131, 136; H. E. Newsom and S. R. Taylor, pages 29-34; Hugh Ross, "Lunar Origin Update," pages 1-3; Jack J. Lissauer, pages 327-328; Sigeru Ida, Robin M. Canup, and Glen R. Stewart, pages 353-357; Louis A. Codispoti, page 237; Kenneth H. Coale, pagges 495-499; P. Jonathan Patchett, page 758; William R. Ward, pages 444-448; Carl D. Murray, pages 586-587; Jacques Laskar and P. Robutel, pages 608-612; Jacques Laskar, F. Joutel, and P. Robutel, pages 615-617; S. H. Rhie, et al., pages 378-391; Ron Cowen, "Less Massive Than Saturn?" pages 220-222; Hugh Ross, "Planet Quest—A Recent Success," pages 1-2; G. Gonzalez, "Spectroscopic Analyses of the Parent Stars of Extrasolar Planetary Systems," pages 221-238; Guillermo Gonzalez, "New Planets Hurt Chances for ETI," pages 2-4; the editors, "The Vacant Interstellar Spaces," *Discover,* April 1996, pages 18, 21; Theodore P. Snow and Adolf N. Witt, "The Interstellar Carbon Budget and the Role of Carbon in Dust and Large Molecules," *Science,* 270 (1995), pages 1455-1457; Richard A. Kerr, "Revised Galileo Data Leave Jupiter Mysteriously Dry," *Science,* 272 (1996), pages 814-815; Adam Burrows and Jonathan Lumine, "Astronomical Questions of Origin and Survival," *Nature,* 378 (1995), page 333; George Wetherill,

"How Special Is Jupiter?" *Nature,* 373 (1995), page 470; B. Zuckerman, T. Forveille, and J. H. Kastner, "Inhibition of Giant-Planet Formation by Rapid Gas Depletion Around Young Stars," *Nature,* 373 (1995), pages 494-496; Hugh Ross, "Our Solar System, the Heavyweight Champion," *Facts & Faith,* vol. 10, n. 2 (1996), page 6; Guillermo Gonzalez, "Solar System Bounces in the Right Range for Life," *Facts & Faith,* vol. 11, n. 1 (1997), pages 4-5; C. R. Brackenridge, "Terrestrial Paleoenvironmental Effects of a Late Quaternary-Age Supernova," *Icarus,* 46 (1981), pages 81-93; M. A. Ruderman, "Possible Consequences of Nearby Supernova Explosions for Atmospheric Ozone and Terrestrial Life," *Science,* 184 (1974), pages 1079-1081; G. C. Reid et al., "Effects of Intense Stratospheric Ionization Events," *Nature,* 275 (1978), pages 489-492; B. Edvardsson et al., "The Chemical Evolution of the Galactic Disk. I. Analysis and Results," *Astronomy & Astrophysics,* 275 (1993), pages 101-152; J. J. Maltese et al., "Periodic Modulation of the Oort Cloud Comet Flux by the Adiabatically Changed Galactic Tide," *Icarus,* 116 (1995), pages 255-268; Paul R. Renne, et al., "Synchrony and Causal Relations Between Permian-Triassic Boundary Crisis and Siberian Flood Volcanism," *Science,* 269 (1995), pages 1413-1416; Hugh Ross, "Sparks in the Deep Freeze," *Facts & Faith,* vol. 11, n. 1 (1997), pages 5-6; T. R. Gabella and T. Oka, "Detection of H_3^+ in Interstellar Space," *Nature,* 384 (1996), pages 334-335; Hugh Ross, "Let There Be Air," *Facts & Faith,* vol. 10, n. 3 (1996), pages 2-3; Davud J. Des Marais, Harold Strauss, Roger E. Summons, and J. M. Hayes, "Carbon Isotope Evidence for the Stepwise Oxidation of the Proterozoic Environment *Nature,* 359 (1992), pages 605-609; Donald E. Canfield and Andreas Teske, "Late Proterozoic Rise in Atmospheric Oxygen Concentration Inferred from Phylogenetic and Sulphur-Isotope Studies," *Nature,* 382 (1996), pages 127-132; Alan Cromer, *UnCommon Sense: The Heretical Nature of Science* (New York: Oxford University Press, 1993), pages 175-176; Hugh Ross, "Drifting Giants Highlights Jupiter's Uniqueness," *Facts & Faith,* vol. 10, n. 4 (1996), page 4; Hugh Ross, "New Planets Raise Unwarranted Speculation About Life," *Facts & Faith,* vol. 10, n.1 (1996), pages 1-3; Hugh Ross, "Jupiter's Stability," *Facts & Faith,* vol. 8, n. 3 (1994), pages 1-2; Christopher Chyba, "Life Beyond Mars," *Nature,* 382 (1996), page 577; E. Skindrad, "Where Is Everybody?" *Science News,* 150 (1996), page 153; Stephen H. Schneider, *Laboratory Earth: The Planetary Gamble We Can't Afford to Lose* (New York: Basic Books, 1997), pages 25, 29-30; Guillermo Gonzalez, "Mini-Comets Write New Chapter in Earth-Science," *Facts & Faith,* vol. 11, n. 3 (197), pages 6-7; Miguel A. Goñi, Kathleen C. Ruttenberg, and Timothy I. Eglinton, "Sources and Contribution of Terrigenous Organic Carbon to Surface Sediments in the Gulf of Mexico," *Nature,* 389 (1997), pages 275-278; Paul G. Falkowski, "Evolution of the Nitrogen Cycle and Its Influence on the Biological Sequestration of CO_2 in the Ocean," *Nature,* 387 (1997), pages 272-274; John S. Lewis, *Physics and Chemistry of the Solar System* (San Diego, CA: Academic Press, 1995), pages 485-492; Hugh Ross, "Earth Design Update: Ozone Times Three," *Facts & Faith,* vol. 11, n. 4 (1997), pages 4-5; W. L. Chameides, P. S. Kasibhatla, J. Yienger, and H. Levy II, "Growth of Continental-Scale Metro-Agro-Plexes, Regional Ozone Pollution, and World Food Production," *Science,* 264 (1994), pages 74-77; Paul Crutzen and Mark Lawrence, "Ozone Clouds Over the Atlantic," *Nature,* 388 (1997), page 625; Paul Crutzen, "Mesospheric Mysteries," *Science,* 277 (1997), pages 1951-1952; M. E. Summers, et al., "Implications of Satellite OH Observations for Middle Atmospheric H_2O and Ozone," *Science,* 277 (1997), pages 1967-1970; K. Suhre, et al., "Ozone-Rich Transients in the Upper Equatorial Atlantic Troposphere," *Nature,* 388 (1997), pages 661-663; L. A. Frank, J. B. Sigwarth, and J. D. Craven, "On the Influx of Small Comets into the Earth's Upper Atmosphere. II. Interpretation," *Geophysical Research Letters,* 13 (1986), pages 307-310; David Deming, "Extraterrestrial Accretion and Earth's Climate," *Geology,* in press; T. A. Muller and G. J. MacDonald, "Simultaneous Presence of Orbital Inclination and Eccentricity in Prozy Climate Records from Ocean Drilling Program Site 806," *Geology,* 25 (1997), pages 3-6; Clare E. Reimers, "Feedback from the Sea Floor," *Nature,* 391 (1998), pages 536-537; Hilairy E. Hartnett, Richard G. Keil, John I. Hedges, and Allan H. Devol, "Influence of Oxygen Exposure Time on Organic Carbon Preservation in Continental Margin Sediments," *Nature,* 391 (1998), pages 572-574; Tina Hesman, "Greenhouse Gassed: Carbon Dioxide Spells Indigestion for Food Chains," *Science News,*

157 (2000), pages 200-202; Claire E. Reimers, "Feedbacks from the Sea Floor," *Nature,* 391 (1998), pages 536-537; S. Sahijpal, et al., "A Stellar Origin for the Short-Lived Nuclides in the Early Solar System," *Nature,* 391 (1998), pages 559-561; Stuart Ross Taylor, *Destiny or Chance: Our Solar System and Its Place in the Cosmos* (New York: Cambridge University Press, 1998); Peter D. Ward and Donald Brownlee, *Rare Earth: Why Complex Life is Uncommon in the Universe* (New York: Springer-Verlag, 2000); Dean L. Overman, *A Case Against Accident and Self-Organization* (New York: Rowman & Littlefield, 1997), pages 31-150; Michael J. Denton, *Nature's Destiny* (New York: The Free Press, 1998), pages 1-208; D. N. C. Lin, P. Bodenheimer, and D. C. Richardson, "Orbital Migration of the Planetary Companion of 51 Pegasi to Its Present Location," *Nature,* 380 (1996), pages 606-607; Stuart J. Weidenschilling and Francesco Mazari, "Gravitational Scattering as a Possible Origin or Giant Planets at Small Stellar Distances," *Nature,* 384 (1996), pages 619-621; Frederic A. Rasio and Eric B. Ford, "Dynamical Instabilities and the Formation of Extrasolar Planetary Systems," *Science,* 274 (1996), pages 954-956; N. Murray, B. Hansen, M. Holman, and S. Tremaine, "Migrating Planets," *Science,* 279 (1998), pages 69-72.

41. There exists, for example, a probability of a little less than one chance in 10^{80} that the hot air molecules arising from the flames on a gas stove instead of dissipating throughout the room could bunch together inside a small volume element, move toward you, and burn a hole through your chest and into your heart. This probability, however, is so tiny that we can safely conclude that such an event can never happen at any time in the history of the universe or at any location throughout the universe.

42. All the references in #40 above apply. What follows are references in addition to those recorded in #40: Yu N. Mishurov and L. A. Zenina, pages 81-85; Guillermo Gonzalez, "Solar System Bounces in the Right Range for Life," pages 4-5; Guillermo Gonzalez, "Is the Sun Anomalous?" in press (2000); Ray White III and William C. Keel, pages 129-130; Raymond E. White III, William C. Keel, and Christopher J. Conselice, pages 761-778; John Vanermeer, et al., pages 788-791; Nicholas R. Bates, Anthony H. Knap, and Anthony F. Michaels, pages 58-61; John Emsley, pages 24, 40, 56, 58, 60, 62, 78, 102, 106, 122, 130, 138, 152, 160, 188, 198, 214, 222, 230; Rob Rye, Phillip H. Kuo, and Heinrich D. Holland, "Atmospheric Carbon Dioxide Concentrations Before 2.2 Billion Years Ago," *Nature,* 378 (1995), pages 603-605; Robert A. Muller and Gordon J. MacDonald, "Glacial Cycles and Orbital Inclination," *Nature,* 377 (1995), pages 107-108; A. Evans, N. J. Beukes, J. L. Kirschvink, "Low Latitude Glaciation in the Palaeoproterozoic Era," *Nature,* 386 (1997), pages 262-266; Hugh Ross, "Rescued From Freeze Up," *Facts & Faith,* vol. 11, n. 2 (1997), page 3; Hugh Ross, "New Developments in Martian Meteorite," *Facts & Faith,* vol. 10, n. 4 (1996), pages 1-3; Paul Parsons, "Dusting Off Panspermia," *Nature,* 383 (1996), pages 221-222; P. Jonathan Patchett, "Scum of the Earth After All," *Nature,* 382 (1996), page 758; Hubert P. Yockey, "The Soup's Not One," *Facts & Faith,* vol. 10, n. 4 (1996), pages 10-11; M. Schlidowski, "A 3,800-million-year Isotopic Record of Life from Carbon in Sedimentary Rocks," *Nature,* 333 (1988), pages 313-318; H. P. Yockey, *Information Theory and Molecular Biology* (Cambridge and New York: Cambridge Univ. Press), 1992); C. De Duve, *Vital Dust* (New York: Basic Books, 1995). See also C. De Duve, *Blueprint for a Cell. The Nature and Origin of Life* (Burlington, N.C.: Neil Patterson Publishers, 1991); Hugh Ross, "Wild Fires Under Control," *Facts & Faith,* vol. 11, n. 1 (1997), pages 1-2; Peter D. Moore, "Fire Damage Soils Our Forest," *Nature,* 384 (1996), pages 312-313; A. U. Mallik, C. H. Gimingham, and A. A. Rahman, "Ecological Effects of Heather Burning I. Water Infiltration, Moisture Retention, and Porosity of Surface Soil," *Journal of Ecology,* 72 (1984), pages 767-776; Hugh Ross, "Evidence for Fine-Tuning," *Facts & Faith,* vol. 11, n. 2 (1997), page 2; Herbert J. Kronzucker, M. Yaeesh Siddiqi, and Anthony D. M. Glass, "Conifer Root Discrimination Against Soil Nitrate and the Ecology of Forest Succession," *Nature,* 385 (1997), pages 59-61; John M. Stark and Stephen C. Hart, "High Rates of Nitrification and Nitrate Turnover in Undisturbed Coniferous Forests," *Nature,* 385 (1997), pages 61-64; Christine Mlot, "Tallying Nitrogen's Increasing Impact," *Science News,* 151 (1997), page 100; Hugh Ross, "Rescued From Freeze Up," *Facts & Faith,* vol. 11, n. 2 (1997), page 3; Hugh Ross, "Life in Extreme Environments," *Facts & Faith,* vol. 11, n. 2 (1997), pages 6-7;

Richard A. Kerr, "Cores Document Ancient Catastrophe," *Science,* 275 (1997), page 1265; Hugh Ross, "'How's the Weather?'—Not a Good Question on Mars," *Facts & Faith,* vol. 11, n. 4 (1997), pages 2-3; Stephen Battersby, "Pathfinder Probes the Weather on Mars," *Nature,* 388 (1997), page 612; Ron Cowen, "Martian Rocks Offer a Windy Tale," *Science News,* 152 (1997), page 84; Hugh Ross, "Earth Design Update: The Cycles Connected to the Cycles, *Facts & Faith,* vol. 11, n. 4 (1997), page 3; Hugh Ross, "Earth Design Update: One Amazing Dynamo," *Facts & Faith,* vol. 11, n. 4 (1997), page 4; Peter Olson, "Probing Earth's Dynamo," *Nature,* 389 (1997), page 337; Weiji Kuang and Jeremy Bloxham, "An Earth-Like Numerical Dynamo Model," *Nature,* 389 (1997), pages 371-374; Xiaodong Song and Paul G. Richards, "Seismologi-cal Evidence for Differential Rotation of the Earth's Inner Core," *Nature,* 382 (1997), pages 221-224; Wei-jia Su, Adam M. Dziewonski, and Raymond Jeanloz, "Planet Within a Planet: Rotation of the Inner Core of the Earth," *Science,* 274 (1996), pages 1883-1887; Stephen H. Kirby, "Taking the Temperature of Slabs," *Nature,* 403 (2000), pages 31-34; James Trefil, "When the Earth Froze," *Smithsonian,* December, 1999, pages 28-30; Arnold L. Miller, "Biotic Transitions in Global Marine Diversity," *Science,* 281 (1998), pages 1157-1160; D. F. Williams, et al, "Lake Baikal Record of Continental Climate Response to Orbital Insolation During the Past 5 Million Years," *Science,* 278 (1997), pages 1114-1117; S. C. Myneni, T. K. Tokunaga, and G. E. Brown Jr., "Abiotic Selenium Redox Transformations in the Presence of Fe (II,III) Oxides," *Science,* 278 (1997), pages 1106-1109; G. P. Zank and P. C. Frisch, "Consequences of a Change in the Galactic Environment of the Sun," *Astrophysical Journal,* 518 (1999), pages 965-973; D. E. Trilling, R. H. Brown, and A. S. Rivkin, "Circumstellar Dust Disks Around Stars with Known Planetary Companions," *Astrophysical Journal,* 529 (2000), pages 499-505; Joseph J. Mohr, Benjamin Mathiesen, and August E. Evrard, "Properties of the Intracluster Medium in an Ensemble of Nearby Galaxy Clusters," *Astrophysical Journal,* 517 (1999), pages 627-649; Gregory W. Henry, et al., "Photomet-ric and Ca II and K Spectroscopic Variations in Nearby Sun-Like Stars with Planets. III," *Astrophysical Journal,* 531 (2000), pages 415-437; Kimmo Innanen, Seppo Mikkola, and Paul Wiegert, "The Earth-Moon System and the Dynamical Stability of the Inner Solar System," *Astronomical Journal,* 116 (1998), pages 2055-2057; J. Q. Zheng and M. J. Valtonen, "On the Probability That a Comet That Has Escaped from Another Solar System Will Collide with the Earth," *Monthly Notices of the Royal Astronomical Society,* 304 (1999), pages 579-582; Gregory Laughlin and Fred C. Adams, "The Modification of Planetary Orbits in Dense Open Clusters," *Astrophysical Journal Letters* (1998), pages L171-L174; Shahid Naeem and Shibin Li, "Biodiversity Enhances Ecosystem Reliability," *Nature,* 390 (1997), pages 507-509; S. H. Rhie, et al., "On Planetary Com-panions to the MACHO 98-BLG-35 Microlens Star," *Astrophysical Journal,* 533 (2000), pages 378-391.

SEVENTEEN—Building Life

1. Christopher Chyba and Carl Sagan, "Endogenous Production, Exogenous Delivery and Impact-shock Synthesis or Organic Molecules: An Inventory for the Origins of Life," *Nature* 355 (1992), pages 125-132.
2. Manfred Schidlowski, "A 3,800-million-year Isotopic Record of Life from Carbon in Sedimentary Rocks," *Nature,* 333 (1988), pages 313-318; S. J. Mojzsis, et al., "Evidence, for Life on Earth Before 3,800 Million Years Ago," *Nature,* 384 (1996), pages 53-59.
3. Kevin A. Maher and David J. Stevenson, "Impact Frustration of the Origin of Life," *Nature* 331 (1988), pages 612-614; Verne R. Oberbeck and Guy Fogleman, "Impacts and the Origin of Life," *Nature,* 339 (1989), page 434; Norman H. Sleep, et al., "Anni-hilation of Ecosystems by Large Asteroid Impacts on the Early Earth," *Nature* 342 (1989), pages 139-142.
4. Maher and Stevenson, pages 612-614.
5. Daniel P. Glavin, Jeffrey L. Bada, Karen L. F. Brinton, and Gene D. McDonald, "Amino Acids in Martian Meteorite Nakla," *9th Meeting of the International Society for the Study of the Origin of Life,* University of California, San Diego, July 11-16, 1999, #c6.4, Book of Abstracts, page 62; Keith A. Kvenvolden, "Chirality of Amino Acids in the Murchison Meteorite—A Historical Perspective," *9th Meeting of the International*

Society for the Study of the Origin of Life, University of California, San Diego, July 11-16, 1999, #i2.1, Book of Abstracts, page 40.

6. Charles B. Thaxton, Walter L. Bradley, and Roger L. Olsen, *The Mystery of Life's Origin: Reassessing Current Theories* (New York: Philosophical Library, 1984), pages 69-98; Walter L. Bradley, private communication (1993).

7. Ivan G. Dragonic, "Oxygen and Oxidizing Free-Radicals in the Hydrosphere of Early Earth," *9th Meeting of the International Society for the Study of the Origin of Life,* University of California, San Diego, July 11-16, 1999, #cA1.3, Book of Abstracts, page 34.

8. Chyba and Sagan, page 128.

9. Gordon Schlesinger and Stanley L. Miller, "Prebiotic Synthesis in Atmospheres Containing CH, CO, and CO_2," *Journal of Molecular Evolution,* 19 (1983), pages 376-382.

10. Robert Shapiro, *Origins: A Skeptic's Guide to the Creation of Life on Earth* (New York: Summit Books, 1986), page 128.

11. Elizabeth Pennisi, "Microbial Genomes Come Tumbling In," *Science,* 277 (1997), page 1433; Colin Patterson, *Evolution,* 2nd edition (Ithaca, NY: Comstock Publishing Associates, 1999), page 23; Gerard Deckert, et al., "The Complete Genome of the Hyperthermophilic Bacterium Aquifex Aeolicus," *Nature,* 392 (1998), pages 353-358; Andreas Ruepp, et al., "The Genome Sequence of the Thermoacidophilic Scavenger Thermoplasma Acidophilum," *Nature,* 407 (2000), pages 508-513; Carol J. Bult, et al., "Complete Genome Sequence of the Methanogenic Archeon, Methanococcus Jannaschii," *Science,* 273 (1996), pages 1058-1073.

12. Michael H. Hart, "Atmospheric Evolution, the Drake Equation, and DNA: Sparse Life in an Infinite Universe," *Physical Cosmology and Philosophy,* ed. John Leslie (New York: Macmillan, 1990), pages 263-264.

13. Hubert P. Yockey, "An Application of Information Theory to the Central Dogma and the Sequence Hypothesis," *Journal of Theoretical Biology,* 46 (1974), pages 369-406; Hubert P. Yockey, "On the Information Content of Cytochrome c," *Journal of Theoretical Biology,* 67 (1977), pages 345-376; Hubert P. Yockey, "A Calculation of the Probability of Spontaneous Biogenesis by Information Theory," *Journal of Theoretical Biology,x* 67 (1977), pages 377-398; Hubert P. Yockey, "Do Overlapping Genes Violate Molecular Biology and the Theory of Evolution?" *Journal of Theoretical Biology,* 80 (1979), pages 21-26; Hubert P. Yockey, "Self Organization Origin of Life Scenarios and Information Theory," *Journal of Theoretical Biology,* 91 (1981), pages 13-31.

14. Hubert P. Yockey, *Information Theory and Molecular Biology* (Cambridge, U.K.: Cambridge University Press, 1992), pages 231-309.

15. M. Mitchell Waldrop, "Finding RNA Makes Proteins Gives 'RNA World' a Big Boost," *Science,* 256 (1992), pages 1396-1397.

16. Thomas R. Cech, "The Chemistry of Self-Splicing RNA and RNA Enzymes," *Science* 236 (1987), pages 1532-1539.

17. Harry F. Noller, Veronita Hoffarth, and Ludwika Zimniak, "Unusual Resistance of Peptidyl Transferase to Protein Extraction Procedures," *Science,* 256 (1992), pages 1416-1419.

18. Joseph A. Piccirilli, et al., "Aminoacyl Esterase Activity of the Tetrahymena Ribozyme," *Science,* 256 (1992), pages 1420-1424.

19. John Horgan, "In the Beginning," *Scientific American* (February 1991), page 119.

20. Robert Shapiro, "Prebiotic Ribose Synthesis: A Critical Analysis," *Origin of Life and Evolution of the Biosphere,* 18 (1988), pages 71-85.

21. Horgan, page 119; Robert Shapiro, "Protometabolism: A Scenario for the Origin of Life," *The American Scientist* (July-August 1992), page 387.

22. Robert Irion, "Ocean Scientists Find Life, Warmth in the Seas: RNA Can't Take the Heat" *Science,* 279 (1998), page 1303.

23. Robert Irion, page 1303.

24. Robert Irion, page 1303

25. Fred Hoyle and Chandra Wickramasinghe, *Evolution from Space* (New York: Simon and Schuster, 1981), pages 39-61; Iosef S. Shklovskii and Carl Sagan, *Intelligent Life in the Universe* (San Francisco, CA: Holden-Day, 1966), pages 207-211; the item on meteorites came from a report of a computer analysis that was presented at the Twentieth Lunar and Planetary Science Conference (1989), Houston, Texas.

26. Shapiro, *Origins.*
27. Yockey, *Information Theory and Molecular Biology.*
28. Charles B. Thaxton, Walter L. Bradley, and Roger L. Olsen, *The Mystery of Life's Origin: Reassessing Current Theories* (New York: Philosophical Library, 1984).
29. Romans 10:18, *New King James Version.*

EIGHTEEN—*Extra-Dimensional Power*

1. Genesis 16:13, 28:16; Deuteronomy 30:14; Psalm 34:18, 119:151, 145:18; Jeremiah 23:24; Acts 17:28; and Romans 10:8 are a few of many examples.
2. Genesis 28:16; Exodus 33:20; Job 9:11, 37:23; and John 6:46 are a few of many examples.
3. 1 Timothy 6:16.
4. Edwin Abbott, *Flatland: A Romance of Many Dimensions,* with notes by David W. Davies (Pasadena, CA: Grant Daehlstrom, 1978).
5. John 16:5-10.
6. John 16:6.
7. John 16:7.
8. Philippians 2:5-9.
9. John 14:12-14.
10. Matthew 28:20.

NINETEEN—*The Point*

1. Hebrews 11:6.
2. Psalm 34:18, 145:18.
3. Ephesians 2:13.
4. J. N. D. Anderson, *The Evidence for the Resurrection* (Downers Grove, IL: InterVarsity Press, 1966).
5. James 4:8.
6. Revelation 3:8.

APPENDIX

1. Hugh Ross, *The Fingerprint of God,* 2nd edition (Orange, CA: Promise Publishing, 1991), pages 84-87.
2. Ralph A. Alpher and Robert C. Herman, "Evolution of the Universe," *Nature,* 162 (1948), pages 774-775.
3. Arno A. Penzias and Robert W. Wilson, "A Measurement of Excess Antenna Temperature at 4080 Mc/s," *Astrophysical Journal,* 142 (1965), pages 419-421.
4. Hugh Ross, *The Creator and the Cosmos,* 2nd edition, pages 22-24, 26-27.
5. John C. Mather, et al., "Measurement of the Cosmic Microwave Background Spectrum by the COBE FIRAS Instrument," *Astrophysical Journal,* 420 (1994), pages 439-444.
6. Hugh Ross, pages 27-28.
7. Antoinette Songaila, et al., "Measurement of the Microwave Background Temperature at Redshift 1.776," *Nature,* 371 (1994), pages 43-45.
8. Hugh Ross, *The Fingerprint of God,* 2nd edition, pages 86-87.
9. Juan M. Uson and David T. Wilkinson, "Improved Limits on Small-Scale Anisotropy in Cosmic Microwave Background," *Nature,* 312 (1984), pages 427-429.
10. Hugh Ross, pages 85-86.
11. George F. Smoot, "Comments and Summary on the Cosmic Background Radiation," Proceedings of the International Astronomical Union Symposium, No. 104, *Early Evolution of the Universe and Its Present Structure,* ed. G. O. Abell and G. Chincarini (Dordrecht-Holland, Boston, U.S.A.: D. Reidel Publishing, 1983), pages 153-158.
12. Hugh Ross, *The Creator and the Cosmos,* 2nd edition, pages 19-26.
13. S. R. D. Hancock, "Direct Observation of Structure in the Cosmic Background Radiation," *Nature,* 367 (1994), pages 333-338.
14. Hugh Ross, "Flat-Out Confirmed! The Flatter-Universe Discovery Affirms the Bible Three Ways," *Facts for Faith,* vol. 1, no. 2 (2000), pages 26-31.

15. P. DeBarnardis, et al., "A Flat Universe from High-Resolution Maps of the Cosmic Microwave Background Radiation," *Nature*, 494 (2000), pages 955-958.
16. Hugh Ross, *The Fingerprint of God*, 2nd edition, pages 79-84.
17. S. Perlmutter, et al, "Measurements of Ω and ∧ from 42 High-Redshift Supernovae," *Astrophysical Journal*, 517 (1999), pages 565-586.
18. Lawrence M. Krauss, "The End of the Age Problem and the Case for a Cosmological Constant Revisited," *Astrophysical Journal*, 501 (1998), pages 461-466.
19. Hugh Ross, *Beyond the Cosmos*, 2nd edition (Colorado Springs, CO: NavPress, 1999), page 219.
20. Hugh Ross, *The Fingerprint of God*, 2nd edition, page 124.
21. Yuri I. Izotov, et al., "Helium Abundance in the Most Metal-Deficient Blue Compact Galaxies: I Zw 18 and SBS 0335-052," *Astrophysical Journal*, 527 (1999), pages 757-777; D. R. Ballantyne, G. J. Ferland, and P. G. Martin, "The Primordial Helium Abundance: Toward Understanding and Removing the Cosmic Scatter in the dY/dZ Relation," *Astrophysical Journal*, 536 (2000), pages 773-777.
22. Scott Burles, David Kirkman, and David Tytler, "Deuterium Toward Quasar Q0014+813," *Astrophysical Journal*, 519 (1999), pages 18-21; David Kirkman, et al., "QSO 0130-4021: A Third QSO Showing a Low Deuterium-To-Hydrogen Abundance Ratio," *Astrophysical Journal*, 529 (2000), pages 655-660; Sergei A. Levshakov, Wilhelm H. Kegel, and Fumio Takahara, "The D/H Ratio at z = 3.57 Toward Q1937-1009," *Astrophysical Journal Letters*, 499 (1998), pages L1-L4; D. A. Lubowich, et al., "Deuterium in the Galactic Centre As a Result of Recent Infall of Low-Metallicity Gas," *Nature*, 405 (2000), pages 1025-1027.
23. E. Casuso and J. E. Beckman, "Deuterium, Lithium, and the Hubble Deep Field," *Astronomical Journal*, 118 (1999), pages 1907-1911; Sylvie Vauclair and Corinne Charbonnel, "Element Segregation in Low-Metallicity Stars and the Primordial Lithium Abundance," *Astrophysical Journal*, 502 (1998), pages 372-377.
24. Hugh Ross, *Beyond the Cosmos*, 2nd edition, pages 29-33.
25. P. Kaaret, et al., "Strong-Field Gravity and X-Ray Observations of AU 1820-30," *Astrophysical Journal Letters*, 520 (1999), pages L37-L40.
26. Hugh Ross, pages 28-29.
27. Stephen Hawking and Roger Penrose, "Singularities of Gravitational Collapse and Cosmology," *Proceedings of the Royal Society of London*, Series A, 314 (1970), pages 529-548.
28. Hugh Ross, "Flat-Out Confirmed!" pages 26-31.
29. P. DeBarnardis, et al., "A Flat Universe from High-Resolution Maps of the Cosmic Microwave Background Radiation, *Nature*, 494 (2000), pages 955-958.
30. Hugh Ross, *Beyond the Cosmos*, 2nd edition, pages 34-45.
31. Gary Taubes, "How Black Holes May Get String Theory Out of a Bind," *Science*, 268 (1995), page 1699; Juan Maldacena and Andrew Strominger, "Statistical Entropy of Four-Dimensional Extremal Black Holes," *Physical Review Letters*, 77 (1996), pages 428-229; Curtis Callan, Jr. and Juan Maldacena, "D-Brane Approach to Black-Hole Quantum Mechanics," *Nuclear Physics B*, 472 (1996), pages 591-608.
32. Hugh Ross, *The Fingerprint of God*, 2nd edition, pages 90-93.
33. Hugh Ross, *The Creator and the Cosmos*, 2nd edition, page 60.
34. Donald Hamilton, "The Spectral Evolution of Galaxies. I. An Observational Approach," *Astrophysical Journal*, 297 (1985), pages 371-389.
35. Hugh Ross, "Hubble Space Telescope Captures Infancy of Cosmos," *Facts & Faith*, vol. 9, no. 2 (1995), pages 1-2.
36. Faye Flam, "The Space Telescope Spies on Ancient Galaxy Menageries," *Science*, 266 (1994), page 1806.
37. Hugh Ross, pages 1-2.
38. Faye Flam, page 1806.
39. Hugh Ross, *The Creator and the Cosmos*, 2nd edition, pages 31-47.
40. A. Melchiorri, et al., "A Measurement of Ω from the North American Test Flight of Boomerang," *Astrophysical Journal Letters*, 536 (2000), pages L63-L66.
41. Hugh Ross, pages 38-40.
42. Douglas K. Duncan, David L. Lambert, and Michael Lemke, "The Abundance of

Boron in Three Halo Stars," *Astrophysical Journal*, 401 (1992), pages 584-595.

43. Masayuki Y. Fujimoto, Yasufumi Ikeda, and Icko Iben, Jr., "The Origin of Extremely Metal-Poor Carbon Stars and the Search for Population III," *Astrophysical Journal Letters*, 529 (2000), pages L25-L28; A. Weiss, S. Cassisi, H. Schlattl, and M. Salaris, "Evolution of Low-Mass Metal-Free Stars Including Effects of Diffusion and External Pollution," *Astrophysical Journal*, 533 (2000), pages 413-423.

44. Hugh Ross, *Beyond the Cosmos*, 2nd edition, pages 30-31.

45. G. S. Bisnovatyi-Kogan, "At the Border of Eternity," *Science*, 279 (1998), page 1321.

46. Hugh Ross, Creation and Time (Colorado Springs, CO: NavPress, 1994), pages 107-108.

47. Hugh Ross, *Beyond the Cosmos*, 2nd edition, pages 29-45.

48. Hugh Ross, "Mass Mystery Nearly Solved," *Facts & Faith*, vol. 11, no. 4 (1997), pages 6-7.

49. Andrew Watson, "Case for Neutrino Mass Gathers Weight," *Science*, 277 (1997), pages 30-31.

50. Joseph Silk, *The Big Bang*, revised and updated edition (New York: W. H. Freeman, 1989), pages 109-167.

51. A. Melchiorri, et al., "A Measurement of Ω from the North American Test Flight of Boomerang," *Astrophysical Journal Letters*, 536 (2000), pages L63-L66; Aaron D. Lewis, E. Ellingson, Simon L. Morris, and R. G. Carlberg, "X-Ray Mass Estimates at z ~ 0.3 for the Canadian Network for Observational Cosmology Cluster Sample," *Astrophysical Journal*, 517 (1999), pages 587-608; Bo Qin and Xiang-Ping Wu, "Baryon Distribution in Galaxy Clusters as a Result of Sedimentation of Helium Nuclei," *Astrophysical Journal Letters*, 529 (2000), pages L1-L4; M. Fukugita, C. J. Hogan, and P. J. E. Peebles, "The Cosmic Baryon Budget," *Astrophysical Journal*, 503 (1998), pages 518-530.

NAME INDEX

SUBJECT INDEX

AUTHOR

HUGH ROSS earned a B.Sc. in physics from the University of British Columbia and an M.Sc. and Ph.D. in astronomy from the University of Toronto. For several years he continued his research on quasars and galaxies as a post-doctoral fellow at the California Institute of Technology. For eleven years he served as minister of evangelism at Sierra Madre Congregational Church.

Today he directs the efforts of Reasons To Believe, an institute founded to research and proclaim the factual basis for faith in God and in His Word, the Bible. He also hosts a weekly television series called "Reasons To Believe" on the Trinity Broadcasting Network. Over the years Hugh has given several hundred lectures, seminars, and courses, both in the United States and abroad, on Christian apologetics. He lives in Southern California with his wife, Kathy, and sons, Joel and David.

REASONS TO BELIEVE

REASONS TO BELIEVE is a nonprofit organization, without denominational affiliation, adhering to the doctrinal statements of the National Association of Evangelicals and of the International Council on Biblical Inerrancy. It provides research and teaching on the harmony of God's revelation in the words of the Bible and in the facts of nature. Speakers are available for churches, business clubs, university outreaches, and so on. A hotline for those with questions or a desire to dialogue on issues pertaining to faith, science, and the Bible operates at (626) 335-1480, seven days a week, 5:00-7:00 P.M. Pacific Time.

A news magazine or a catalog of materials may be obtained by phoning (800) 482-7836 or by writing to: Reasons to Believe, P.O. Box 5978, Pasadena, CA 91117.

The e-mail address is reasons@reasons.org
The web site is http://www.reasons.org